MW00476875

LEE'S
LAST CASUALTY

LEE'S
LAST CASUALTY

The Life and Letters of Sgt. Robert W. Parker, Second Virginia Cavalry

Edited by Catherine M. Wright

Voices of the Civil War
Peter S. Carmichael, Series Editor

The University of Tennessee Press / Knoxville

The Voices of the Civil War series makes available a variety of primary source materials that illuminate issues on the battlefield, the home front, and the western front, as well as other aspects of this historic era. The series contextualizes the personal accounts within the framework of the latest scholarship and expands established knowledge by offering new perspectives, new materials, and new voices.

Copyright © 2008 by The University of Tennessee Press / Knoxville.
All Rights Reserved. Manufactured in the United States of America.
Cloth: First printing, 2008.
Paper: First printing, 2012.

LIBRARY OF CONGRESS CATALOGING-IN-PUBLICATION DATA

Parker, Robert W., 1838–1865.
  Lee's last casualty : the life and letters of Sgt. Robert W. Parker,
Second Virginia Cavalry / edited by Catherine M. Wright. — 1st ed.
    p. cm. — (Voices of the Civil War)
  Includes bibliographical references and index.
  ISBN-13: 978-1-57233-957-6
  ISBN-10: 1-57233-957-8
  1. Parker, Robert W., 1838–1865—Correspondence.
  2. Soldiers—Virginia—Correspondence.
  3. Confederate States of America. Army. Virginia Cavalry Regiment, 2nd.
  4. Virginia—History—Civil War, 1861–1865—Personal narratives.
  5. United States—History—Civil War, 1861–1865—Personal narratives, Confederate.
  6. United States—History—Civil War, 1861–1865—Campaigns.
  I. Wright, Catherine M., 1981–
  II. Title.
  E581.62nd .P37 2008
  973.7'455—dc22   2008000424

CONTENTS

ILLUSTRATIONS

FOREWORD

Not long after Robert Parker's 1861 enlistment in the Second Virginia Cavalry, he received a letter from his mother, imploring him to accept Jesus Christ as his savior. She wanted him to understand that the conflict with the North would be bloody and unpredictable and that the popular idea of Southern invincibility was a youthful illusion many young men would not discover until it was too late. Most of all, she impressed upon her son to remember that the war would not be decided on the battlefield. God would grant victory to the side that expressed the purest faith and showed the highest principles. Parker's mother, like countless other Southern women, conveyed a critical message that every Confederate soldier confronted at some point during his enlistment: How could one live as a Christian in an army that taught men to kill, in camps where immorality flourished, and in military units where unbelievers cursed and drank with impunity? The struggle to live as a Christian had nearly defeated Parker before the war, and his mother deeply regretted that her boy had dodged God's loving embrace. "I have often wished you had read the bible more," she wrote, "and recollected more His inscrutable providences." Now that Parker was in the ranks, risking his life for Southern independence, his mother was hopeful that he would undergo a "change of heart" and put his "trust in a stronger power than this poor uncertain world and its perishing objects."

How Parker responded to his mother's entreaty is not known, but his subsequent letters make it clear that his mother, as well as Parker's wife, Beck, shaped Robert's thinking about what it meant to be a Confederate. Women, especially those of the slaveholding class, made sure that men in the ranks understood that more than politics or manly honor was at stake in fighting the Yankees. Parker recognized this point, just as his mother and wife had hoped, believing that war was a supreme test in which God would look deep into the souls of Northerners and Southerners. His private beliefs had broader ramifications. They informed his public views on how Southerners should act as citizens of a Confederate nation. People of all classes, Parker reasoned, had to give themselves both to country and God if Southern armies were to succeed on the battlefield. Such a view was typical of most white Southerners, and Parker's letters underscore how members of the rank and file needed to believe that those behind the lines were devoted to the cause. The correspondence that Parker received from home, some of which is published in *Lee's Last Casualty*, is exceptionally rare and exceedingly important in showing how women shaped public notions of Confederate loyalty. Parker's steadfastness can be partially attributed to the words of his family, who instilled in him just cause and comfort to continue fighting. He represents, both in words and actions, that reliable class of Confederate soldiers that anchored every Southern army.

There were times, however, when Parker became frustrated and depressed about the war, his mood turning dark, almost to the point of demoralization. In 1864 he informed his wife that he would like to buy a substitute so that he could return home. This crisis reveals the contradictory consciousness that every Civil War soldier endured. Issues of loyalty were not black and white. They were fluid and constantly changing in relation to a host of factors. What stands out is that his moments of despair were not the simple consequence of military reverses. Problems within the army, suffering on the home front, separation from his loved ones, and the army's inability to properly equip and feed him pushed him to the brink. Moreover, when a crisis hit Parker, he did not analyze the problem as a question of nationalism versus community. The problem was far more complicated as Parker saw it. Editor Catherine Wright offers us a brilliant exploration into how Parker reconciled himself to the conflicting demands of serving in the Southern ranks while also being an absentee husband and father. Wright makes it clear that Parker's morale and commitment to the Confederacy drew from a complicated set of relationships that merged family, community, and nation together. Rarely did Parker feel conflicted between his responsibilities to home and those to the army. Living in Virginia, as Wright suggests, probably eased tensions in Parker who, unlike Confederates fighting outside of their native states, was protecting his wife and children from a Union foe that posed an immediate physical threat.

Although metaphysical matters were of undeniable interest to Parker, most of his letters center on the grinding tasks of being a Confederate cavalryman. Too often we dismiss practical issues as mundane and of secondary importance to questions of ideology or politics. This is an unfortunate perspective because it overlooks how ordinary matters of survival influenced the ways in which soldiers negotiated their duties to both home and country. Lee's Army of Northern Virginia, for instance, could not sustain the rank and file. Shortages of food and clothing left most men destitute and starving, but Parker relied on his family for boxes of necessities. Consequently, in his letters to his family, he wrote a great deal about clothes, food, and other articles, but this dialogue contributed to his perception that a collective endeavor existed between soldier and civilian in a war against a Northern invader. Sending a handwoven shirt, a pair of mittens, or a batch of apples gave the women in Parker's life a tangible way of contributing to the war effort. Parker was effusive in praising their efforts, not only as confirmations that people back home loved him but also as demonstrations of their patriotism. Material and spiritual support from his wife reassured him that he was fighting in a just cause. We can only wonder about the impact of Parker's death at Appomattox on his family. He was probably the last Confederate in Lee's army to be killed in action. Did news of this heroic final act give comfort to Beck, knowing that her husband had been dutiful to the bitter end? Or was she resentful that her beloved husband had died needlessly for an army that was surrounded and in the process of surrendering? Her private reaction will remain a mystery, but we do know that she was about to enter a new world after Appomattox—one in which there was no choice but to mourn every fallen Southern soldier as a noble Confederate martyr.

Peter S. Carmichael
West Virginia University

ACKNOWLEDGMENTS

Many people and organizations contributed to this book in a variety of essential ways. I would like to thank Bradley Bereitschaft, Beth Carmichael, Peter S. Carmichael, David Ickes, Julie Krick, Robert E. L. Krick, Patrick A. Schroeder, Emily Schweninger, Jane Sugarman, Cheryl Wright, and Jeffrey Wright, as well as the staff of Appomattox Court House National Historic Park, the Bedford City/County Museum, the Library of Virginia, and the Stonewall Jackson House for their expertise, assistance, and support during this project.

A distinct thanks goes to Robert T. Dooley for making these documents available to scholarly study, and for his generous support of this project.

A final and special thanks to Matthew S. Harvey for his unfailing belief in this project—this book also belongs to you.

INTRODUCTION

In the bitter depths of a Virginia winter in January 1865, a Confederate cavalry-man named Robert W. Parker huddled against the cold, writing a letter to his wife Rebecca. Having just returned to the front lines from a furlough home, he confided that he presently felt "more despondent than I ever was in my life, prospects are so gloomy here."The men and horses of his regiment, the Second Regiment Virginia Cavalry, were on the brink of starvation; news from the battlefront was disheartening, as Gen. Ulysses S. Grant's siege continued at Petersburg and Gen. William T. Sherman marched north from Georgia; and his treasured pocket watch"stopped last night and won't run a tick."But worst of all, he lamented,"I have not heard or gotten a line from any of you since I left. Hearing from you and the children often is one of my greatest comforts in camp."In closing his letter, he plaintively reminded his wife to"remember your promise to write me twice a week."[1] This lack of correspondence left Robert feeling isolated from and forgotten by his family and community, which shook the foundations of his morale and his support for the Confederacy.

Letters such as Robert Parker's constitute rich and unique historical sources, for they candidly relate the thoughts, emotions, and experiences of American Civil War soldiers. Correspondence was an integral part of creating strong relationships in the mid-nineteenth century United States, but the Civil War transformed this modest form of communication into a vital support network for Confederate morale.[2] The war presented Southerners with numerous tensions and challenges, both tangible and intangible. Letters could ease or exacerbate these conflicts by communicating information and sentiments that affected morale between soldiers on the battlefront and their family and friends back home, thus powerfully influencing the outcome of the Civil War. Far more than the mere"residual substance"of ruptured relationships, letters served as a means of maintaining personal and communal ties, transmitting information, and reinforcing morale and Confederate nationalism.[3] Often intended to be shared with numerous members of the community, soldiers' letters communicated information from camp and the front lines; in return, civilian letters related the neighborhood news, "down to the chickens, cats, and dogs."[4] These letters played a crucial role in sustaining morale and ultimately shaped the fate of the Confederacy.

The letters of Robert W. Parker contribute in significant ways to our understanding of the Civil War. Since cavalrymen composed only 20 percent of the Confederate army, correspondence from this branch of the service is comparatively scarce.[5] Parker's letters belie "the essential unity of the homefront and the battlefront," revealing critical aspects of the Confederate wartime experience that affected Southerners on both fronts.[6] They expose the extreme pressures that the war placed on soldiers and civilians alike. More important, they reveal the ways Southerners surmounted these pressures and maintained their morale and sense of nationalism, with particular emphasis on the role of correspondence, communities, and religion in providing solace and sustaining morale. Understanding private relationships are the key to understanding public actions, and the Parker letters demonstrate how Southerners maintained sufficient commitment to the Confederacy that, even in the darkest days of the war, most soldiers still believed, "If I should fall, I think 'twill be in a good and just cause."[7]

Robert William Parker was born in Pittsylvania County, Virginia, on August 31, 1838.[8] His parents, Ammon and Frances Parker, were slaveholders on the make who moved to Bedford County, Virginia, shortly after his birth. By 1850 they had four children together, of whom Robert was the eldest, and owned seven slaves and real estate valued at approximately four thousand dollars.[9] Ten years later, they had nearly achieved their planter aspirations, with real estate worth about seven thousand dollars and seventeen slaves.[10] They had also replaced their modest cedar-roofed log house with a more sumptuous pine-frame house named Lone Aspen, complete with three fireplaces, paneled wainscoting, and a two-story porch supported by square columns.[11] With the labor of their slaves, they cultivated oats, corn, and wheat and raised pigs, cows, and sheep on nearly seven hundred acres of land.[12]

Although somewhat different from many well-to-do Southern men in the 1850s, Robert Parker's early life illustrates numerous developments in antebellum Southern society. Perhaps most significant, the road that led his parents to prosperity was largely closed to members of his generation. Virginia's political and economic decline through the middle of the nineteenth century placed land and slave prices far beyond the means of most young men. Productive land was still the key to prominence, and many Virginians left their native state for more fertile acres in the Deep South and West.[13] With the traditional routes to becoming a head of household through slave ownership and farming closed, most wealthy young men worked as professionals, delayed marriage, and lived in their family home.[14]

Robert experienced these socioeconomic trends, although his responses to them differed from those of most other wealthy young men. He received

Lone Aspen, the parental home of Robert W. Parker in Bedford County, Virginia. Courtesy of David A. Ickes.

some schooling, but unlike the sons of most large slaveholders, he did not attend college. Like many young Virginians, he remained in his father's household at least until his marriage to Rebecca Walker in December 1860.[15] After this point he appears to have farmed and set up his own household on his father's land, perhaps in the log house his parents had lived in while building Lone Aspen.[16] Thus while Robert's early marriage, education, and profession differentiated him from most well-off young men, his options were nonetheless circumscribed by the bleak realities of the Virginian economy in the years immediately before the Civil War.

Yet it would be mistaken to assume that the economic limitations of the antebellum South detracted from Southerners' devotion to their way of life, which involved state rights, agrarianism, racial slavery, aristocracy, and habits of mind.[17] On the contrary, as Northerners increased their attacks on the institution of slavery, Southerners only intensified their defense of the system that significantly shaped their society. In defending slavery, Southerners argued they were truly defending what Robert termed "liberty and rights"—to own and dispose of their property as they wished, to ensure the freedom of white Americans, and to secede from a government that they believed no longer represented their interests.[18] Even if Southern white men could not always identify the forces that threatened their freedom, their patriotic response was to go to war to protect it.[19]

On May 23, 1861, Virginians approved the Secession Ordinance and eagerly began mobilizing their resources for war. Voluntary military service was the ultimate patriotic wartime contribution and a much-welcomed test for young men eager to finally assert their manhood.[20] Thousands of enthusiastic white men of all classes rushed to enlist in community-based regiments. On May 28, Bedford County organized the Bedford Southside Dragoons.[21] Most of these men had little or no prior military experience; they were wartime volunteers from civilian life who remained rooted in the homes and communities from which they sprang to arms and to which they longed to return.[22] Ironically, it was the very values and beliefs held by the members of those communities that impelled men to enlist. For Virginians, convictions of defending home and hearth from rapacious Yankee invaders were particularly strong motivators.[23] "I hope every man that thinks enough of his country to defend it, will volunteer," Robert told Rebecca, then insisted that if her brother Jimmie had "taken unto himself a wife . . . he must volunteer to protect her."[24]

Most citizens who did not volunteer themselves viewed soldiers from their families and communities as extensions of themselves, the embodiment of their own unselfish dedication to the cause.[25] Since units were almost always composed of men from a single town or county, they represented their communities in a very real sense, and the population at large wanted soldiers to believe this.[26] Women could even contribute manpower to the war effort in various ways, from sewing regimental flags to "raising soldiers to defend our southern homes," as Robert put it.[27]

Soldiers' enlistment and subsequent deployment caused them to be physically absent from their homes for most of the war, but they remained emotionally rooted with the families and communities that supported them. Robert demonstrated this when he told Rebecca, "I will try and be content and do my duty as a soldier for my beloved country, [but] my greatest wish and anxiety is to see my loved little family, the theme of my earthly thoughts."[28] A sense of national community certainly helped anchor Confederate nationalism and tenacious will.[29] Yet most Southerners depended primarily upon their local communities, not the Confederate nation, for material and emotional support. Southerners had always relied upon nearby neighbors for aid in times of need, a custom reinforced by evangelism's focus on mutual support among Christian followers.[30] During the Civil War they continued to rely on informal local support networks established in the prewar years.

Most visibly, civilians provided tangible support for soldiers in the form of food, clothing, and equipment. Civilians attempted "to keep the war a community affair by supporting their 'boys' with minimal help from outsiders."[31] By providing supplies to supplement those issued by the Confederate national government, local communities ultimately enabled Confederate soldiers to remain in the field far longer than they could have otherwise. Some communities pooled their resources and sent enough supplies for many men, even an entire company. Such displays of support could hardly have failed to lift soldiers' spirits and strengthen their resolve to carry on the war. In early 1864 a private in Robert's company "received a box with a good many little goodies in it." He apparently shared the contents of his box with Robert and his other messmates, for Robert reported, "We have had plenty [to eat] since its arrival. Every little is a help."[32] Although this private may have been particularly generous in sharing the contents his box, it is far more likely that it was intended to provide supplementary provisions for several men. Speaking of the contents of another box, Robert wrote, "We have plenty to eat since the box came to hand and have a good deal of its contents yet, which we use with our rations and live as good as soldiers could wish."[33] Military rations and other supplies became inadequate just a few months into the war, which made communities all the more instrumental in providing material support for their troops.

Families and individuals also helped provide necessary items and services to keep their soldiers in the field. Robert's wife and parents sent him several boxes of food throughout the war, some stocked with such luxuries as peas, bacon, ham, butter, sausage, and dried fruit.[34] He also relied on Rebecca to provide much of his clothing throughout the war. After her repeated inquiries about the status of his clothing, he said, "You seem quite uneasy as to my suffering for want of my clothes."[35] Her concern should come as no surprise, for when the Confederate blockade made it all but impossible to import cloth, the Confederate government and Southern media exhorted women to perform their patriotic duty and take up textile production.[36] Rebecca mended and altered Robert's clothing, as in the prewar years, but now she also spun and wove.[37] Like many Southern women, she eagerly assisted the war effort in any way that she could, including contributing her labor to help clothe a Confederate soldier and keep him in the field.

Food, clothing, and gifts from family and friends also aided the Confederacy in a less tangible way. By providing physical evidence of their love and support, they helped sustain soldiers' morale. For instance, food was a daily concern for Confederate soldiers, and insufficient rations fostered desperation and depression.[38] Robert reported that "several of the boys" wanted the good cotton shirts Rebecca sent him, "but I guess they will never get them, for I hate to part with any thing you send me from home."[39] He appreciated the shirts not only for their functional value but also for the affection and devotion that impelled her to make and send them. Similarly, he said he was "very thankful for Mory's tin cup; tell him I will try and keep it for his sake."[40] Although his toddler's cup was probably of limited usefulness, Robert nonetheless treasured it because it reminded him of his beloved family. For men like Robert, who enlisted to protect his family as well as his nation and liberty, such reminders also served to bolster his morale and commitment to the Confederacy.

These examples demonstrate that emotional support was at least as essential as material support in continuing the war. All the supplies in the world would have been inconsequential without the will to fight, which was reinforced via emotional sustenance from absent loves ones. Soldiers and civilians strengthened the intangible support that they provided for one another through continuous interaction. Bedford civilians visited campsites often, taking advantage of their relative proximity to locations where their soldiers were stationed to provide supplies and news from home; as Robert wrote, "Some of our Bedford friends are in camp almost every day."[41] Coveted furloughs enabled soldiers to occasionally reciprocate these visits.

The most common method of communication between soldiers and civilians was correspondence. By embodying and conveying localized communal support, letters played a pivotal role in sustaining the Confederate war effort. They did so by combining sheer number of letters with nineteenth-century cultural expressions of intimacy.[42] Civil War armies were the most literate in history to that time, with a literacy rate of more than 80 percent among Confederate soldiers.[43] This widespread literacy under wartime circumstances resulted in a flood of letter writing from all classes across the South, for on no other occasion had so large a proportion of the people been away from home for so long a time.[44] Furthermore, romantic correspondence between nineteenth-century men and women often contained exchanges of self-criticism and praise, which worked to enhance self-esteem and provide strong doses of reassurance.[45]

Robert Parker wrote letters to many loved ones back home; in return he received letters from several family and friends, providing information about his home community and, more important, offering moral support. Merely receiving a letter from home could help boost morale, while not receiving one could have the opposite effect. "Please write soon and often," Robert begged his wife. "I almost get out of heart sometimes."[46] One modern military scholar has convincingly argued that letters represent soldiers' major contact with the social unit that reinforces their desire to serve faithfully and under great hardship.[47] This was certainly true during the Civil War, but it is imperative to recognize that letters from the battlefront shaped civilian morale in a reciprocal fashion. Through their content and very existence, letters played a key role in sustaining morale on both fronts.

Letters provided a vital means of transmitting information. They often contained news of regional, national, or global interest, but even more important, they contained information specifically about or of interest to members of their community. As the only available means of contact, "communication, professions of love and support, and even the simplest exchanges of information occurred almost exclusively through the mail."[48] Due to illiteracy, the unreliable mail service, paper scarcity, and variations among letter-writing frequency, soldiers and civilians often included information about and messages for various members of their community.[49] Information could take the form of gossip, highly personal messages, troop movements, battle reports, political developments, or even the mundane details of daily life. Thus letters usually served as both private and public documents, relating information of an intimate nature to the addressee but also containing news for a larger community.

Correspondents usually did not provide such information in response to a direct inquiry. Rather, they understood that their letters often served as the only source of news on individuals and events that their loved ones on the other front were likely to receive. For instance, after Robert briefly related recent troop movements and details of the Battle of Stanardsville in 1864, he admitted that "our losses has not ascertained yet," but "the only one of our regiment wounded bad that I have heard of and since reported dead is Lieut. William Parker, shot through the bowels"—his own cousin.[50] The battle had occurred only two days prior, and Robert's letter may have been the first news of it to reach Bedford. If not, it was most certainly among the first eyewitness accounts they received and, more important, contained information about the welfare of soldiers from the Bedford community.

Correspondents sometimes directly responded to community remarks and questions. Although mail was the principal form of communication during the war for most Confederate soldiers, reciprocal exchanges demonstrate that soldiers and civilians strove together to over come the limitations intrinsic to the written word. They also underscore the public and communal nature of Civil War correspondence. In response to a letter from Rebecca, Robert wrote, "You and many others have laughed and asked me how I could wash and cook. I can tell you this morning was the first time I ever took my cloths to the creek to wash them . . . [but I] washed them right and can cook so we can eat it."[51] It would thus appear that Rebecca read some portions of Robert's letters aloud for a wider audience of family and friends and then incorporated their verbal responses into her return letter.

Other segments of Robert's letters were intended for his wife's eyes alone. Letter writing was a crucial aspect of romantic love in nineteenth-century America. Though letters were never an adequate substitute for absent loved ones, they were symbolically akin to personal presence.[52] This symbolic presence was essential during the Civil War, when husbands and wives reflected and reinforced one another's morale. Like most Southern women, Rebecca endured many hardships during the war, including anxiety for loved ones on the battlefront, food shortages, financial difficulties, loneliness, multiple pregnancies, and perhaps problems managing slaves. But like most Confederates of her generation, she also displayed a deep commitment to the Confederacy that only intensified as the war became more physically grueling and emotionally demanding.[53]

Like most letters written by women to their enlisted husbands or lovers, only a handful of Rebecca's survive; however, it would be erroneous to conclude, as some historians have, that most evidence of their support is "lost to history."[54] Much can be inferred about the content of Rebecca's letters by carefully analyzing Robert's responses. A close examination of his letters supplies strong evidence that their correspondence provided her with crucial emotional support that enabled her to maintain her devotion to the Confederacy, which in turn allowed her to bolster his morale and will to fight.[55]

The unreliability of the Confederate mail service and general limitations of correspondence greatly impeded "the mass of almost trivial details that comprise the emotional intimacy of married life."[56] Perhaps most obviously, Robert was absent for the births of their children, and his parental involvement was largely limited to statements such as "Tell him to be a good boy and mind Marmy."[57] In a thousand ways, whether in the mere absence of a loved one or a hardship distinctive to war, reliance on correspondence naturally restricted emotional intimacy. Furthermore, Southerners did not always do everything in their power to support and comfort their spouses. Bad news, low spirits, long response times, and comments such as "I have a lively time here where I go for grog [alcohol]; I tell the ladies I am a married man but they don't believe it" undoubtedly damaged marriages and morale.[58]

However, it is inaccurate to conclude that these factors demoralized Confederates throughout the war, drained their will, and ultimately led to the fall of the Confederacy.[59] Like many Civil War soldiers and their wives, Robert and Rebecca usually strove to mitigate, if not overcome, the limitations inherent in correspondence. They wrote frequently, exchanged new information of everything from national politics to the minutiae of their everyday lives, provided updates on family and friends, openly expressed their affection, hesitatingly admitted their fears, and professed their faith—all of which helped sustain the bonds of their relationship and, ultimately, their morale. Robert illustrated this when he wrote, "To tell the truth my health seems to have improved since I heard from you the first time, for I never was more uneasy in my life. And since I received your last [letter] I have felt almost like a new creature, I have felt so much relieved about home affairs."[60]

Although good news and affectionate remembrances from absent loved ones were always welcome and did much to raise spirits, letters possessed the power of boosting morale by their very existence. Letters had mass, dimension, substance, and—most important—a point of origin a world away. Small and frail though they were, they proved the existence of a place far removed from the brutal battlefront.[61] Soldiers and civilians alike mirrored Robert's sentiments when he wrote, "It would afford me the greatest pleasure just to know that you get my letters, and I would [will?] try to write to you every week."[62]

It was not until late in the war that soldiers and civilians encountered severe obstacles to calming one another's anxiety, tension, fear, and loneliness. By mid-1864 Union forces had heavily crippled Confederate transportation routes, bringing the postal service to a standstill. Without the letters they had so long relied upon to counter the demoralizing effects of"the deadly missiles of the enemy, disease, death, and the privations of camp," some Confederate soldiers began to lose hope that they could ever prevail.[63] Many soldiers echoed Robert's sentiments when he plaintively wrote,"If life lasts, I hope to see you. . . . Were it not for hope, it seems to me I would have to give up in despair."[64]

Yet even despite these obstacles, most Southerners remained devoted to the Confederacy. After Richmond's surrender on April 3 and Robert's death and Lee's surrender at Appomattox Court House on April 9, a family member professed to Rebecca, "I can't believe but what we are yet to enjoy that for which there has been so much sacrifice and blood shed."She also hoped that Rebecca's"dear little boys"long enjoyed"the freedom and independence their Father fought and bled and died for."[65] Resistance was clearly burning brightly in the hearts of more than a few civilians.[66] These true believers in the Confederacy faithfully held onto a hope that, though increasing feeble, enabled them to press on with the war.

Soldiers remained no less committed than civilians in the waning months of the war. In March 1865 Robert was hungry, on foot, and had not received a letter from Rebecca in weeks.Yet he still spoke of trying to take care of himself, keeping"in fine spirits," and doing his"duty"for the Confederacy.[67] He was not a fanatic blinded to the bleak Confederate military situation by hatred, religious zeal, or fear of enduring the humiliation of defeat.[68] On the contrary, Robert's letters reveal a rational man who, despite hardship and trauma, still deeply believed that his nation was worth fighting for. Without military victories and loved ones'letters to offer moral support, most Confederate soldiers relied upon such internalized values as honor and duty to sustain their motivation through the end of the war.[69]

But when hardship, hunger, disease, and death obliterated lofty notions of courage, honor, and obligation, Confederates turned to religion to give meaning and order to the war.[70] Religion had always constituted a vital element of life in the South, but it became increasingly central in antebellum culture and politics as a means of justifying the institution of slavery and providing an impetus for war. During the war, Southerners enshrined their Christian identity by"invoking the favor and guidance of Almighty God"in the Confederate Constitution.[71] But religion's significance in justifying the war was matched by its role in providing comfort and maintaining morale.[72] As the Parker letters demonstrate, religion reinforced Confederate commitment to the war even more than correspondence did."May the good Lord comfort and sustain her

[Rebecca] in this great affliction,"wrote one of Rebecca's relatives, evincing the widely held belief that only religious faith could provide solace through the most severe trials.[73]

Many Southerners came to regard the war as a sort of crusade: So long as they remained faithful and pure, God would personally guide the Christian South to victory over the sinful, materialistic North. Before the First Battle of Manassas, Robert wrote,"I hope by the help of God we may meet with success when we have to meet our foes on the field of battle."[74] Southerners believed military victories would prove that the creation of an independent Confederate nation was divinely sanctioned.[75] Convinced that they were more Christian than Northerners and favored by God, most Confederates harbored few doubts about the outcome of the war. Their commitment to Christ flowed into their commitment to their nation; forsaking their government became equivalent to forsaking their God.[76] Indeed, many Southerners remained convinced until the very end of the war that God would deliver a last-minute victory against all odds.[77] As Robert told Rebecca, "'Tis Him who rules on high that can fix the destinies of a nation."[78]

Because Confederates believed that Christianity embodied the same values that would bring Southern victory, soldiers and civilians alike strove to live as true Christians.[79] First and foremost, this involved conversion to Christianity. Some soldiers were relatively apathetic in their religious convictions in the antebellum years, but the horrors of war and the imminence of death induced many of them to embrace Christianity.[80] Because the death of an unconverted soldier meant eternal separation and damnation, civilians also expressed great concern over the spiritual welfare of their enlisted men.[81] Although Robert's letters indicate that he possessed strong religious convictions, his mother still expressed great concern for the state of his soul:"I have hoped for years past you had experienced a change of heart and had tried to put your trust in a stronger power. . . . Our lives at best are short and uncertain here—the important part is to secure that rest that remains to all the people of God."[82] Even if soldiers were content with the state of their own souls, Southern evangelism made it acceptable for them to attempt to convince their peers of their sinfulness and the need for conversion."Let your light shine as a believer,"Robert's mother implored."It might be that you would save some friend a great evil."[83]

Many Christians believed that every aspect of their lives, not merely their souls, was consigned to God. As the suffering and death attendant to war scathed every community in the South, many Confederates found great comfort in trusting that all was beyond their control and in the hands of God. Fatalism helped many Civil War soldiers face the dangers of disease and combat without giving way to fear, for if fate decreed one's death, there was nothing one could do about it.[84] When a dying soldier in Robert's company said, "The Lord's will be done,"he revealed the role of fatalism in rationalizing even the greatest of wartime sacrifices. Fatalism also eased their minds regarding the welfare of loved ones back home they were unable to directly assist or defend. Fatalism served an analogous function for some civilians by fortifying their courage in uncertain times and offering explanations for wartime hardships. When Rebecca expressed concern for his physical safety, Robert advised her to adopt his fatalistic attitude, saying, "I try not to think so much about it, for 'twill do no good. . . . I generally try each day to do my duty and leave the rest to Him who rules on high."[85]

Although many Confederates believed that God's will ultimately determined the course of their lives, they also believed in the power of prayer to protect loved ones and shape the outcome of some events. Confederates' fervent belief that God heard and responded to their entreaties eased their concerns for absent family and friends, thereby helping bolster their morale and allowing them to perpetuate the fight. Because distance limited the protection and assistance that soldiers and civilians were directly able to provide for one another, they often appealed to a higher power to do so in their stead. Robert asked God to do just this when he wrote, "May you all be blessed with good health and have the kind protection of Providence."[86] Confederates also prayed for their own personal protection and were quick to ascribe their safety to divine intervention. Robert described a fairly common sentiment among devout soldiers when he wrote: "I am thankful to almighty God that . . . He has protected me. Different times in within [sic] the past few days, while confronting the foe on the field of battle, it seemed as if He was directing the balls [on] either side of me. And none has, so far as I know, touched my clothes."[87] Believing as they did in the Christian superiority of the Confederacy, it should come as no surprise that Southerners also prayed for their nation. Confederates not only asked God to grant them battlefield triumphs but also remembered to offer thanks when they achieved victory. "We should be more than thankful to almighty God that, through His kind favor, our troops have been able to drive the invader from the front of our capitol," Robert reported after Confederates pushed Union forces away from Richmond in July 1862.[88]

Southerners further cultivated God's favor and strengthened their morale by attending religious gatherings. Revivals proliferated among Confederate soldiers, especially late in the war when suffering and carnage reached devastating proportions.[89] However, Robert never so much as mentioned one, although it is unclear if this was because he was disinterested in attending or because his company never experienced one. In any case, he practiced his faith in a variety of other ways. Just days after enlisting, he informed Rebecca that he and his messmates were the only ones that had "a [Bible] chapter read and prayer every night before retiring."[90] He also reported the arrival of Chaplain Bowls, whose presence allowed them to properly observe Sundays with sermons and prayer meetings.[91] Robert attended church whenever he could, even attending different denominations; after his first Quaker service, he praised the "excellent sermons" that were delivered by "two Quaker ladies" but found their manner of worship "quite strange" overall.[92] Correspondence with his family, particularly his pious mother, also allowed him to discuss and express his religious beliefs. Many soldiers used these same avenues of religious expression to reinforce their faith. Robert found them so enjoyable that he was "surprised" to learn Rebecca "had been to church but twice since I left; I expected you had been frequently."[93] Religious expression provided comfort and support; because of the close association of Christianity and the Confederacy in the minds of many Southerners, those contributions ultimately strengthened Southerners' commitment to the Confederacy and the war.

Many Confederates feared that religion would not be enough to protect soldiers from the sinful aspects of the military. Rebecca apparently wrote "of many people being afraid their husbands or brothers would be led astray" once removed from the moral influence of their families.[94] The monotony of camp life encouraged every conceivable vice, from playing cards to drinking to consorting with prostitutes.[95] Not only were such behaviors sinful, but they could potentially harm those back home. Speaking of a Bedford soldier who had taken to drinking and gambling, Robert feared it would be "almost enough to kill his wife to know how he is going on."[96]

Resisting such temptations was especially important for Confederate soldiers because their moral purity would determine the outcome of the war and the fate of the Confederacy. If God had ordained the Confederacy to win, they had to denunciate sinful behavior and prove themselves worthy of His trust.[97] Feeling thus, Robert's mother wrote, "I fear sin on the part of our Confederacy more than the sword."[98] She and many other Confederates attributed Confederate military failures to God's displeasure at their unabated wickedness: "I feel that this great calamity is permitted to be on account of the great disobedience, ungratefulness, [and] unthankfulness of us as a nation. And if we are engaged as we should be in the right kind of a spirit—call on God clothed as it were in sack cloth and ashes—He is able to avert this great calamity . . . when we are sufficiently humbled."[99] These biblical allusions to repentance were widely echoed by Confederates later in the war, when numerous military defeats caused many Confederates to ponder possible sins for which God was punishing them—even the institution of slavery, the very foundation of their Southern identity.[100]

It was not sin that shook Confederate faith and morale to their very core but the ever-present fear and reality of death. Just one year into the war Robert soberly reflected, "It seems strange but nevertheless true that most of the boys from our neighborhood have either been killed, wounded, or have died of sickness."[101] Losing so many men not only decimated the ranks and weakened some soldiers' resolve but also wounded the heart and soul of each intimate community to which the men of those companies had belonged to since boyhood. The toll that battlefield losses and homefront destitution had taken on Robert's morale was apparent by 1863, when he told Rebecca that he "would be perfectly willing" to hire a substitute for twenty-five hundred dollars or "even more if I could get out of this war, even if it didn't last six months longer."[102] The harsh reality of war had set in. Gone were the days when brash, untried Confederate soldiers were "for going to see the Yankee as soon as possible."[103] They were no longer the "tigers and lions" who had "completely overturned . . . old Abe's intentions."[104] As hardened combat veterans, they expressed relief at avoiding skirmishes and hoped it would be "some time now" before they were forced to fight again in "this unholy war."[105] The names of the killed and wounded, once so carefully recorded for the benefit of anxious loved ones back home, had become "too tedious to mention."[106] Soldiers' morale suffered under the strain of prolonged combat, exhausting marches, sleep deprivation, poor or inadequate food and water, lack of shelter, exposure to the elements, the torments of insects, diseases, injuries, and death.[107] Like most Confederates, Robert acknowledged that Confederate soldiers "have stood up to the struggle beyond all expectation" but desperately hoped "we may finally be successful, for I think this is the last struggle."[108]

Young Confederate soldiers may have grown desensitized to the ravages of war and occasionally grew frustrated with unfaithful civilians, but they did not question the existence of God, the virtue of the cause, or whether the Confederacy would be successful.[109] The hardships and destruction of war certainly threatened their morale, but factors such as correspondence and religion were sufficient to sustain their morale and their commitment to the war. Like many Confederate soldiers, Robert occasionally slipped into melancholy introspection, but he remained predominantly optimistic and encouraging. "I am well as common and getting on finely," he assured Rebecca in mid-March 1865. "Have not had to stay out of doors . . . a night since I left home, and have met with the greatest kindness every where."[110] Indeed, his words and actions indicate that, despite dismal military failures and ever-increasing privations, Robert remained staunchly committed to the Confederacy. Although he apparently returned home on a furlough in late 1864 or early 1865, he promptly returned to his command and intended to "join the [Lynchburg] city battalion or local forces of this place" if he could not locate his company.[111] "Many that won't fight now ain't worthy [of] the name of a man," he passionately confided to Rebecca.[112]

Like many Confederate soldiers, Robert relied heavily upon interpersonal relationships and religious faith to uphold his morale and loyalty. Christianity not only helped sustain their commitment and justify the war but also mitigated their fears of making the ultimate sacrifice for their country. Christian soldiers could boldly and confidently face the enemy because their eternal destinies were secure and their most important battle already won.[113] Robert frequently signed his letters, "Yours until death" and told Rebecca that if he died in battle and they did not see each other again, "let us try and prepare to meet in heaven."[114] On one level he was encouraging them both to live as true Christians so that they could reunite in the afterlife. On another level he was expressing his willingness to make great sacrifices, even unto his very life, if it ultimately benefited the Confederacy. He was prepared to do so because he did not believe death entailed an eternal separation from his friends and family; rather, bodily death was merely the entry of the soul into a better world, where it would dwell in peace and happiness with loved ones for eternity.[115]

When Robert's furlough ended in early 1865 and he departed Bedford to return to the military, he did not know it would be the last time he saw the family and home he was fighting to protect. After locating his regiment and his horse near Mechanicsville, he and the mounted portion of the Second Virginia Cavalry, under the command of Col. Thomas Munford, rode steadily south and west. In the early morning hours of April 9, they arrived near Appomattox Court House.[116] They attacked and routed Union cavalry from the road that led north to Oakville—the only remaining route for the Army of Northern Virginia to escape the enemy's tightening snare. They rode southwest, through fog, fields, and forests, eventually encountering Col. Samuel B. M. Young's Union brigade near the road west to Lynchburg and Bedford. Fighting in the woods just a few dozen years behind a house, Robert was shot and killed.[117] Moments later, Confederates learned from the bearer of a white flag that Gen. Robert E. Lee had surrendered his army.[118] Robert may have been the last man killed in action in the Army of Northern Virginia.

Several differing versions of the story of Robert's death merely emphasize the unique ability of letters to communicate the true way any individual experienced the Civil War. He had not, as one soldier in another company recalled, returned to the front lines just five minutes before, having gotten married while on a furlough home.[119] Nor did "officers and men of both lines" meet and bury him "just as news of Lee's surrender came."[120] It is not known who buried Robert in the woods behind the modest two-story home belonging to widow Elizabeth Robertson. The grave was not marked, and during the year that followed, the soldier's name was forgotten. One year later, the Ladies Memorial Association in Appomattox organized and funded the reinterment of "Confederate soldiers killed or deceased" in their area. The anonymous soldier behind the Widow Robertson's house was buried along with seventeen other Confederates on December 1, 1866, on a green windswept hill just west of Appomattox Court House.[121] The tombstone placed over his grave—the sixth from the left, as one faces east—reads, "C.S.A.: Unknown."

Rebecca was two months pregnant at the time of Robert's death. They had probably conceived when he was home on his final furlough; neither of them knew she was pregnant. Nothing documents who told Rebecca of Robert's death, and she never learned what became of her husband's body. One of her relatives remarked that her"soul seemed centered in her dear Robert, who was worthy of her love,"and this may have been true: She died on January 5, 1867, a little more than a year after giving birth to their daughter, Fannie Rebecca.[122]

Thousands of Southerners believed in the dream of an independent nation too fervently to recognize the truth of their reality, even after the fall of Richmond and Lee's surrender. They believed God was merely chastising them, testing their faith before delivering a glorious triumph when they were humbled.[123] Shortly after Robert's death, Rebecca's relative hoped the Parker children would"long live to enjoy the freedom and independence their father fought and bled and died for."[124] Her distress, confusion, and dogged trust in the Confederacy were all evident when she wrote in another letter,"What is to become of us, we know not; [w]e can do nothing but stand still and see the Salvation of the Lord."[125] Statements such as these prove that Confederates were not a disillusioned, demoralized mass, as so many historians have claimed. Such assertions overlook or ignore the voices of devoted Southerners such as the Parkers and the sacrificial actions made by soldiers such as Robert, voices and actions that prove that many Confederate soldiers and civilians continued to fervently believe that the war was sacred, just, and winnable. Such voices also emphasize the vital role of correspondence, communities, and religion in sustaining Confederate morale and nationalism throughout the war, and even beyond.

The letters of soldiers such as Robert Parker serve as important reminders of the human aspect of the oftentimes-overwhelming story of the Civil War. Too often the war is portrayed through the names of famous generals, massive troop movements, a nameless mass of restless civilians, and momentous clashes on the battlefield. But the true story of the war was played out on a stage far smaller and more modest, but just as crucial. It was in a mother praying for her absent son, a wife sewing shirts for a husband who may be dead, and a shivering soldier finding warmth in memories of home. These intimate, compelling moments reveal how soldiers and civilians truly experienced the war on a daily basis. Only the intimate, communal nature of correspondence could allow these personal stories to be told.

METHODOLOGY

The letters of Robert W. Parker exemplify the problems and promises of Civil War soldiers' letters. As noted historian Bell Irvin Wiley observed, the larger part of these letters were badly written from every standpoint of external form. Because of their prevalence, unique insights, and rich detail, however, these humble letters deserve attention.[1]

The Parker collection consists of approximately 350 documents. Most of these are letters written from Robert W. Parker to his wife, Rebecca L. Parker, from 1861 to 1865. The remaining documents consist of letters written by Robert Parker to other members of his family, or to Robert Parker by family and friends, as well as a few miscellaneous documents. Letters not written by Robert Parker can be found in the appendix; for the sake of clarity, the author and recipient's names are given in brackets at the beginning of each letter in the appendix.

Every attempt has been made to present these letters in an accurate and historically useful manner. When letters were undated, their sequential placement was determined by their content and context. Editorial comments are placed within brackets. This includes estimations of illegible text, ellipses where there are missing or illegible sections of a letter, and explanations for large gaps in the letter sequence. Spelling and punctuation were standardized to simplify readability. Every word of every letter was transcribed, except when a letter or portions of a letter were illegible, deteriorated beyond readability, or missing.

The Parker letters were owned by his descendents until donated to the Southern Historical Collection in the Wilson Library at the University of North Carolina at Chapel Hill in 2006. The letters were transcribed by Emily Schweninger, and I began editing the letters as my graduate assistantship project for the 2005–6 academic year at the University of North Carolina at Greensboro.

1861

Robert W. Parker enlisted in Capt. James Wilson's company of Mounted Rangers, Bedford Southside Dragoons, Thirtieth Regiment Virginia Volunteers, on May 28, 1861, for one year's service under Col. Richard C. W. Radford. They were among the first mounted units to defend Bull Run, and they fought in the First Battle of Manassas. They were transferred under the command of Brig. Gen. J. E. B. Stuart in the autumn of 1861. They engaged with and defeated Union cavalry in a series of engagements between early August and year's end.[1]

May the 29, '61
Dear Wife,[2]

I am glad to inform you that I am well as common with the exception of my ear, which has improved very much, and soreness from my trip. We arrived in camp[3] yesterday near 4 o'clock, all our company are on foot. I was appointed officer of the guard[4] yesterday evening and also this morning. They keep me busy. We do not expect to [be] marched into service till tomorrow. Our horses look mighty badly. I regret I had not bought a finer horse, for they take the day.

May the 30 even. We are not mustered into service yet but expect to be this evening. The Arkansas regiment left here yesterday for Richmond. Soldiers are coming in and leaving every day. Several of our men are sick, Alick[5] very much complaining but on foot. The officers have a house to stay in. Our provisions from home are not out yet. Duty calls me. I must close though I am not half done. Nothing more very interesting.

My best love to you and all. Write soon. Direct your letter to the care of Captain Wilson[6] BSSD.[7]

From your devoted husband.

Presentation Flag of Company F, Second Virginia Cavalry. Courtesy of the Bedford City/County Museum.

June the first

Dear Wife,

Hoping to have the opportunity of sending you a few lines. As I have the chance to write I cannot let it pass. I have no news very interesting. I have rest today for the first day since I've been here from guard duty. I do not stand guard myself but [as] officer of the guard, which is almost as hard. I hope I'll not serve again for several days. We muster four times a day: twice on foot in the morning, on horseback in the even[ing].[8] Nine cavalry comps in our camp, which is Camp Lee. Two of our companies have orders to leave tomorrow, Terry's[9] and [?]. The best news I have is I think I've the best mess in our company, as good as any. They are Goggin,[10] Lipscombs Jim[11] and George,[12] Burroughs Jo,[13] and several others, ten in all. We are the only mess in our company that has prayers so far as I heard. We have a chapter read and prayer every night before retiring.[14] Mr. Bowls[15] a young preacher joined our company, I suppose as chaplain. Several sick in our regiment; two from the Franklin troop have the fever. I wish you, Ma,[16] and Pa[17] and as many of my relations and friend as possible would come down and see us. Some do come in to see us almost every day. I saw your uncle Thomas Joplin and I suppose his wife.[18] All of you come down and see our dress parade. It is worth coming down just to see six hundred of the best looking men and horses that our old mother state can afford. The Fork company got in Thursday, I saw several of them this morning. Booker Robertson brought me those letters.[19] They could not have come in better time, for I wished very much to hear from hear from you all. We get plenty to eat and tolerable good, some as good fat beef as I ever saw, bacon, sugar, coffee, rice, and light bread.[20] Every mess cooks in an iron kettle and frying pan. I never knew what strict orders were till I was mustered in service.[21] Rise at four, feed and water our horses, then drill for an hour, then return and eat breakfast, and soon through the day. You wished to know how I slept. We have plenty of straw to put in our tents. I throw down my oilcloth on the straw, then myself on that, cover with my shawl and blanket, and generally sleep till next morning without waking. As to coming home, I don't know when; perhaps I may come in a few days or a few weeks. I like the camp life equally as well as I expected. Alick and I stayed together when we first got here, but now I am head of a mess and he stays with the officers.[22] I think the camp life does not agree with Alick much but we will soon get use to it.

3 June. This leaves me on foot. Several of our men are sick but not dangerous. I think we will soon get use to it.[23] Two of our companies left this morning for Culpeper Court House. We do not know how long [. . .]

Morning, June the Seventh
Dear Wife,

As Jimmie expects to go up this morning, I must drop you a few lines. I am tolerable well this morning and had a fine night's sleep. I did intend writing to you by Alick,[24] but as I was on duty, he was gone before I knew it. I have no important news. Skirmishes are taking place almost every day on the frontier of VA.[25] A call for us is expected every day but I hope we will not go till we know more about the saber exercise. We commenced that yesterday. We are all in tolerable good spirits, and I hope by the help of God we may meet with success when we have to meet our foes on the field of battle. I wish you all— that is, you and all that are near and dear to me—to remember me when you approach Him who rules on high in your petitions.[26] I wish to see you all very much and still hope I may see you all again before I leave this campground. If you, Pa, Ma, or any of my near relations get sick write to me immediately, as that is part of a good excuse to ask for a furlough, as none can leave with out a good one.

I saw Elias Clemmon yesterday. I heard no complaint from home. He said they were getting on very well and my corn looked well.[27] Mr. Barford, Ginnie, and Jane [. . .] were in camp today. Some of our Bedford friends are in camp almost every day. Soldiers are coming everyday down the train and but few stop; they average near seven hundred per day.

Friday evening. I heard this evening privately that it is believed we will leave in the course of a week. Tommy Phelps arrived here this evening, and

Robert William Parker, Company F, Second Virginia Cavalry, ca. 1861. Courtesy of the Bedford City/County Museum.

as Jimmy left while I was on parade, I'll send this letter by Tommy in the morning.

Saturday morning. Nothing has occurred of importance since yesterday. I was rather unwell this morning but hope to be better in a few hours. I wish if you have the chance you would send me that bed tick. If you can't, I can have one made at short notice. I received ten dollars of the county contribution and sent it up to you by Uncle T. C. Goggin,[28] as I had enough for the present. Tell Missouri Pullen I will answer her letter in a few days. Tell Ma I'll try and answer her letter soon. If you have the chance, send me any little thing you think I'll need. I must close.

Tell all to write to me.

From your devoted husband

R. W. Parker

Sunday evening

Dear Wife,

As Alick is going up home this evening, I must drop you a few lines. I have no news of interest to give you. This leaves me tolerable well. I have improved very much since yesterday. I missed only one drill on account of sickness since I've been here.

I went to church today for the first time since I've been here. It was at Fourth Street Church. We marched in town on horseback, tied our horses, then marched up to church. When the sermon was over, we marched out to our camp. The most of our sick men are getting better. I have no more news that will interest, if what I have written does. I must close, as Alick is waiting. As to begging Colonel to let me come home, it would be of no use, for if he would, Colonel Radford would not. I expect to offer no excuse, for they are considered disgraces unless they are good ones, and they have to be very good ones.

My best love to you and all. I'll try and come home yet to see you before I leave here.

From your devoted husband,
R. W. Parker

June the 19
Dear Beck,

Wednesday morning, before day. I have [just] got up to feed and prepare to start for the Junction. There is considerable stir here to be ready to start at six. The most of our valises gone out, guns packed, and but little to do but strike our tents. I have but little news to give you. We heard here last evening that another little skirmish took place near Alexandria in which there were seven Yankees killed and no southerners. Also that two of Capt. Terry's men were taken near Alexandria by their own imprudence, following the enemy to near their camp.

I send two likenesses, the small one for sister,[29] the other one for you or Ma, taken in my everyday suit. The most of our company are in for going to see the Yankees as soon as possible.[30] I sent Price Writer's gun back by Tommy Phelps. It is said that it will take six or seven day to get there. The trip will be very fatiguing to our horses. I must close, as they are taking down the tent. I expect this will be the last note you'll get from me for the next week.

This leaves me well. Remember me when far away. My love to you and all.

From your devoted husband,
R. W. Parker

Manassas Junction
June the 26, '61
Dear Wife,

As we have stopped to rest and wash up, I must drop you a few lines. We are now camped in Broad Run campground in three miles of the Junction. As I gave you in my last letter some few points of our march up to the 23, I'll now try to extend them up to the 26 June. We started the 23, Sunday morning 7½ o'cl. Our breakfast was given to us—that is, our mess—by Miss Julia Neuman; who could forget such kindness? Arrived at Orange CH 10 o'cl., took dinner at Wentzdale 12½ o'cl., [and] arrived at Culpeper CH 6½ even. There were near four hundred soldiers there with the measles. I hear of none being dangerous. [On the] 24th, started at 7 o'cl., passed Rixlyville 10 o'cl., passed Hayle River 11 o'cl., passed Jeffersonville 11½ o'cl., and took up camp at White Sulpher Springs in Fauquier Co. at 2¾ o'cl. [On the] 25th, started 6½, passed Warrenton, Fauquier CH [11] o'cl., passed New Baltimore [11] o'cl., took dinner, passed Green Village at 2½ o'cl., arrived at this camp near 6 o'cl. yesterday evening. The second squadron left here the day before we got here, Captain Pitzer[31] and Capt. Hale,[32] for some point near Alexandria. We expect to leave here for some place near Alexandria, but know not where.

Something about the country. We've passed through 8 counties to get here: Amherst, Nelson, Albemarle, Madison, Orange, Culpeper, Fauquier, and now in Prince William, the poorest county I've ever seen so far. Albemarle and a portion Orange is as fine land as I ever saw; as for the remaining counties, they looked quite thin. As for the people, they are generally the finest people I ever saw or read of. I had but little idea of meeting with so much kindness, and had but little hope of so much enjoyment in a march of such length. We enjoyed ourselves as well as we could ask, with the exception of the dust, which rose sometimes like a cloud so that you could not see anything for you might see the dust for a mile. Beck, you and many others have laughed and asked me how I could wash and cook. I can tell you this morning was the first time I ever took my clothes to the creek to wash them. I this morning washed a pair of drawers, shirt, two pair gloves, and hanker[chief], and washed them right and can cook so we can eat it. We are drinking and cooking out of the creek.

Wednesday evening. I've just heard from the Junction they expect a fight at any time. There are near twelve thousand soldiers there. The armies are advancing on each other. Our cavalry are in four miles of [them], some seventeen or eighteen miles below the Junction. We have just received our valises and guns from the Junction, much better luck than I was afraid we'd have. Since I commenced this letter this evening, we have had a very hard storm of wind and rain which blew off the fly of our tent. I would like camp life better if the wind didn't blow so hard sometimes. It blew this letter off, got it very wet and dirty; but as paper and time is so scarce I must send it. There is a report in camp that Colonel Radford[33] is or will be promoted to brigadier general. I must close as we are wet and must try to dry some. I believe I have given you the principal news. When you write direct your letters to: Manassas Junction, Care of Colonel Radford. This leaves me and the company generally well and tolerably well satisfied. You and all must write. Write soon, direct your letters as above mentioned. Beck, I should like to have some two or three colored shirts made of calico or something of the kind, if they could be sent to me. But do not pester yourself—all those I have are well yet and tolerable clean.[34] If anything is sent to us, send it to the care of Colonel Radford. I must close as it is near suppertime. My best love to you and all. Tell all my friends and connection to write. May the Lord bless, strengthen, and protect you in these your days of trouble, is my sincere wishes.

R. W. Parker

P.S. I, being misinformed this evening, directed you to direct everything [to] Colonel Radford, which was a mistake. Direct everything you send to the care of Captain Wilson. Let it be understood, Captain Wilson, Manassas Junction.

Clifford Mill
June the 29, 1861
Dear Beck,

As my promise was, so shall I endeavor to fulfill. As to news that will interest you, I have but little. I have a pen and ink in hand for the first time to write a letter since I left Lynchburg. We are still in Broad Run camp, cooking with creek water and getting drinking water out of about [a] half-dozen little springs, which are kept well drained by us. One of the springs is [?] water and has I think the taste of salts. The water generally seems to agree very well with me, but a great many of the soldiers say that it will kill them to drink it long and are very anxious to leave. We are still getting plenty to eat: bacon, flour or cornmeal, coffee, sugar, rice, and our bucket of butter is about to give out that we brought from Lynchburg, made up of a portion of that you brought me. Our mess had plenty of cups and plates when we left Lynchburg, but they are quite scarce now, having three or four cups and that number of plates. We do our cooking in a frying pan and sit or stand on the ground to eat, as we have no seats unless we take rocks.

I must give you an idea of the fences down here. A great portion of them are made of cedar brush and stakes like that one you have seen on Stony Fork. I say now, as I said in my last letter, this is I think the poorest land I ever saw, hardly worth fighting for and would not be if it was not Virginian land. It reminds me very much of the meadows land, as to being level. Its color I can hardly describe, a sort of red purple and after getting a few feet in the ground has a sort of rock bottom of the same color, and so level the earth has to be thrown up to make the railroads. I was down at the Junction day before yesterday, and hardly know how to describe the appearance of things there. It is a very level place with the exception of the breastworks, which are thrown up in almost every direction, some of them with cannon planted and others ready for them to be planted at any time. There are about fifty cannon there, some of the longest lying about there like logs in a new ground. I saw also the flying artillery.[35] One company, each cannon having four horses to it, a saddle on every horse, having two drivers generally, one for when necessary; they could change their fronts almost as quick as infantry or cavalry. All the soldiers have left the Junction except three thousand left to guard it. General Beauregard is there. The most of the soldiers, from what I can learn, are placed near Alexandria. Our pickets are taking in some of the Yankee pickets every few days.

The Franklin and Fincastle Troops killed one Yankee, took 2 prisoners, one fine horse, four six-shooter minie rifles—this is a fact. None of our troops hurt. There were two Yankee prisoners at the Junction yesterday to be forwarded to Richmond.[36] The report reached here yesterday that ten thousand South Carolinians had surrounded 8 thousand Yankees; two tried to make their escape but were taken prisoners. Before I forget it, we received orders from the colonel to send all of our clothes home except a change. I bundled up 1 shirt, 1 pair drawers, bed tick, your [. . .] I get cartridges for them. My bundle was forwarded with several others to Billie Burford, so you must send to him for them. I let Jim Lipscomb have one pair of socks. If I should want any shirts, I'll get colored ones. Or any other clothes. I reckon I can get them down here. If not, I'll let you know to have me some forwarded.

My gun was appraised at twenty dollars. The pair of pistols your Pa[37] let me have were appraised to him at thirty dollars, and as there is such a scarcity of horseman's pistols, no trooper has but one pistol or can draw cartridges for but one. So I had to part with one of them. I let Captain Wilson have the other, with the understanding that if we had no bad luck and returned home, I was to return them. We have received no sabers yet and hardly expect to get any as we are to be scouts or [?] which are the same.

Saturday evening four o'clock. We have just received orders to leave here tomorrow morning at 6 o'cl. for Fairfax Court House 8 miles from the Potomac River. Ready for the fourth of July, from what I can hear, as Maryland has seceded or as it reported.[38] If Congress declares war, Alexandria and Washington City are to be taken immediately, if not sooner. I heard this evening that the Wise Troop[39] from Lynchburg had a skirmish a few days since; had four of their horses killed, none of their men hurt, and took two horses with several side arms.

I have given you all the news I can think of at this time, and as it is getting late I must close. This leaves our company generally well. Whit Johnson[40] is a little complaining. The most of our soldiers seem quite cheerful and anxious to leave. I am well as usual this evening.

I received your letter written the first of June this evening. My love to you and all. Write soon, goodbye. Ever yours devotedly,

R. W. Parker

Manassas Junction
Direct to Manassas Junction
Direct your letters 30th Regiment VA[41]
Care of Capt. Wilson

Camp Radford, Fairfax CH
July the 8, '61
My Dear Beck,

As I have not heard from you since I left you three weeks tomorrow, I now commence the fifth letter to you since I left Lynchburg. I spend the greater portion of my leisure hours in writing to you, for I never knew what it was to want to hear from anybody till now. I never till now knew what it was to be deprived of kind wives, parents, and friends round our firesides at home till now. I do not say this to make you think I have no friends here—far from it, for I believe I've as kind soldierly friends in this camp as any soldier could wish. But you know they can't be like friends at home. I must stop this for fear I trouble you.

We have plenty to eat and tolerable good water. We had Sunday[42] yesterday for the first time since I was mustered into service. All we did Saturday [was] we went through inspection in the morning, had preaching at four in the evening (Mr. Bowles preached), had dress parade, and prayer meeting near six in the evening. I was put on picket Saturday and yesterday night on the little river turnpike with 8 men with me. We took in one Yankee. All he had to say for himself was that he had deserted the northern company and wished to join our army. He was an Irishman, and a rough one at that; he could not give us much news of the northern forces, but said unless there was a move for peace on the part of the South, that old Scott[43] would advance on us in the course of ten days. He also said that he had been a Texas Ranger for the last five years. He was sent on to headquarters. Sandy Wilson[44] and a South Carolinian standing picket took a Yankee the other day; Sandy is entitled to the saddle as a prize. I wrote to you several days ago that two of Captain Pitzer's [men] had been taken prisoners. They took the oath of allegiance to never fight against the United States. They said it was either the oath or starvation; they were put in jail as soon as they got to Washington and had one herring each for supper. They arrived here last night.

There happened a considerable accident just below here. We heard that some of Abe's forces intended advancing, and several hundred of our boys went down to meet them. Our men were stationed, and by mistake, two of our pickets that were sent out to learn something of the enemy, not knowing that there were any pickets before them, fired on them and retreated at full speed—this giving of course the signal to fire. The firing commenced and continued through the whole line of infantry, killing two men. Sad accident. Our boys never knew what it was to play a tune with rifle balls before.

I believe I've given you the general war news so far as I know. You can hear more news that we can hear in camp. Archibald Vance[45] leaves here to day for the hospital at Culpeper Court House, his disease I know not. There are several others sick in our company: Lieut. Johnson, Peter Rucker,[46] and others. Bad news: I think my horse has gone blind in one eye.

Monday evening. Dear Beck, I feel much refreshed, having just dispatched a splendid dinner of rice and sugar for the first time for a week. We had a very hard rain here a few days ago, and from all appearance we'll have another this evening. I should like to hear how the seasons are in old Bedford, also the crops. Corn looks badly here, about eighteen inches high. There are a great many farms vacated round here by the Yankees; some have gone to Washington, some to Alexandria. I would not be surprised to hear the alarm, "To arms, to arms!" at any time. I've spent several nights with my cartridge box and belt round me, my saber and gun under my head, and everything ready to start at a moment's warning. For all this I sleep sound and a slight alarm will wake me. I must close and prepare for duty. I expect to go out this evening on picket duty. I learnt yesterday that Lieut. T. H. Vance has resigned his commission, and if the governor recognizes it [he will] return home soon. No more at present [. . .]

I hope we have all the flies down here and that you may not be pestered with them. For if you have any there, [it] is certainly more this year than ever was before. If you want to see lazy men, come to camp. This leaves me well as common. Write soon. My love to you and all.

From your ever devoted husband,
R. W. Parker

Stephen Goggin [blotted] this.

Direct your letters to Manassas Junction, care of Capt. J. Wilson, 30th Regiment VA Volunteers.

Tell Alick our company has the mustache worse than any company he ever saw.

Tell George[47] if I had the chance he has to write, I would write to him if I never got an answer. This is the place to try friends; if one has true friends, they will not forget him as soon as he is gone. I would write to my friend if I had the chance, [even] if they never answered them. Farewell Beck.

Fairfax CH
July the 14, '61
Dear Beck,

I must write to you again, as I have the opportunity of doing so, though I do not know whether it is worth while or not, as this is the sixth or seventh letter to you and one to Ma since I left you, and I know not whether you have ever received one of them or not. I haven't received a letter from you, Ma, or any friend since I left Bedford, and unless you get mine and I get some of those written to me, if any there be, I had better stop writing or it is a waste [of] time and paper. Beck, it would afford me the greatest pleasure just to know that you get my letters, and I would try to write to you every week, but as it is I know not what to do. I was much relieved yesterday evening to learn that you was at church last first Sunday, through a letter Mr. Phelps received from his wife. This is the first I've heard from you since I left. Coly Adams[48] received a letter yesterday from Jimmie and I suppose if any of you was sick he would have told me.

I have no news to interest you, as there is nothing of interest occurring. There is a good deal of sickness in our company. We have sent three to the hospital at Culpeper Court House: Arch Vance, John E. Jones,[49] and Peter Rucker. Rucker was very low with the typhoid fever when he left here. Several of us here are too unwell for duty. Lieut. Johnson has been very unwell for some time; George and Jimmie Lipscomb and I have been unwell for the last two days with something like the flux, which weakened me very much. I hope I'll be ready for duty by tomorrow. Our camp is badly situated for such weather as we have had for the last week, as it's rather low and we have had any quantity of rain and mud. The fare for our horses is rather rough; nearly enough grain and but little hay, and plenty [of] mud to stand in.[50] As to the war news, you hear more than we do. We hear but little that happens out of camp. This and several adjoining counties have been drafted and have commenced mustering. It is their property we are protecting and of course they aught to help protect it, though there are numbers of men who have property here and have left it and gone to Yankee-dom. Some have quantities of hay and will not stay at home and cut it, for fear our soldiers would get it.

I was out on picket last Friday and got a dinner that reminded of summer time and vegetables at home. We had bacon and snaps, roast chicken, milk and butter, light bread, and good warm corn bread this dinner. We have very good friends down here but they are not numerous; there might be more if they were not afraid of the Yankees. News reached camp this morning that four Mississippians were taken prisoners. We have not had the chance to overhaul any Yankees lately. They are like wild turkey to inhabit pine thickets. As to getting shot, I fear more danger from our men. Their guns go off frequently here in camp. One of our near rank men's gun went off the other day[. . . .] No one shot as it happened. I heard from Captain Hale's company at Leesburg. He with some of his men went over to the Potomac and captured a packet boat with something considerable. Whether this be true or not I can't say.

We get word every few days that the Yankees intend to advance on us, but I have not seen them yet.[51] No more news at present. Write soon. My love to you and all.

From your ever-devoted husband,
R. W. Parker

Direct your letters to Manassas Junction on Prince William Co., care of Capt. James Wilson, Colonel Radford's regiment.

[. . .] that there near 30 of men company down with measles.

Coly Adams sends his best respects to you all and Bet. He looks tolerable well and well satisfied.

Fairfax Station

July the 16, '61

Dear Father and Mother,

As our company has moved to Fairfax Station, I must try to give you the news. Our company came here yesterday. This is a station on the Orange and Alexandria Railroad, some fourteen miles this side [of] Alexandria, as far down as our cars run. This [is] only about three miles from the Court House. We are much more agreeably situated than at the Court House. We are camped in a beautiful grove about 100 and fifty of the railroad and have splendid water. We are here for a few days under the command of General Ewell,[52] an infantry general. Twenty of our company were detailed to Colonel [Roades] soon after they got here. This camp is only two or three miles from here. So our company is divided, only I suppose for a few days. While I think of it, the news has reached here from Bedford that our company has happened to very bad luck: some shot, Whit Johnson's horse shot from under him. All these reports are false. The first one was not hurt up to yesterday evening. Also, that several of [Minter's] comp. had been killed. I think this false but several are sick; some 8 or 9 are at the hospital [at] Culpeper CH. Several of our company are complaining, two or three too unwell for duty. Among the rest, I am very unwell, have been so for some few days with something like the diarrhea. Although sick, I was on camp duty last night. I am too unwell to go on picket. This evening I feel very weak and feeble, but hope I'll be well soon. I've seen nothing too hard for me yet, if I can only have health. I fear bad health more than the Yankees. I have wished frequently for some good cornbread from home. We have plenty flour and sea bread, but cornbread suits me best.

I wrote in my last letter that three of [the] company were at the hospital: Rucker, Jones, and Vance. Vance returned here this morning on his way home. The doctor advised him to return home. He says he does not want to return, but as the doctor thinks he had better, he will do [so]. The doctor done nothing for him. I understand the doc says there is no chance for him; so do I, he has the dropsy. Vance states that there are some nine hundred or a thousand sick at the Court House. Death occurs frequently. Most from measles and whooping cough.

As to the war news, you get more now than we do. I got hold of a late paper this morning for the first since I left Lynchburg; paid only one dime for it. Some few little skirmishes are taking place every few days. Four Yankees were near our pickets last evening. Our pickets fired on them in the thicket as they made their retreat, supposing to have killed the rear man, as he was heard to halt at the crack of the guns, and when they passed out of the thicket only three was seen. The Yankees down here remind me very much of wild turkeys slipping through the thickets. I learn they are making their boasts how easy they can make us retreat to the Junction and hardly expect us to do any thing there. Our pickets went down to day to the stations of the Yankee pickets but saw none.

A little change of subject. I have not heard a word from Goose Creek[53] since I left you. I should be very glad to hear how my crop is getting on and whether they have enjoyed health since I left. I have not heard whether the bundle I sent home has ever reached there yet or not, nor whether any of my letters have ever reached you. I directed them to Liberty; they ought to get there in twenty-four hours. Some of our company have received letters in a day from Liberty. Some get letters almost every day, and why I can't get a word from home is strange, something I can't account for. This is, if I mistake not, the ninth letter to you and Beck since I left you four weeks today. It does seem to me my health would improve some if I could hear from you all. Direct your next letter to R. W. Parker, care of Capt. James Wilson, Colonel Radford's regiment, Manassas.

Before I forget, received Beck's letter of July the 9 yesterday, the 18—all I've received—which relieved me very much. I never received a letter that did me more good. That one by Daniel Robertson I've never received.

July the 20, '61, evening. Union Mills. I'll attempt to give you some of our news since the morning of the seventeenth. On the morning of the seventeenth, I left camp early to water my horse some distance from camp. Just before I reached camp, I received the alarm, "To haste!" in camp. The Yankees were approaching. With all haste, we struck our tents and packed for retreat. Our company was called together as soon as possible, wagons loaded and started for the Junction. We there mounted and prepared for action. Prayer was offered by one of our squadron for our heavenly Father's protection. By this time our pickets came in, bringing the news that the Yankees were advancing in great numbers, one column up by the station, the other by the Court House, numbering from 30,000 to 50,000—this the report. Our forces received orders from General Beauregard to retreat, which was obeyed immediately at both points, Station and Court House. Only a few of one of our regiments fired on the enemy, killing eighteen, the number wounded not known. The loss on our side: two wounded, one flesh wound in the leg, the other a part of his ear cut off by a ball. All our forces retreated; all from the station, up the station road toward the pines, those from the Court House, up the turnpike toward the Junction. Our squadron took the rear of the infantry from the station. Never before did I see such a day, the poor infantry wore down with their guns and knapsacks. It being so warm, many threw away their knapsacks, overcoats, and almost anything they had. A good many just out of the measles, almost too weak to travel; one or two poor fellows, I heard, died on the road. It is thought one or two thousand dollars worth of one thing or other was thrown away. Our division retreated to Union Mills on the east side of Bull Run. As we retreated, a good many ladies left their homes and marched in advance of us. No one could tell the feeling some of us had to see some of the ladies in so much distress. We stopped in an oat field and let our horses eat the oats, not getting off our horse. We stayed on the east side of the run till next morning about sunup, lying out that night in a clover field on hay. Had nothing to eat but a few crackers and but little meat, which we were glad to get, our wagons having on our baggage and several miles in advance. Early the morning of the 18, we crossed the run and came to where we are now, in the woods this side the run. Some of the soldiers gone without eating twenty-four hours at once. We took several prisoners during the 17 day. I must tell you how the Yankees did when they took possession our breast works at the Court House. As it happened, four of our troopers and a corporal were on picket between the two roads. The Yankees came up and didn't know of their advance till they had taken possession of the town.[54] They then made their escape through the farms, the Yankees being at one time in two hundred yards of them, but so overjoyed they never noticed them. Our troops said of the whooping, halloring, and waving swords they never heard, and dancing on top the breast works they had taken possession, and made the rebels run without fighting.

The 18. Memorable day. The Yankees pursued us and came in sight on the morning of the 18th on the opposite side of the run, but didn't attack us. Their number was not known [although] their advance pickets came it sight, or suppose to be. We are here on the opposite side to whip them, many or few, God being our helper. The column that advanced up the other road, twenty thousand strong, attacked our little band of heroes at a ford on Bull Run[55] two miles and a half above here. Our force amounted to three regiments about three thousand strong. Our heroes repulsed them three times. The fight commenced near seven o'clock. Our artillery soon made them retreat. They rallied and gone again. They soon found too much hot balls meeting them. The third time, they returned with double resolution, if possible, to roust our little band and attempted to cross the creek, in short range of our cannon and rifle, and they swept them as they came until they were obliged to give back the third time. Our boys mounted the breast works, and with their bayonets slew them rank and file, some of them having three or four holes through them by the bayonets. A singular occurrence happened. It is said while our men were killing them with the bayonets, two seized each other's guns from [their fist to kill] and another ran up and killed the Yankee. Our loss was twelve killed and a good many wounded.

The Yankees' loss is not exactly known, believed to be from 900 to fifteen [hundred], took several prisoners. One that was taken saw that when he fell it seemed that the whole column fell. One rifled cannon and reported 500 stands of arms. During the cannonading, a ball passed through the house where General Beauregard[56] was eating dinner, it is said. The general says he never heard or read of such a battle. Three thousand whipping 20,000 around and at the [Manassas] Junction. I believe [it] will be the great battle to decide either for or against us. But God being our helper, I don't think we can be whipped. Thousands of us may fall but still I think we will prevail. Beck wished to know whether [I've] seen any Yankees or not. I've seen some, but not in shooting distance except prisoners. [I] have been in no fight. I saw fifty-seven Yankees prisoners yesterday, the fight of the 18. No cavalry were called in.

We are hourly expecting old Abe's boys over to see us. I have heard the cannons firing since I've been writing this letter, above here on the run. I've learnt the Yankees intend to attack us at the same place again. I have written this so scattering I fear it will weary you to read it. Look it over and give it to Beck. Tell her to keep them that I may see them when I come home, if it should fall to my lot to do so. And if I do not, I wish to sell my life as dearly as possible.

I've been unwell for several days but think I am improving. We have to lay out in the open air as we have no tents down here, for fear Abe's boys might get them. Write soon. Tell all to write to me. I've never received but one letter from any of you. That was from Beck, dated July 11th.

From [your] devoted son,

R. W. Parker

I send a pair of epaulettes to Beck. Presented to me as I came down by a lady. Beck, you must take care of them to remember me. Farewell beloved wife.

From your devoted husband

R. W. Parker

Union Mills
July the 22, '61
My Dear Beck,

As Uncle Johnson is here and expects to return in the morning, I must give you some of the points, but hardly know where to commence. It is now ten o'cl. in the night. I don't have the chance to give you all the points. I wrote a long letter to you and Ma three or four days ago, with a pair of little epaulettes presented to me by a lady as I came down. I gave you the particulars of the battle of the 18 in which the enemy's loss was great. Our loss, as I learn, 11 killed, 14 badly wounded, 16 slightly wounded. I was only in hearing of that battle, 2½ [miles] off. The greatest battle ever fought: 3,000 whipped 20,000.

We had a great battle fought near here yesterday, a little above the other.[57] I was not in the midst [of] this battle either. We were under General Ewell's command here at the mill, expecting an attack at any time, but did not have any. A while after twelve o'cl., General Ewell's command had orders to flank the enemy. We started to do so, and after marching a mile or two received orders to change our course toward where the battle was then going on. Just at this time I was detailed as courier to General Beauregard, who was then leading the left wing. I reached the next hill to the battleground a few minutes before the enemy ceased firing. There was one cannon fired at us as we passed in sight of the enemy; no damage done. Soon after I reached our cannon, I saw thousands of Yankees retreating. Our cannon commenced firing at them, and it did me good to the bottom of my heart to see them retreat at double-quick in the utmost confusion. I sat on Logan right by our artillery while it was firing, and he would hardly throw up his head, and the first time he ever was near the firing. In this retreat, all the cavalry companies near the battleground, except those belonging to General Ewell's command (of which we were a part), made a charge with great effect and losing but few men. Captain Terry's men did honor to themselves. Just as we were leaving for our quarters, they came in with near 80 prisoners and lost two men, I think Whit Fuqua[58] and our Mitchel. We lost Eddy Erving and Captain Radford. We have lost a few men, but God be praised, we completely routed the Yankees, and up to this evening, we learn that the Yankee loss was great. General Johnson[59] pursued them to Fairfax Court House. The dead Yankees are from the battleground to Fairfax CH. We have a secession flag waving out there now, where the Yankees danced and whooped [and] waved their swords on our breastworks at our retreat. But I imagine they know something of a retreat now. Up to this evening, if no mistake, we have near one thousand prisoners, I have just been informed by a friend; he counted 500 marched to the cars for Richmond. We have taken every piece of the artillery they had except two; we have about seventy pieces now in possession, Sherman's[60] brag battery of the North, the best rifle cannon known. Our forces also took 18 baggage wagons, 140 splendid horses, number of arms not known. The battle of General Johnson you spoke of in which our men were so badly cut up is not so, as I have heard that fifteen hundred killed is not so, if I am rightly informed.

I saw General Johnson yesterday; General Jackson[61] was in command also, but I did not find him out. I saw also President Davis.[62] I forgot—there was thirty-one Yankee officers marched into the Junction this morning as prisoners of war. A few more rounds of this sort, God being our helper, we will come out victorious. I must close, as it is going on twelve o'cl.

Direct your letters to Manassas Junction, care of Captain James Wilson, Colonel Radford's Regiment. Beck, we are in good spirits, doing tolerably well, and get plenty to eat, and good water when we get sick. Fair as we get now, we ought not to grumble. Beck, I wish that you and all of my friends could visit the Junction just for curiosity, to see the big cannon breastworks. I don't think one hundred thousand men could take it at once. And the number of soldiers I know not. You wished to know if had been in any fight. I've never fired my gun at one yet. But I hope, if I do have to be in one, to get you a prize of some sort. We would have been in the battle if we had not been joined to Ewell's command. Jo Burroughs sends his love to Bet and says all that grieves him is he broke his bowie knife. Tom Johnson[63] sends his love to you. I wish you could hear from down home and give me the news about my crop.

Beck, if you just knew how my whiskers and mustache looks, you would laugh—they stand in most any direction. If you have the chance to send that package of shirts by private hand, send me some paper and envelopes. I have some yet. This leaves me tolerably well and I hope it may reach you enjoying good health and enjoying yourself finely. May God bless and protect you, is my great wish.

Mr. Phelps is getting on very well. Tell all to write to me. You all will know where to direct you letters to now. [. . .]

From your devoted husband,
R. W. Parker

Tilghman Scott[64] has your pa's gun. I think it was valued at $18.

Union Mills
July the 25, '61
Dear Beck,

As Ike Cundiff[65] expects to leave here in the morning for Bedford, I must try and give you some more of the points. I hardly know where to commence. In the first and foremost place, I am tolerably well and have had quite an easy time since the great battle on Sunday last. All of our company that are here are tolerably well.

Three more of our company left today for Culpeper hospital: George Lipscomb, Hen Bond with the measles, [and] Mr. Phelps with deep cold and something like neuralgia (some of the boys say homesick, too). I don't know about that. No doubt he would like to see home, as [a] good many of us would no doubt. I feel very much relieved since I've received two letters from you and you are getting on so well. I have your last letter yet and expect to keep it to read till I receive another from you. Do not be afraid of my losing it. It makes me think of the happy hours we've spent together, and hope the time is not far distant when we will spend some more of the same sort.

Something of the battle. I sincerely wish it was in my power to give you the true statement of the battle. One thing is certain: we won the greatest ever won on the American continent, in the way of arms, July the 26. We are not done gathering up arms and prisoners yet, some say twenty-five thousand stands of arms. I think this is handy. Where the Yankees crossed Bull Run, the guns are very thick—thrown in to get us from getting them. The number [of] cartridges is hundreds of thousands. A great many boxes were thrown in the well to destroy them. I saw great piles of wet cartridges, all ruined but the lead. We are not done yet hauling guns from Fairfax Court House. I expect there are 5,000 knapsacks at the Court House. I never expected to see such a sight—the knapsacks are new ones, never used. It is said we have every piece of their cannon except one—a two-pounder belonging to a private man. All their very best. Their baggage and baggage wagons with out quantity or quality, and hundreds of horses—some say twelve hundred, I think not more than half the number. We have taken, without a doubt, 2,000 prisoners and [are] still catching them. It is said a good many got drowned trying to cross the Potomac. The great Zouave Regiment of [1,700] marched back with 200. We are called by the name of tigers and lions. We took a great quantity of wine and everything of the sort, prepared and fired at Centreville for a feast when we took the Junction. The wine did our soldiers a great deal of good. I have just got half quire of paper and envelopes. We are camped near where we were when [. . .]

Guess at the balance, as Cundiff is leaving. My love to you and all.

R. W. Parker

Jo Burrough sends his love and best respects to all.

Our report is 5,000 killed, 1,500 wounded, the Yankees between five and six thousand killed.

Centreville, Fairfax Co.
July the 31, '61
Dear Wife,

I received yours of the 28 yesterday the 30, and I assure you it has been perused again and again with the greatest pleasure. I have had great luck in the last few days. If not mistaken, I received five letters the 28—1 from you, three from Ma, 1 from Cousin Missouri[66]—and to tell the truth, my health seems to have improved since I heard from you the first time, for I never was more uneasy in my life. And since I received your last I have felt almost like a new creature, I have felt so much relieved about our home affairs to know you are able to go down once and awhile and see how they are getting on.

I was very much pleased to hear our crop and stock looked so well. Was somewhat surprised to hear our number of hogs had been increased, and cats also. I am sorry you had such bad luck gathering seed tick, and hope you may next time gather the berries and leave the ticks. I haven't caught the first tick down here yet. Tell Nannie[67] she must go down with you again soon, but not to catch all the seed tick, for I want to see one, as I am not acquainted with them.

As to clothes, I am doing very well yet. Have no holes in any of my clothes yet that I know of, except the heel of one sock. Have two shirts, two pair drawers, 3 pair socks, 2 pair pants, 2 staple jackets, and about as many clothes as I can take care of yet. I reckon you had better wait till I wear out some of these I have on hand before sending them. Make me two pair of drawers and have them ready. I could get some Yankee clothes, but I don't think a Yankee suit would fit. I must tell you what happened to me a few days since. I went down to the creek to wash, and while my damp clothes were drying I concluded to wash the others and did so, getting considerably sunburnt. That wash made me think of the old revolution. As to what clothes I ought to have, you can [be judge] of that. I am very glad indeed to hear your health is improving and that there is some chance of having a big fat wife.[68] And I assure you there will be no time spared on my part in trying to come home and see you. There is no danger of you getting so large I won't know you. As to your knowing me, just imagine, when you hear I am coming, of seeing one of the ugliest men in Bedford and you won't be disappointed much, for I am getting to be a sight.

It is somewhat distressing times in our company now. Our good old Captain with twelve or fifteen of our men, are too sick to perform duty. The Captain is down on Bull Run, very sick; I am afraid he may not recover soon. Waddy Burton,[69] John and George Lipscomb, Alfred Creasy[70] with measles. Payne,[71] Bond, Zimmerman, Phelps have left for the hospital. Leftwich,[72] 2 Johnsons, or 2 or 3 others haven't left yet. Beck, tell George from me not to join any company unless his health has improved greatly, for I am sure he can't stand the soldier's life unless he's greatly improved. The exposure we undergo, fatigue, and food would soon fix him. I see but little of so many volunteers now anyway, though it may be for the best. Our men have whipped five to one, so far from what I understand. Our heavenly Father be praised for such a glorious victory.

The 31st, evening. I've just received a letter from Ma of the 26th, in which I was sorry to learn George had joined a volunteer comp[any]. I think he had better waited a while, though every man has to stand for himself. I forgot to inform you about that gun. Scott has it and I think it was appraised at $18 dollars. As to the war news, we have nothing of late interest. I rejoice that I can inform you our loss is nothing like what it was first thought to be. Not much over five hundred killed and wounded, in the last news we received. Still catching a few pickets. Nothing like done hauling in the plunder yet, carrying loads of guns yet. The last news, we had taken twenty thousand stands of arms. We have soldiers guarding Yankee property at different points. There is no doubt they were completely routed. They say we took their cannon and turned them on them, and they were obliged to retreat. The soldiers continue to come down. There will be another great move, some think. Old Abe's intentions have been completely overturned, and he wishes Jeff Davis give him sixty days, but I learn Jeff has given him ten days to withdraw his forces from VA, which I don't think he will do till they are driven off. They are leaving Alexandria and going to Arlington Heights. If we go there, we'll have a time. But the cavalry won't do much there if it is attacked.

We have quite an easy time since the battle. Every day seems almost like Sunday. We drill sometimes once or twice, sometimes not at all. We have the chance now to pull off our boots and spurs of a night. I have, if no mistake, slept with all my clothes on two weeks at a time without pulling them off more than twice. I have paper and envelopes enough for a while. I happened to very good luck in getting it at the Junction. I haven't had the chance to see Daniel Robertson yet to get any paper. I intend going to see him in a few days. Several of our company were detailed day before yesterday with rations for three days for some purpose unknown to any of our company. They will be due here Aug. the 1st. It is reported the property taken from the Yankees is rated at three million. I wrote you word I had seen the great men: Jeff Davis, Beauregard, [and] Johnson, and Beauregard has the quickest expression of countenance of any man I ever saw. I have given you the most important points in general. As to the battle, some of the papers tell nearly the truth. Some of the northern papers give a better description of the battle than I ever expected to see in the public of the North.

Whit Vance has left for home. May joy go with him and may he spend a pleasant life at home. There was not a tear shed in camp when he left. He can tell of the fairytales some when he reaches home. He had a Yankee musket given him—I know this for I was with him. He has told one or two men that he captured the Yankee and took it from him. He has never taken one or helped to take one. I have never sent in but one Yankee when out on picket. Our company has not taken many prisoners, but we are here, God being our helper, to try our hand with them at any moment. They dread our cavalry I believe more than the infantry. I don't believe that there is any columns of Yankee infantry that will stand a charge of our cavalry.[73] I must close. It is raining very hard indeed, round our tent is in a complete float. I intend answering Ma's letters today if I have the chance. Give my love to your pa, ma, and all the family, and [tell them] that we have a lively time down here in our cloth houses, especially when it rains as the wind blows very hard.

Tell Bet Coly is as tall and dark-skinned as ever. He got a letter from your uncle that the Yankees have him, but he will [. . .] He says the people up in Bedford have heard no Yankee has him yet. Tell Bet I say if anybody's legs saves him it will [be] Adams, for he [. . .] legs as any man.

Tel Bet Jo Burroughs is here, as well as ever. He sends his love and respects to her. He is one of the best messmates I ever saw, he is so accommodating. I shall ever esteem him highly as a friend and soldier.

My love to you, dear Beck. May the Lord guide, govern, protect, and bless you is the prayer of your sincere but unworthy,

Robert

Camp Cable
August the 7, '61
My Dear Beck,

I wrote you a short note two or three days since by our captain, expecting you would have received it before this time. But our capt., when having reached the Junction, learnt that the papers for his furlough and those that were with him were misplaced by some means or other, and I don't know now when he will leave, but in a few days I hope, for I think a trip home would help him very much, though he is now improving some. I am sorry for some of our men, they look so badly; John Lipscomb and Tom Johnson look comparatively like shadows. Several others are in very bad health now in camp. It is very hard indeed now for anybody to get a furlough. It has to go through so many hands and so many have been leaving without the proper authority that there is a guard appointed to search the cars to know who is leaving, so none can leave now without proper authority.

Beck, there was something took place here in camp, something that hasn't taken place before since we were mustered into service. I guess your curiosity is up now. Well, I must tell you we had an excellent sermon last night by the Rev. J. C. [Cranbery]. I assure you it was a quite a treat to us soldiers.

I can never be grateful enough to our heavenly Father for the easy times we have now, blessing us with so many blessings not deserved by us, such good and kind officers, especially our captain and colonel. Colonel Munford[74] is one of the finest men I know. We can have preaching and Sabbath days now, drill only twice a day, have no guards only of a night. Haven't been under Colonel Radford since the battle, and I hope we will not be under him again soon. Have plenty to eat and that is good, and excellent water. We see such a good time I fear it will not last long. As to the war fever, it very quiet with us now. I learn the Yankees are getting rather daring again, have crossed over the Potomac above here and caught some of our pickets. They have also caught a few down near Falls Church just above Alexandria, this is the report. We had an election the other day to fill the vacancy of Lieut. Vance. Billie Graves[75] was elected Lieutenant, and I orderly sergeant.

I understand Uncle Tom Robertson is at Preston's Regiment and I intend sending this note by him, as he is to leave this evening for home. A report has reached here that Mr. Phelps is now at home healing up, come another that he is very unwell. I should like to hear from him, and if he is sick, give him my respects. Tell him we have quite an easy time now and he must get well soon as possible and come back. Our company is getting very small [with] so many sick.

August 8th. Dear Beck, I guess you will think this is the most scattering letter you ever read. I went up to Preston's regiment yesterday, intending to finish it and send it up by Uncle Tom Robertson, but he was gone before I got there, so I'll finish it for the mail. I have nothing to interest you this morning. Jim Robertson is here in camp. He came down with us yesterday evening. He is nearly well enough for duty. One of the Wise Troopers [had] a considerable accident a day or two since. His gun went off by accident and shot off his little toe. We had one of the nicest drill parades last Monday I've ever seen. Near 11 thousand soldiers were out and splendid music. I must close as Sam is nearly ready to start to [the] Junction. Write soon. I've received two letters since the 28th of July. Excuse this scattering letter and bad writing. Write all the news. Write long letters, write about anything and everything.[76] The report, I understand, has reached the [. . .] that our letters are broken open and read. This is not so. Farewell, dear Beck. My love to you and all. From your unworthy husband,

R. W. Parker

I have just learnt the name of this camp.

Fairfax CH
Aug. the 15, '61
My Dear Beck,

I take the present opportunity of answering your very interesting letter, which was received a few days since and was perused with the greatest interest, though I feel but little like writing, having been up all night. I intended writing to you yesterday, but as we had to move I had not the chance. We moved half mile out of the mud, as we have had a great deal rain for the last few days. I must tell you about my night's work. Last night near nine o'cl., after we had fixed dow[n] our beds and I had lain down on mine—and thought to myself I had a better one than usual, having it made down on some good plank to keep me off the damp ground—a detail was sent to our company for six men and a noncommissioned officer with them, and it fell to my lot to go with them. We fixed and started as soon as possible to the Seventeenth Regiment Va., where I received orders for the infantry captains of the pickets stationed on the Little River Turnpike. The pike leads directly from here to Alexandria. We went down to the outside picket station at Annandale, some five miles this side Alexandria, farther down than our pickets stood since the Bull Run battle. I stood there until this morning sunup without lying down, which you know was hard, but what seemed much harder [is that] the night seemed almost as cold as winter. I had to keep striking my feet against the ground to keep at all warm, but such as this is but light on a soldier.

I should like very much to give you something interesting this evening, but 'tis out of my power. This place though much infused by soldiers is much more interesting to me than before the battle of the 2. A great many persons have returned to their homes. The ladies and little children make it seem a great deal more like home. I saw more ladies here last evening than I saw in the two or three weeks before the battle.

As to the news of the war, I have nothing that reliable. I've heard of reports of battles in western Va. and other places, but nothing reliable. I guess you hear more of the particulars than I. The report reached here that a battle took place yesterday or day before a[t] Leesburg, our men gaining a great victory, killing some 5 or 6 hundred, and took near that number prisoners. The report is they came across the Potomac and the swell of the river prevented their escape. As to the truth I know not. I have just learnt this battle is false. Our pickets and the Yankees are in sight of each other every day. They do no damage so far as I learn.

Something as to our company. From what I learn, our captain is sure to resign his office and return home on account of his health. I don't think he mends any at all and is very weak indeed. It will be a source of considerable grief to the company for him to leave, but to prolong his life we will try to give him up. The members of our company in camp are mending except Lil Board.[77] He is quite sick. Tom Bernard[78] is nearly ready for duty.

Aug. the 16, morning. Nothing of interest has occurred up to this time down this way. I have heard something like distant cannonading this morning in a south east direction. We are among advance forces down here and so many of our men being absent, our duty is rather hard sometimes. But that is but a small matter with us if we can have good health.

I guess you think by this time I am quite changeable as to my clothes. The reason I wrote you word to send them by Mr. Phelps was perhaps it was the last good chance you would have soon. As to sending them down by him, I am not particular. My clothes are fair, tolerable good. The pants and draws, have them ready; the shirts use your own pleasure about that. As to the paper, I have just bought a quire of very good fools cap at twenty-five cts. I don't care for you to send me but little as one paper, as I learn it is higher up home than down here, though it was an accident I got it. Send me some envelopes and pens and a hat by Mr. Phelps if you can, as this I have will hardly stay on my head. If you can't send it by him, let me know soon as possible so that I may strike one down here. I must close as I have written nothing interesting nor have nothing to write. Please excuse such scrawl. I had a very good night's sleep on my new bed and feel quite well with the exception of a cold. Our men that are here are in good health and high spirits. Give my love to Mr. Phelps and family. Tell him we are getting on very well. Our three month [. . .] will soon be out and some of us may have the chance then to go home.

Tell Bet Jo is yet alive and one of the strongest living men I ever saw. He has an old white coat he used to wear for a summer one but now he uses it for an apron. He wears it wrong side up hind part foremost, or any way a coat can be worn. He told me something to tell you, but have forgotten it. I must quit and get ready for washing today. I guess Beck you would be much amused to see us washing. We get on very fast but don't wash very nice. My love to you and all.

Farewell from your devoted husband,

R. W. Parker

I pay the postage to all my letter[s] before sending them.

The last letter I received from you was mailed the 11. I received it the 12. It made a quick trip.

Camp Harrison, Fairfax CH
Aug the 18, '61
My Very Dear Beck,

As I learn there is a chance to send you a letter by Uncle T. C. Goggin, I can't let the opportunity pass without dropping you a few lines, though uninteresting they may be. We are looking for him, George Johnson, and old Mr. Lipscomb in our camp at anytime, as they left Manassas yesterday to see us. They went to Camp Cable last night to see the sick, as we left them there till they recovered.

Uncle Tommy and Mr. Johnson have just arrived from the camp of our sick. They say some of them are improving but that Tom Johnson, John Lipscomb, [and] Lil Board are no better and ought to go home. The captain is but little better, and I expect he will leave soon for home. We have but one sick in this camp, Tommy Nichols,[79] he is very much complaining. We have some twenty-eight men fit for service who are getting on fine with the exception of hard duty, though harder on our horses than men.

I with twenty men had a fine trip yesterday, going round with the officer of the day to our outside pickets, which were stationed at Falls Church and Annandale. We went from here to Annandale to our pickets, then down the pike, near a mile and a half below, in sight of the Yankees' picket. We made a kind of charge toward them to see what they would do. We learnt they were supported by several companies of infantry just to their rear, so we stopped some five hundred yds. from them and returned. During the charge they scattered considerably. There was not a shot passed. From Annandale we went across to Falls Church. Here the day before, ours and the Yankee pickets had a sort of skirmish fight over a peach orchard. Our men, I learnt, killed three, having none of our men hurt. They fired several shots yesterday morning from each side but no damage done. I guess the Yankees will soon learn that southerners are as fond of good fruit as they are. Falls Church is some seven miles from Washington City. Our pickets can hear their drum beat for roll call very distinctly, as their camps are only some three miles below, that is, the Yankee camp. If it was not so far to bring roasting ears and peaches, we could fare finely on Yankee corn and peaches, as they are fine down there. A great many of the citizens in the vicinity of Falls Church and Annandale came up with the Yankees on the 21 to enjoy the anticipated victory, and on the retreat of their Yankee brethren they retreated also to Alexandria and Washington City for protection.[80] So a great many of their farms and dwelling houses are left solely to our care. Their houses seemed to be thrown open to the mercy of man and brute, and I assure you our boys take pretty good care of their corn, peaches and honey. I've learnt from the pickets a day or so since [that] a Yankee took a stand of bees near our pickets, and as good luck would have it, the bees stung him. So he had to drop them with his blanket and soon learnt if he didn't leave, and that quick, our boys would sting him. He made his escape but our boys took the honey.

Aug 19th. I've nothing yet to interest you. Our boys have taken possession of the peach orchard they were fighting over a day before yesterday. Our boys gave them another race out of a roasting ear patch yesterday; shot at them but saw none fall. As to the next move of our advance, I know not, but I expect we will move farther toward Yankee-dom soon so as to annoy them as much as possible [and] not to expose us. I've heard of several little battles lately in which reports say we have gained several victories. As to the battle, I know not; we hear hundreds of reports but I pay but little attention to them.

Enough of this. I'll tell you something of our fare. We have splendid living for soldiers: flour, pickles, pork and beef, coffee, sugar, roasting ears, and Irish potatoes by the barrel. Some of the corn fields fare badly down here. In some of them there is but few ears to be found. We fare finely now, with the exception of rainy weather. We have that all the time now, but two or three clear days in the last fourteen and still cloudy. I fear this weather will cause a great deal of sickness in camp, for the land is so flat in many places the water can't run off.

Aug 20th. Nothing new has happened up to this time. Uncle Tommy and Mr. Johnson has been with us for the last two days. Old Mr. Lipscomb hasn't been down to see us yet, he is still staying with John at Camp Cable. We expect him down to see us today. They intend starting for the Junction tomorrow. We have heard Mr. Phelps and Waddy were on their way down here for the last few days but have not seen them yet. None of our men have returned to camp yet but John E. L. Jones. Haven't heard from the others for some time. We begin to think it is time some of them were returning.

I've received no letters since yours of the 12. Jo Burrough received one from Ma a few days since in which was one from Cousin Ann Tate. I've been looking for a letter from Ma for some time, also cousin Missouri Pullen, Uncle John Goggin,[81] and any other relation or friend that thinks proper to write to me. Tell Bet, Lucy[82] and Charley[83] I think they could write one letter between them to me if they would half try.

I must close this scrawl, as I am sure it has pained you to read it. This leaves me well except a little cold, which I hope will leave me soon. My love to you and all.

From your

R. W. Parker

Camp Cable

August the 19, '61

My Dear Beck,

I must answer your kind letters tonight. As I am sergeant of the guard, I have the chance to write till midnight. I received two letters from you yesterday, one mailed the 4th, the other the 6th of this month, and never received letters that interested me more, and thank kind Providence that you are blessed with good health. I wish you—if this reaches you before Mr. Phelps leaves—to send me one quire and a half of paper. Also, one package of $1/3$ envelopes and the price. Those shirts, as to the color, it makes no difference, [just] so they won't be white. The weather is so warm I can hardly keep on any. If you can get me a good hat and send it by Mr. Phelps, do so; as to the color, it makes but little difference, so it is not white. If [you] can do so, let me know in your next letter. If you can't get it and send it by him, I can get me down here as there are some bought in some of the camps. If you make me any drawers or pants, make one pocket in each on the left-inside to hold my pocketbook, as that is the most convenient way of carrying it. Put in the other pockets in the pants.

As to the general news, there is nothing very interesting. The best I have is that Prince Napoleon of France[84] visited Manassas yesterday and had a private interview with Beauregard and Johnson. It is thought he will recognize the southern Confederacy.[85] And on his return to Washington today, our troops at and near Centreville were called out for review, he being out on the field. I saw him at a distance not near enough to describe his features. Our squadron had orders to escort him to Fairfax, but went only a mile or two and returned to camp by some misunderstanding. There were more men together than I ever saw before, with bands of the very best music. There were said to be twelve thousand out besides the bystanders, which were numerous.

The 10 Aug. Nothing new or very interesting this morning, but have a quantity of sickness. We have, I believe, ten sick here now besides those that have left for the hospital and homes. Some of those that are sick: John Garrett,[86] Jim Franklin,[87] Morgan,[88] G. Leftwich, [and] Tom Bernard with the measles, besides those getting well. Tom Bernard has been very sick but is improving some. Gran Leftwich is very low, and unless a change soon, he must die. Lil Board is down with the fever in his tent. Those I mentioned above are in a house. Tom Johnson, John Lipscomb, and the captain are here yet and have given up the hopes getting home soon. I hope they are mending. They can walk the encampment now and stay with us through the day.

We have hardly enough well men now to take care of the sick and the horses. We have received orders to move this morning, but don't know yet whether we will move or not. The captain has sent to the colonel to know if he could not remain here a short time. You wished to know what had become of Arch Vance. He left here a few days since for home with a discharge. No Yankee has him unless they have taken [him] since he left. I am sorry Mr. Phelps has given you all such a horrid opinion of camp life and that he should ever think of having no friends in this company, for I don't think any of our company had such thoughts, much more expressing them. I didn't think I have ever hurt his [feelings] intentionally. Just between you and I, he happened to fall a little under the weather, and some of the boys took delight in teasing him.

Dear Beck, the hard time has come at last on the poor sick boys. I learned this morning that the sick can't get certificates signed at the Junction to go to the hospital. I have just learnt we are to leave today. The sick are to remain here. We are to march for Fairfax CH, a place I don't love much. Skirmishes are taking place on the Potomac every few days. We had 6 men taken prisoners, one killed, and lost 20 horses. The reason this happened [was] an old traitor led the Yankees in and informed them how to take them. Some of our men caught the old traitor and hanged him in sight of the enemy. This is what I heard this morning.

I must close and commence to pack up. I have given you the most of the particulars. Three regiments passed here this morning for Leesburg. There seems to be a move toward Maryland. This leaves me well and I can never be as thankful as I ought for this blessing. Let us remember, dear wife, that all our help comes from God. Let us put our trust in Him, for He can protect and no man can hinder.

From your unworthy husband,
R. W. Parker

My love to you, dear wife. Farewell.
Let nothing I have written make you uneasy. I am doing finely. Robert
Send me a few steel pens.

Camp Harrison, Fairfax CH
Aug. the 29 [1861]
My Dear Beck,

I take my pen in hand to drop you a few lines to inform you that I am well and have just eaten a very hearty dinner of corn, batter cakes, and molasses.

Had also fine Irish potatoes, and yesterday we had some of the best beef steak I ever saw in camp. Such a dinner as we had, with molasses and batter cakes, is good enough for any soldier. We drawed molasses yesterday for the first [time]. We have splendid fresh beef, pickles, pork, sugar, coffee, rice, flour— enough good things for any soldiers. Such things all are brought to camp by the farmers [and] are extremely high: butter 25 cts., chickens 25 cts., eggs 20 to 25 cts. the dozen. I paid, a few minutes ago, 10 cts. for five pears; I guess you will think this high.[89] I've paid as high as ten cts. a garment for washing. Mr. Phelps reached camp a few days since looking very well indeed. He brought me the paper and envelopes, also five or six letters. He has rather been teasing me since he came back, and if he does not mind I'll get to teasing him. On a new string, one or two have rather [cut] at him since he arrived. Some of the boys received a letter not long since and says he wants to get a substitute. If he should succeed in getting one and return home, the boys would be sure to tease him about his great bravery when he left Davis Mills.

Give my best wishes to Clem.[90] Tell her I don't know how the chickens can get on without her to feed them. Tell her she must go down and gather chestnuts and save me some. I was very glad indeed to hear Job[91] and his folks came up and that they are getting on so well, and sorry to hear they are so lonesome. Beck, you must write Jake a letter for me. Give him all the points as nigh as you can: that I am well and doing well, [that] we have whipped the Yankees, [and] that I am glad to hear he is getting on so well. I hope he will do the best he can. Tell him I hope I can come and see him soon. Give my love to him and Elva. Tell them I would have written to them before this but was afraid the letter would get misplaced. Tell him to do the best he can at home and I will here. I would have written to [Bossy] Newman, but thought it doubtful about his ever getting it. Give my best wishes to him. I don't know when I ever was as glad to hear from any brute as I was Bossy. Sis wrote me word Bossy came up with Job. I received a letter by Mr. Phelps from Ma, Sis, and George. I received a note from Jimmie Walker a few days since. I will answer them soon. Tell Ma I've received several letters from her. I believe I have given you and Alick all the news. Read his and send it to him. Give my love to your ma[92]—tell her I am glad to hear there is such good corn in Bedford—also to your pa and all the children. Tell Bet that Billie Fields[93] says if his name was Bettie W., Coly Adams would write to him. Tell Sarah I think she might write to me sometimes as well as Coly. Tell Bet and Sarah to write to me, also Charley and Lucy. My love to you and all.

From your sincere but unworthy husband,
R. W. Parker

The 28. As to the direction of my letters, it does not make much difference anyway, either place, Fairfax CH or Manassas. Our men have had another fight yesterday. Three of our companies ran in three Yankee regiments some two miles. Their loss was not ascertained; our loss was two killed, 4 wounded, and took 8 prisoners.

Farewell this morning, the 28 Aug., '61.

R. W. Parker

Camp Harrison, Fairfax CH
Sept. the 3, '61
My Dear Wife,

As I have the opportunity and have just dispatched with a splendid dinner of beef steak, bread, and coffee with sugar in it, I feel like writing you a short note, as it has been some time since my last to you. This leaves me enjoying very good health and hope it may reach you enjoying the same. I think I have fleshened up considerably within the last month, and with the addition of my new hat look some better. I have no very good news but plenty of bad. I am sorry to inform you of the death [of] Tom Nichols. He died and was buried the last Sunday. It was his last request to be sent home to old Bedford to be buried, but could not be. He wished to be buried at one of the updikes where his wife and children could see the last of him. Kind Providence spared our company a good while without taking any of its members. He will be greatly missed by his company as a kind and friendly soldier, and we buried him as such in the honors of war.

All of our sick seem to be improving, all able to walk about. We have [had] fine weather for sick soldiers for the last few days. Our good old captain is still with us and I hope he is improving. His resignation has been forwarded to the governor but hasn't been returned to him yet. I guess he will leave soon for home.

As to the progress of the war down this way, I know but little. Our pickets are fighting almost continually day and night; killed four yesterday and six today, I understand, of the enemy. We lost none. I had the pleasure yesterday, with many others, of escorting General Beauregard in sight of Washington and Alexandria. The trip was quite an agreeable one to me. I was in sight of the enemy and their embankments. From all appearances, they seem quite busy throwing them up. They send up a balloon almost every day to take a peek at us.[94]

I received yours of the 25 a few days since and was truly glad to hear you was enjoying such good health, and do sincerely wish the continuance of the same. You wrote of dreaming about me and that we were at home and were so happy. Dear Beck, I have dreamed of you frequently since we parted and that we were at home enjoying our selves. But lo, 'twas but a dream. The moments are few that pass but what I think of you, the last at night and first in the morning, and I try to ask Him who rules over all to spare us, protect and permit us to meet again soon. It seems to me now the greatest pleasure that earth could afford to me would to be with you, if but for a few minutes. And when I am out on duty, it is one of my greatest pleasures to think of you and the happy hours we've spent together.

I was surprised to learn from your letter you had been to church but twice since I left. I expected you had been frequently. You have had a good chance since I left to visit our relations. If you haven't, you must do so; if you don't, they will think hard of you. Visit our relations and the time won't seem so long to you. And perhaps [so] it is the best chance you will ever have, let times be as they may. As to circumstances being as they are, it is nothing more than your relations and friends expect.[95] Go see our relations and enjoy yourself the best you can. Some of our company have been trying to tease me since Mr. Phelps came to camp, but it makes no difference with me, for it is nothing more than I expected.

You write about clothes. I don't know as it makes much difference, so they are good thick ones [. . .] flannel shirts and drawers. As to the coat, I don't know what to say about that yet, but will let you know soon. I shall want a good pair of boots, tolerable heavy with long legs [that] come up to the knees with a piece to come up over the knee and tie.[96] Alick knows what I want, he has seen them frequently. Tell Pa about them, he will have them made. I should like very much to come home and get them, but think it doubtful. There will be someone appointed to go for them. As to the shirts being sent by Mr. Phelps, that made no difference. I am getting on finely yet as to clothes. My pants are good yet; my shorts and drawers also; have a hole in the heel of one sock; have one or two pair I've never worn yet. I am doing well in almost everything, hope it may continue so with me.

I send you some *Arborvitae*[97] that I took yesterday from a Yankee yard just this side [of] our outside pickets above Alexandria. Give your ma and my ma a piece, and others if you can spare it.

I have given you all the news I can think of now. Let Ma and Pa hear from me whenever you do. If you can't let them see the letter, write them how I am. I received a letter from Pa's a few days since and they are anxious to hear from me frequently. I guess I have received every letter you have written. Write often and long letters. I am glad to [hear] from anything at home, down to the chickens, cats, and dogs. Tell my friends to write to [me]. They have the chance to write while I am on duty. My love to you, also to my new Pa and Ma, and all inquiring friends.

Tell Bet all the boys say Coly will do more for me than anybody in the company. I think she might write to me once and not to Coly all. Direct your letters to Manassas, though I can get them from the Court House. Farewell. Ever your devoted husband,

R. W. Parker

Sept. the 4, '61. Everything quiet here this morning. It is a little cloudy this morning and has rained a little. All my mess are getting on finely except Steve Goggin. He is a little complaining this morning with headache and cold. This leaves me well this morning, hoping to hear from you soon. My warmest love to you. Tell Clem to be a smart girl; my best wishes to her. We have not drawed any money yet, nor do I know when we will; expect during this month sometime. I am not in need of any money yet, have all the silver and gold and one note yet in my belt, and a little besides.

Excuse this unconnected and badly written note, for it is hard for me to write an interesting letter at any time. Farewell, dear wife.

From R. W. Parker

Mr. Phelps is well as common and looks very well.

Camp Harrison, Fairfax CH
Sept. the 8, [1861]
Dear Wife,

Your letter of Sept. the 1 was received a few days since and read with the greatest interest. It was mailed for the CH and came directly to hand. You can direct your letters there if you wish, as we get the mail from the Junction and CH everyday.

News. I am nearly well as common. I had an attack of something like cholera morbus a few nights since, which weakened me down considerably, but am nearly stout as ever now. And Captain is still with us but expects to receive his resignation from the Governor at any day. It has been sent to him some time. All our sick, I think, is improving some. J. M. Garrett is the worst off; he has not recovered his strength from the measles and the boys tease and fret him till he can't rest. They have him mad constantly. Three of our men left for home a day or two since. Thomas and Lewis Martin[98] and Samuel Nichols[99] on a sick furlough. Some of their sickness, I think, is homesick[ness]. I think another will get a furlough today: Whit Vance. He will leave on a furlough of [the] expected sickness of his wife. I hope the men of our company who are leaving on account of sickness and other business will return soon and my time will come soon.

I know none of them wants to see their wives and friends worse than I do mine wife.

Payday has reached us at last. We were paid a day or two since for one month's wages. I received $49.33 dollars: thirteen dollars for myself, twelve for my horse, and the remainder for clothes. When I get all due me [it] will amount to fifty dollars, as this is a little remnant of the amount at Lynchburg due yet. I want to send you forty-five dollars and then I'll have some twelve or fifteen dollars left. You must take it and use it when you want it. If Pa wants

Rebecca Walker Parker, wife of Robert W. Parker. Reproduced from Ackerly and Parker, *"Our Kin."*

some to pay for my clothes and taxes, let him have it or anything else. Try and keep everything straight as possible. Try and keep out of debt [in] these hard times, if possible. I will want the clothes I named: drawers, shirts, pants, and [. . .] It does not make much difference as to the colors of the pants, so they are good, strong, warm ones. I have not worn the flannel belts for a month or two, but expect to try them soon. I'll want a good pair of boots suitable for winter made by a good shoemaker. Tell Pa he will attend them. I am not needing any clothes yet, and hope if the weather keeps fine I will stand a chance to come after them, if nothing happens. As to the coat, I want to find out of the company what sort of coat the majority intend getting before I send you word to make it. And if they don't have a uniform coat, it makes but little difference with me what sort it is.

Well, Duck,[100] I shall attempt to answer some questions asked in your kind letter. I am very glad to hear you are so fat once in your life.[101] 'Twould be one of the greatest pleasures for me to see you, for I have always wished to see you a big fat woman.

You wished to know if I had burnt your letters. I kept all of them till a week or so since, when I had a bonfire. [I] burnt up all I've received from you except the two last, and expect to burn them when I get through answering them. Don't lie uneasy about them, for I am as particular with them as you would be. Write what you please. I'll take care of the letters if they reach me.

I am not very afraid of the boys teasing me, and if they did, little would the difference be. I am glad the prospect is favorable of good luck and hope it may continue so.

You wished to know if that certain letter with you-know-what in it was sent by hand or mail—I think by mail. I don't think the report of Lil Johnson[102] being fretted when he saw the news from home can be true, but don't know. He is a very strange fellow. To show you, he sold his three months' wages for forty dollars just before payday—and his first month's wages was forty-eight dollars. The three months wages was worth ninety-five dollars, so you see he lost $55. You see what sort of fellow. He is odd; he takes a notion [and] 'tis not worthwhile to try to turn him. If the report be true of his saying what he did about his wife, he surely hasn't got good sense, for I don't think anybody with good sense would even think, so much more speak, it.

You spoke of many people being afraid their husbands or brothers would be led astray. There is no doubt there will be many led far from the path they trod when they left home. I thank kind Providence that I have taken no bad habits since I left you and have only increased one, that the use of tobacco. I chew some more than I did when we parted, but can quit at any time. I think it does me good sometimes, but may be disappointed. Never fear of my yielding to dissipations of a dissipated kind. Remember my promise to you when we parted.

I received a letter from Ma yesterday by Billie Wells. He looks tolerable well. Ma wrote principally of George leaving. I wish he had come and joined our company. I know something of the hardships of the infantry soldiers. Let others do as they wish, I'll always go with my horse, if possible; if not, give me artillery next. There are hundreds, and I might say thousands, that say if ever they reach home, they will come into service on horse back.[103]

If you could see one force march, it would satisfy you [to] see the poor infantry lying on the sides of the roads, broke down with their knapsacks, blankets, cartridge box, and gun, all for them to carry on their back. And when they come to fighting, they have the hardest to do: all the roads to make, all the fortifications to make, all the cutting to do. While this is going on, the troopers are doing but little. You need not tell George this, for it's too late now. I should like very much to see him before he leaves and have a long talk with him. Give him my best wishes. Tell him not to expose himself no more than he can help.

The [. . .] are doing but little down here anyway now. Pickets fighting, taking a Yankee frequently. We have lost but few in the skirmishes we have. The report reached here yesterday that our troops had taken possession of the Chain Bridge near Georgetown. There has nothing of particular interest taken place since I wrote to you last. Daniel Robertson was in our camp today. [He] looks well; says he is writing a letter to Ma. He wishes to give her a full description of this part of the world. I carried Jimmie R. part of the way to

Manassas a few days since on his way home. He looked rather badly. I must close, as I have given you the news, all I think of now.

My belt is getting on very well. I have all the money in it yet except my notes. You wished to know about the postage. I receive all my letters "post paid" and send all mine "post paid." Write soon and a long letter. I must quit with the promise of writing soon. I had much rather received the kiss from your lips than in ink and paper, but am glad to get it anyway. Goodbye, my dear Duck. Accept the best love and a kiss from your ever affectionate,

R. W. Parker

Fairfax CH
Sunday morning, Sept. the 15, '61
Dear Duck,

Just as I took my pen and paper in hand this morning to answer your kind letter of the 10 this month, I was called on camp duty, so I am now writing in the guard tent. It is quite pleasant here, but the flies bite most prodigiously. I am in good health with the exception of a bad cold that is some better. Hope I will be well in a few days. There is nothing new in camp this evening. Our company is getting on very well. Our Captain is here, will leave next Tuesday for home on a furlough if his discharge does not come to hand in that time. Mr. Phelps is out on camp guard today. He looks quite well and I think he enjoys camp much better than before he went home. John Garrett has a furlough to stay up in Loudoun County a few days for his health.

Sept. the 16. Nothing fresh this morning. Steve Goggin came in off duty yesterday evening very much complaining. I rather think Jim Hughs is taking the fever but hope is not so. He is very unwell.

Well, dear Duck, I must give you some of the war news, so far as I know. I had to stop writing just now to listen to the cannononading down near Falls Church. There is considerable firing down there. I am very anxious to hear the result.

The little fight our men had the other day in taking Hall Hill resulted in our taking sixteen prisoners, killing seven of the enemy and perhaps many others. Our loss was none killed. We sent twelve prisoners to Manassas yesterday. Our pickets are fighting almost everyday. I have not been in any of the skirmishes yet, but have been out in readiness several times lately. But the little fights are over, all won before we get there.

I think the time is not far distant when we will all be engaged in a fight—not one of the little skirmishes, but a regular battle. The Yankees are making great preparations: cutting and burning the timber around Alexandria and Washington; throwing up breastworks in almost every direction around this side Alexandria, so as to prevent, if possible, our ever getting there, if we should attempt it.[104] I think the chance is very good for us to try the enemy's blockades and breastworks soon, for the general move of our forces is onward [and] outward to that point. By the help of Him who rules over all, if they will come out from their breastworks, we will give them a fair fight.

We have heard here in camp that General Lee[105] gained a considerable victory in western Virginia, killing two hundred of the enemy, one hundred wounded, [and] taking fifteen hundred prisoners.[106] I hope it is true. About my clothes, I hardly know what to say in regard to getting them. Whit Vance went home partly on that business but will do but little towards getting them, and it makes but little difference with me whether any of them are sent by him or not. You can be getting them nearly every chance. Put a watch pocket in my pants, for I have frequently to keep the time. I have not yet found out yet what sort of dress coat our company intends having. As to the overcoat, I'll wait a little longer before I order one. I may get one down here. Some of our boys have been buying some of the Yankee overcoats that have been taken by our men at from eight to ten dollars—excellent coats—and have ordered some from home also, so I may get one that way. And it is too warm yet for overcoats. I'll wait a little longer anyway.

As to the blankets, I have all I brought from home and have bought an excellent Yankee blanket, one as good as any I have seen, for one dollar. So I have two excellent blankets, shawl, and oilcloth. I am doing well yet as to clothes.

Duck, Mr. Phelps says he is an excellent hand to guess, and guesswork is good as any when it hits wrong. I think Ms. Mitchell is one of the fast women. I must close, having given the news generally. Write soon a long letter and all the news.

Sept. the 17, '61. Dear Wife, I have nothing new yet. The firing on yesterday was the Yankees firing off their guns. No harm done. The captain expects to start today for home. Nothing more at present. My best love to you. My best wishes to your Pa, Ma, and family.

Nothing new at present. From your ever devoted but unworthy,

Robert

This leaves me well as usual this [morning]. Duck, the news came to camp yesterday [that] we were to be connected to the main body of Col. Radford's regiment. If we are, I guess times will be a little closer. Will Parker[107] was to see me yesterday; he and George were well as usual. Jo B[urroughs] sends his best wishes to you all, especially to B[et]. I showed him the word written in the envelope. Farewell, dear wife. I accept the kiss with thanks and hope the time is not far distant when I can receive it in reality. Write soon, Duck.

Robert

Vienna, Fairfax CH
Sept. the 19, '61
My Dear Wife,

I received your very interesting letter a few minutes ago which afforded me great relief. I had been looking with unusual anxiety for a letter from you, as it had been going on two weeks since I heard from you. I was more than glad to hear you was enjoying such good health and sincerely wish its continuance. It affords me great pleasure to hear from Pa, Ma, and all the neighbors. Sorry to hear Ma is so much grieved about Brother G[eorge]'s leaving. It would be much better for our parents and wives if they could be perfectly resigned as to the leaving of their children and husbands. Though greatly relieved by your letter, I was somewhat disappointed also at hearing whether Clem was well or not; also to hear whether the money I sent you had ever reached you or not. I started 45 dollars to you and a letter to you and Ma by Mr. Vance.

I have nothing interesting for you this evening. I came in from twenty-four hours picketing [the] day before yesterday evening. I was on picket some two-and-a-half miles from the Potomac; had an excellent time, with the exception of being a little cool at night. I had plenty of the best for myself and horse and felt in but little danger. I was on camp duty last night. Had an alarm in camp about nine o'clock and kept our horses saddled all night. The camp is quiet today. I think we will be roused tonight and perhaps move our encampment towards the Court House, as we are now some 8 miles northeast of that. Some of our boys took a Yankee last night. The old fellow got lost from his regiment at Falls [Church] and fell into our troop.

I learnt today our men had fell in back from Falls Church and our men were fighting in that vicinity today, which is below us, and some of our forces are fighting at [Big Falls] above us. I think our generals are doing all they can to attract the enemy's attention at this point and near here so as to give our forces [. . .] a chance to cross to Maryland. I understand we have the river blockaded at one or two points now below Alexandria. A fight would not surprise us at any time. You must not be uneasy. The same God is here to protect us that would if we were at home.

I received a letter from your aunt Caroline yesterday and was quite glad to hear from her and family and will answer soon. We had an election a few days since in our company for a captain. Lieut. Graves was elected our captain; Waddy Burton sick, no Lieut.

The sick in our company seems to be improving, with the exception of our Captain; he is very much complaining. Steven G. is improving some. W. N. Morgan left last night for home by putting in his brother as substitute.

Oct. the 1. I am well this morning. You wished to know about my coat. Make me a frock after the fashion of my dress coat. I don't know what to say of my coming home, but will come soon as possible. I am doing well as to clothes yet.

I am writing in the woods. We struck our tents [on] a river last night. Our tents are some distance from theirs towards the Court House from [. . .] The Yankees are arriving toward our lines. Mr. Chalmers was shot and thought to be dying last night; Dr. Saunders soon came. He was shot, I understand by one of our soldiers.[108]

Soon be ten o'clock—no breakfast yet. Don't often wait for me write.

I must close have [. . .] interesting. I want some of you to write me word where Brother G[eorge] is. I wish to correspond with him as soon as possible. My best wishes to you, Pa and Ma, and the children. My best love to you. Farewell, dear Duck.

Yours,

R. W. Parker

Camp Harrison, Fairfax CH
Sept the 24, [1861]
My Dear Wife,

I received yours of the 17 which I assure you was read with the greatest interest. I was more than glad to hear you was well as assumed. Hope your health may continue good. This leaves me enjoying very good health. I have fattened several pounds within the last two months. I weighed 160 lbs. a week or two since. I have nothing new for you this morning. There is but little doing down this way. Nothing here or but little but the move of soldiers busily drilling. There is not so much sickness in camp as was a week or two since. Jim [. . .] left for home on a sick furlough a day or two since, and another will leave soon, I think, to see his family. I hope my time will come soon. I'll do all I can to come soon. I am confident you don't want to see me worse than I do you. I would do anything in reason to go home.

Duck, don't get low spirited—look to the bright side of everything. I sincerely hope you will not take trouble or interest, for persons may make themselves almost miserable in this way. Duck, look to Him who is able to take care and protect you. Write me word when you think I had better come as nigh as you can, and I will do all in my power to come. Don't be too backward in letting your ma and my ma know how you are, for they have had experience in such things and might save you of a great deal of pain and uneasiness. Don't be too backward, dear wife. Write often, for I am anxious to hear from you often, especially for the future.[109] Please write often. I have given you all the news I can think of now. Farewell, dear wife. I remain, as ever, your devoted but unworthy husband,

R. W. Parker

May the Lord bless and protect you is my sincere prayers. Robt.

Let me know whether you have received the money I sent you by Whit Vance [. . .] I sent 45 dollars.

Coly has heard that Bet does not intend writing to him anymore. Suppose his father was the man to write him of that; no gentleman would be guilty of such a trick. Coly's feelings is considerably roused and rather lays it on me. I have never written anything there corresponding that I recollect, and if he has ever received a letter from her I don't know, as he has never exposed them to me or anybody else that I know of. If I have ever written anything about it I want to know it. I aim to attend to my own business strictly. Mr. Phelps is well as usual. Stephen Goggin is improving, I think.

Farewell, dear wife. I send a letter for you and Ma in the same envelope by Mr. Milton Cumming.

Cavalry Camp, New Fairfax CH
Oct. the 9, '61

Your letter of the first was received with the greatest pleasure yesterday. You can't imagine the relief it afforded me to hear from you and that you was up and doing well. I was also glad to hear our neighbors and friends were well. I have nothing that will interest you. I am enjoying very good health and doing well. Night before last was, I think, one of the rainiest nights I ever saw with hard wind with it. I think over half of the tents in our encampment blew down. Kind Providence blessed me with the good luck of not being turned out of doors. As good luck would have it, we happened to pitch our tent better than common [and] ditched 'round it well, which saved us from a dreadful night's rest. I threw down my oil cloth and blankets on the ground and had a very good night's rest while a good many of our company were out taking it fair and easy.

There is but little excitement in camp at this time. Some of our pickets were run in last night, which caused us to be roused up before day and get breakfast. No harm done as yet. Our camp has become quiet.

I understand a few days since some four or six of our soldiers were getting chestnuts near Falls Church [and] were surprised and taken by the Yankees at one tree. A lieutenant was at the threshing and three privates picking up. I guess they felt rather singular when the Yankees rode up.

We are now situated three miles northeast of the CH, a very poor-looking part of the world. We are expecting to move soon two or three miles north of this, and I think, from the general move of the regiment, we will be apt to go to Leesburg soon. I hope we will. There has been a good deal of heavy cannonading for the last two or three days in the direction of Falls Church and

Alexandria. It has been quite heavy this morning. It may be just the enemy firing off their guns.

There has been such news in camp of some of our forces having a fight near Falls Church day before yesterday, which resulted in our forces whipping the enemy. My information was not definite. As to the number killed or wounded, I know not.

The great fever in regard to the expected fight at or near Alexandria is somewhat abating. I don't think there is half the excitement down here in regard to the war that there is up in Bedford. We have to serve one day and night in every four or five on picket, generally. I prefer it to camp duty. I must stop this. You may make me a homespun jacket and send it down when you have the chance. As to my clothes, I am doing very well. My clothes are tolerably good yet. When it turns a little, I put on both my jackets, so I get on finely. I am sorry to hear old [Pit] has been acting so badly. He will ruin his character if he does not change. I don't know what name to give you for your puppy. I reckon you had better name him Beauregard or Beale.[110] Beale is the name of an officer in this regiment and a fine young man.

The general health of our company is tolerably good. Jo Burroughs and Tom Bernard are about ready for duty again. I have not heard from Captain Graves since he left. Hope he is improving. Colonel Radford has returned to camp, though not entirely well; he looks better than he did before he went home. He seems a great deal more mild than he use to be. I was somewhat surprised to hear of such luck from Mrs. B. I should like to see her with that little creature in her arms. Don't you think she could settle a sick stomach with her soft talk, for she could always use enough when she [. . .] before she was married. You asked me if I didn't think I would feel quite strange to have one of those lovely little creatures to greet me home. No indeed—I am more and more attached to the little creatures. Coming off of picket the other day I saw one, and could hardly keep from stopping to have a romp with it. Some of the boys saw me notice it and said they expected I would have a young Beauregard before long, as they call every one of the little creatures young Beauregards. You asked me to kiss myself for you. I think that will [be] rather hard to do but I'll try. My whiskers and mustache are quite short yet.

I must close. Kiss yourself for me. I have wished so often I had your likeness. I wish I could get it some way or other. I've given you all the news. Write, don't wait for me. I'll try and write often. I get a letter generally every six or eight days. Give my love to your pa, ma, and family, and a large portion in fact all for yourself. Farewell, dear wife. I remain, as ever, your devoted but unworthy husband.

R. W. Parker

Centreville, Fairfax Co.

Oct. the 19, '61

As I haven't heard from you for over a week, I'll endeavor to drop you a few lines this morning anyway. I am somewhat disappointed on not hearing from you in the last few days but hope you are doing well. I should like to give you something interesting this morning, but it is impossible as the tent is full and busy talking. Captain Graves, John Lipscomb, and old Mr. Lipscomb arrived in camp yesterday with the latest news from Bedford. The Captain and John look very well. The Capt. has his new uniform and looks better than I ever saw him.

I have nothing very interesting for you. It is quite a rainy damp morning and very warm—a good sign for more rain. I guess you will [be] surprised to hear of our retreating from below Fairfax CH up to Centreville a few days ago. I was down on picket on the Leesburg and Alexandria Turnpike 6 or 8 miles north of the CH, and when I returned, all our camps had been moved up near Centreville. What I might say a general retreat. The general move of our forces is back toward the Junction. The enemy are following us but slowly and very particularly. They came up to the Court House a night or two ago but was run back. I think the intentions of our generals is to try and get them to follow us back to Centreville. If they follow us, Centreville will, I think, be the next battleground, as our forces are fortifying it in a hurry, and also building up the fortifications at Manassas higher. As to the use of all this work, time only can tell. We are camped about one mile and a half north of Centreville on a very nice situation where we will stay for some time, I hope, for I am really tired [of] moving so much. We have moved two or three times in the last week and packed up almost every night. I came to this camp last night with the last load from our other camp, and as soon as I unloaded had orders to keep on the harness, ready to start at any moment. I think it will be rather hard for the Yankees to surprise us now, for we are constantly on the lookout. We have but few now sick in our regiment, none but can get about in our company. Lil Johnson left camp sick the other day for the Richmond hospital. The most of the complaints is cold.

I am glad that I can say to you I am enjoying excellent health and fattening. Get plenty to eat and that is good. Good fat beef, bacon, flour, sugar, and sometimes coffee, with the addition of sweet and Irish potatoes. And we have splendid eating when we go out on picketing, but pay our money for it at a quarter a meal generally. Sometimes meet with a good old friend that gives us a meal or two

I must tell you what took place with me on picket the other day. I had two old friends on picket that had treated me very kindly, and on my last picket tour I was going on in a glee with my men to my post, and to my great surprise met the old lady some distance from home going at the top of her speed afoot.

When I got in speaking distance I spoke to her, and she offered me her hand and gushed into tears and said, "Mr. P., they have taken my husband." And it was some time before she told me who had taken him, for I feared the Yankees had him and he lived near my post. I soon found out what was the [in]fraction. Mr. Sherman (as that was his name) had gone to mill outside of our lines without a pass,[111] and our pickets had taken him up to the Court House. She remained in the greatest distress all the time I was on picket. I went to see her twice, told her he would be sent back to her soon, but did no good. She said it hurt her feelings to think they took her husband just because he went to get some meal for his poor grandchildren. I went to see her just before I left my post. She seemed in greater distress, if possible, than at first. She asked me my name and those that were with me, which I did. She said if she was stripped of what little she had, she intended to go and see her friends in Bedford and Franklin. She asked all of us to remember her and treated us on the very best she had: chestnuts, apples, and pears. To my great joy we met her husband returning home the evening we left Mr. Sherman going home. Mr. Phelps and I took breakfast there once together. They were both professors. They asked him to pray with them, which he did, and I to ask a blessing at breakfast, which took me on surprise, and you know I had to let it pass to someone else. You can imagine how I felt.

I fear I shall never see them again, as the Yankees has that section in their hands now. And I don't hardly expect to go on picket again soon, as I am now acting as quartermaster for our company, which exempts me from that duty. Our [. . .] Murrill[112] is promoted to assistant quartermaster of the regiments. I must close, as I have given you the general news. Send this to Ma and Pa. I have not received a letter since those sent by Samuel Pollard. Write soon and give all the news. Farewell.

From your affectionate but unworthy husband,
R. W. Parker

I am getting on very well as to clothes yet.

Cavalry camp, near Centreville, Fairfax Co.
Oct. the 30, '61
Dear Brother [George Parker],

I have waited to receive a letter from you until I've lost all hopes, and shall attempt to drop you a few lines though they may never reach you. I understood through a letter I received from Ma that you was at Staunton.

I have nothing to interest you, nor do I feel like writing a letter, for my jaw bone seems almost like bursting with the toothache which I have had for the last two or three days. Tried to have it pulled yesterday evening but the doctor broke it off at the gums, so it is no better.

I received a letter from Beck yesterday. All were well as usual at Pa's and the Doctor's. In that letter was the sad news of the death of Cousin Missouri Pullen. She died of diphtheria the 22 of this month [and] was buried in the corner of the garden. Aunt Polly says she is broken up, poor woman; I reckon she thinks so. Uncle Pullen seems to take her death harder than any of them.

I guess you would like to hear something of the news of our army. It is doing but little but picketing, had no move lately, indicating a fight. Our men are fortifying Centreville but I don't think the Yankees will ever sum up courage enough to fight us there. I think the center of the Manassas army is at Centreville. It is quite an interesting view to be at Centreville and look at the camps. Our regiment is kept quite busy picketing. We picket some twelve or fifteen miles from camp, and these cold nights almost freeze us. I reckon you have had all of the particulars of the Leesburg fight[113] before this; it was quite a victorious fight on our part. Our loss was light compared with the enemy's.

Our company is getting on quite well now. We have had a good deal of sickness in our company, but through the blessing of kind Providence we have but few men, and none so but what they can go about camp. Tom Bernard is one of the sickest. His complaint is rather a strange one; the most he complains of is pain and fullness of the stomach.

I've given you the most of the news I have and must bring my note to a close. Well, Brother, I understand you are doing very well and are corporal. If you have a chance for a higher office, run for it. You must never get mad or fretted; just determine you won't get mad at anything, for if you suffer yourself to get fretted, you are sure to say something you ought not. Any is liable to do so; take everything patiently. I am acting quartermaster for our company now, which exempts me from all duty, so I have no picket duty to perform. The paymaster paid us a visit yesterday evening and also two months wages. My two months amounted to fifty dollars. I've received, since in service, about one hundred dollars.

I must quit, as it is nearly time to draw provisions. You must write to me as soon as you get this, if ever you do, for I am quite anxious to hear from you. You have never wrote me but one little note that I've ever received. Uncle Jo Parker left here last Sunday morning; told me Sallie[114] had received a letter from you a day or two before he left home.

Mr. Phelps wants you to inquire where his brothers are, John, Henry and Ammon. He has heard that Ammon was dead. Try to find out where they are.

Farewell, Brother. Try and do your duty. Don't suffer yourself drawn off by the reckless, for there is always something up in camp to draw one off from the path of rectitude. Always be on the lookout. Great success to your efforts and a happy return to home is the sincere wish of your devoted but unworthy brother,

R. W. Parker

Write me word where to direct my letter. Direct yours to Manassas Junction, care of Capt. Wm. F. Graves, 30th Regiment Va. Cav.

Cavalry Camp near Centreville
Thursday, Oct the 31, '61
Dear Wife,

I seize this opportunity of answering your very interesting letter of the 25, which arrived a few days since with the sad news of the death of my dear cousin Missouri, one of my dearest friends on earth. Great was the shock of that sad news to me, for she has ever proved to be one of my warmer friends ever since we knew what friendship was. She was ever punctual, when I was far from home and friends, to write to me. Lasting will her memory be to me. Oh, I shall miss her so much; wish I could have seen her. But dear as she is to us, we will have to give her up. Hope through the blessing of kind Providence she is better off than when here in this troublesome world.

Dear Duck, I would have answered your letter before this had it not been for several reasons, and when I give them to you I am sure you will forgive me for not answering sooner. Ever since the reception of your letter I have been laid up with the toothache. I [have] been to have it pulled, but being nothing but a shell it broke off at the gums, which made it no better. On yesterday evening I was taken with neuralgia and toothache, and this morning my jaw was a sight—all swollen up. It has pained me but little comparatively today; hope it is a good deal better. As to my general health, it is very good. I have no news interesting for you this evening, but such as I have give I thee. All our company are out on picket except those that are sick and live or those well ones to take care of things.

They left this evening and as they were paid yesterday for two months wages left a good part of it with me. I think I have somewhere from five hundred to a thousand dollars now in my pocket—a good time to run with a pocketful, if I wished to. My two months wages amounted to the even sum of fifty dollars. I wish you had about forty-five of it. I have never used the first piece out of my belt yet. Silver and gold is quite scarce in camp. If the boys know I had it, they would soon tease me out of it, I guess.

Our army seems very quiet now; haven't heard of any late move of the enemy as definite. We have an alarm every few nights and have to pack up, but all prove to be false so far. I think it very doubtful about their attack[ing] us this winter, though they may at any time, which would not surprise us. I have no late news from Leesburg; the last was all quiet.

You wished to know about the clothes. They suit very well. The coat fits well and I am very well pleased. The suit you have at home—color it. Hickory bark will color them very nice. Any color suits better than light in camp. I wish you could go down home, but reckon you can't. You seem to have rather a bad opinion of Mr. Newman. Don't wish the [Yankees] to take him, for they are not fit to have any southerners.

Duck, you must not get fretted at anything that happens; do like I try to do, not to get fretted [at] anything. I try to take everything fair and easy. Since I have been quartermaster, some of the boys say I suit better than anybody in the company except Sam Murrill because we don't get mad at anything. I knew before I commenced it it required almost the patience of Job.[115] Duck, I have one of the best fellows in the company for my bed fellow. It is Sam Murrill. He is one of the best fellows I ever saw. I don't think Mr. Phelps will succeed in getting in his substitute, as I learn the Colonel has refused to take him. Fields is driving the wagon now.

You must excuse this short note. I have given you all the news I have. I haven't half the news you have around home. I've written you two letters; the last I wrote and sent them by hand by Uncle [Job W.] Lipscomb.

Farewell, dear wife. My love to you and all. Mr. Phelps well as usual. Accept the best love and a kiss from [your] devoted but unworthy husband,

R. W. Parker

Write soon. Robert
My jaw pains me but li'l.

Waterford, Loudoun Co.
Nov. the 11, '61
Dear Wife,

It affords me one of the greatest pleasures of my life to have the chance to drop you a few lines, for it has been a long time since I had the chance to do so. I have been so busy going all day and sometimes in the night. Quartermaster keeps me engaged all the time except night. I would have laid up if I had had time, but my business called me and I had to go. I have gone several times when I ought to have been in camp. I have no news of interest to give you. A good many of our company are sick. When we left Centreville, we sent four to the Lynchburg hospital, and when we left Leesburg, left four or five there in the hospital, and several in camp not fit for duty. So I think near two-thirds of our company are sick. Will and First Lt. sick at home and Captain very unwell in camp. We are certainly in a bad fix.

This is a little town of several hundred inhabitants when they are all in, but several have gone over to Yankee-dom. It is a real Union hole, and the greater portion of this end of Loudoun County is quite northern, which makes us have to treat all as Yankees. Then some are true to the South. This is an excellent portion of our native state, as good as any portion I have seen. We have to picket on the river between Point of Rocks above Leesburg and the

Shenandoah River. Also keep up communication with Colonel Josh by near Harper's Ferry. Capt. Meed's company of this are here with [us]. It's quite a nice company. The Yankees seem to be very quiet since the Leesburg fight, have interrupted us but little. I hope they will remain so. They are doing but little anyway, so far as I can learn. I forgot to tell you, another of our men has just been discharged: Tom Franklin. He will leave for home tomorrow, making the fourth or fifth of our company that has been discharged.

I hardly know what to give you next. They keep up such a fuss in this church. I am writing up in the gallery. It is an excellent Quaker church with three or four good fireplaces and one or two stoves. It has two rooms like our old Quaker church. We all stay in the church of a night. They have preaching twice a week. I guess it would seem quite strange to you to hear an old Quaker woman preach. I've given you all the news I can think of now. I received a letter from Brother G. a day or two since. He was getting on very well, with the exception of the toothache. He has left Staunton, has made a march of four or five days. He is now near Monterey, Highland County; says it is very rough and the mountains were white with snow the 4 of this month. I fear he will see a hard time this winter.

I received a letter a few days since from you, also one from Ma. Was glad to hear from you all and that you all were doing so well. Your letter was the answer to mine of the 19 of last month. I received a letter the 8 from Ma written the 4 which rather surprised me. The reason it did [was] it was received the day after I received the two above-named and informed me of the great change that had taken place with you.[116] It did my heart good to hear all was over and you was doing so well. The way Ma introduced it rather surprised me. She said she and Pa was sent for that morning to go up to the Dr.'s[117] to see the young soldier just at that place. I thought, "What young soldier?" but soon I knew. You seemed so confident that it would be the reverse, I had almost come to that conclusion. I thank kind Providence for His protecting hand over you, that He has protected and blessed you in the great change that has taken place. Hope He will ever overshadow you with His merciful hand. A tongue cannot express the pleasure it would offer me to be with you and the sweet little babe, if to stay but a few minutes. You can't imagine how bad I want to see you both. I received the little lock of his hair you sent me in Ma's letter. I think it the prettiest little lock I ever saw. I hardly know what color to call it. It is not very light or dark, it seems to be between the two. Take good care of him, which I know you will, and kiss him for me.

I must close. I have not had the toothache this week. I feel a good deal better this evening. Hope I will be well soon. The most of my sickness is griping. I have had a bad cold and think it is passing off and soon will be well. I am doing well yet as to clothes yet. Have not put on my flannel yet, will put it on soon. My boots got very thin. I had them half-soled a day or two since, so they do very well now and keep my feet quite warm. Don't have my boots sent unless you have a good chance. I expect I could have a pair made here easier than at home. There are three or four shoe shops in this place and work as cheap as any I know. I could have the best of boots in this market made to order at ten dollars.

I must close. Write soon [and] give all the news. I'll answer Ma's letter in a few days. I wrote her a letter a few days since. Tell all to write.

Direct your letters to Leesburg, Loudoun Co., care of Capt. Graves. Farewell, dear Beck, and kiss the babe for me. May kind Providence bless and protect you both is my sincere wish.

Robert

Waterford, Loudoun Co.
Nov. the 11, 1861
Dear Brother [George Parker],

I received your kind letter a day or two since, which relieved me very much to hear you was well with the exception of toothache. I hope you are doing well now and have gotten over your long march, for I guess you was quite tired walking with your knapsack and musket, for I think it would lay me up to march a day on foot.

I have nothing interesting for you. I have gotten over the toothache but have a bad cold and touch of diarrhea; hope it will be well soon. I received a letter from home a few days since, all tolerably well. The press master[118] had pressed Sam[119] and the two mules for service in western Virginia, Sam for a driver. Ma seemed very much hurt about Sam's leaving.

You wished to know the particulars of the Leesburg fight. It was quite a hot fight. We had about fifteen hundred men engage the enemy, several thousand; our loss was from two to three hundred killed and wounded. The enemy's loss was near two thousand killed, wounded, and prisoners. Our forces took 7 hundred prisoners, several hundred stands of arms, 6 pieces of artillery. It is believed the enemy also lost from three to six hundred drowned trying to recross the river. Among the killed of the enemy, if I mistake not, was Generals Butler[120] and Baker.[121] Several colonels among the prisoners; the officers taken prisoners was, I think, from twenty-five to thirty.

Nov. the 12. Everything quiet this morning, so far as I know, from Parkers Ferry down to the Point of Rocks, as that is our line of pickets on the [Potomac] River. You spoke of the cold weather. We have had no snow but some very cool weather for the season. The country through here is generally tolerably level and quantities of forage. I am nearly always going for forage or provisions. We have plenty to eat and that is good: fresh beef, bacon, flour, sugar, coffee, molasses. Draw such candles and I draw provisions at Leesburg. Before I forget it, direct your letters to Leesburg, care of Capt. Graves, if you ever get this. I've lost your letter and will have to direct this by guess. Tom Bernard has been sent to Lynchburg hospital. Jo Burroughs is out on picket. Near two thirds [. . .] our company is sick. We left from at Leesburg a day or two since. I have not been home yet, nor do I know when I will have the chance to go, but hope it will be soon. I have been in service soon six months.

I must close, as I have given you the news generally. This leaves me unwell with a touch of the bellyache. Give my best wishes to Ed, Will, and all inquiring friends. My love to you. May the God that rules in all guide, govern, and protect you is the sincere wish of your devoted but unworthy brother,

Brother R. W. Parker

Brother, don't give way [to] the temptations of camp life.[122] Write soon. Give all the news. Farewell, brother. R. Parker

Waterford, Loudoun County
Nov. the 17, '61
Dear Wife,

I have not heard from you for the last eight or ten days and will attempt to drop you a few lines informing you that I am yet alive and doing well. I am improving considerably, feel nearly well as ever now. Heard two excellent Quaker sermons today delivered by two Quaker ladies. The first one's text was (by their fruits ye shall know them).[123] The second was (the kingdom of heaven is liken to a merchant seeking godly pearls).[124] I assure you they were excellent sermons. They were the first I ever heard from the Quakers. Their manner of worship seemed quite strange to me. All came in, took their seats, and remained still until the spirit moved them, and when through they remained still for sometime, then commenced shaking hands and broke up. Had no singing or praying. Nearly all the old ladies had bonnets alike. The men did nothing in the services.

I have no news to interest you. The enemy seems quiet, so far as I know, for the last few days. They gave some of our pickets a close race for their lives several days ago. They were on both sides of the river and had crossfire at our men, but didn't hurt a man nor horse. 'Twas a miracle, for they were about nigh enough to touch our men with their bayonets. Providence only provided for them. Go out on the high hills and one can see several Yankee camps. I heard from Centreville a day or two since they are, I understand, expecting a fight to take place there in a few days. But I think it very doubtful indeed, for I think they have but [little] idea of advancing on that place. If they do so, I am sure they will be met with a warm reception. We have Centreville well prepared for them now. It is as well or better fortified than Manassas, for they are so fixed as to have crossfire in almost any direction at the Yankees.

I understand the Yankees are doing some little toward winter quarters in the way of making dirt houses for their pickets. I guess they intend keeping up their line of pickets up the river. I am afraid they will pester us through the winter.

I have not heard of any preparation for winter quarters for our men yet. I think if they intend to have any winter quarters, it is time they were about them, for the weather is getting tolerably cooler a little that way now.

I have given you all the Yankee news, so I'll change the topic. I tried my flannel for the first time today. It feels quite agreeable. I think it will help the cause considerably. Am getting on tolerably well yet as to clothes. Hope I can come home before they give out, but fear they will have to last some time, as there is but little chance to go home now.

I must close, as it is getting late and there is such a fuss I can't hear my ears. Write soon. I have given you the news. Write a long letter. Take good care of the little babe. Kiss him for me. Farewell, dear wife.

From your devoted but unworthy husband,
R. W. Parker

Direct your letter to Leesburg, Loudoun Co.

Waterford, Loudoun County
Nov. 19, 1861
Dear Wife,

I have not heard from you since [the] 4th, but will endeavor to drop you a few lines informing you that I am still at this place and getting on quite well and think [. . .] I am enjoying tolerably good health [. . .] company is still in rather a bad condition. Several sick, none dangerous, I hope, but Cousin Bob Johnson. He is very low with typhoid pneumonia. His recovery is given out.

Nothing new or interesting taking place up here. The enemy seem quiet in this vicinity.

I heard of a skirmish or foraging expedition down near Falls Church took place a day or two since.[125] A party of Yankees with five wagons were getting corn and was surprised by a party of our men. Several killed, the remainder taken prisoners with their teams. The enemy is believed to be advancing in direction of Centreville, but nothing certain. The news has reached us of a late battle in Kentucky in which the enemy proved victorious.[126] As to the truth, I know not. I think our forces are expecting an attack at several points. Kind Providence alone can tell what our success may be in the future. Let us look to Him who has the power in His own hand for our success. I guess you have heard before this of the captain of our navy taken to England by order of Lincoln's ships. They were on board.[127]

Well Duck, I must tell you something more of this country. I like it much better than I expected when I first came up here. It is a beautiful county, and the most of the citizens I have formed an acquaintance with seem to be very fine people. It would be a nice place for us if it were not for the [enemies] but we have too many of them to contend with to be safe.

Write soon and tell me how you, Pa, Ma, and family, your pa, ma, and family, and all my old friends are getting on; how they are getting on down home; how Mr. Pullen, Aunt Polly are getting on since the death of Cousin Missouri. It seems that all my correspondents have stopped writing to me and I would be forgotten in old Bedford if it were not for you and Ma. I have hardly expected a letter from you for the last two weeks, knowing you are sick.[128] Hope you will soon be able to write to me, for before you was sick I heard from you and home regularly nearly every week.

I must close as it is getting late and I am confident my notes are not interesting, for it seems to me of all notes mine is the most uninteresting. Kiss the babe for me. Tell him I have a beautiful little dog for him. Farewell to you both.

R. W. Parker

Direct your letters to Leesburg, care of Capt. Graves.
Don't be uneasy about me. I am getting on quite well. R. W. Parker.

Leesburg
Dec. the 1, 1861
Dear Wife,

It affords me one the greatest pleasure that camp can give to have the chance to drop you a few lines. I have, if I mistake not, written to you every week since I have been up here, but have received but one letter mailed the 15 of last month. I received a letter from Ma a few days since which gave me great relief to hear you and the little darling babe were doing so well. I was quite uneasy about you both till I received that note. My greatest desire is that you both may have good health and do well. The greater portion of my time when not busily engaged is spent in thinking about you and to see you. I am a little unwell this morning, but don't be uneasy about me; I have not stopped duty and hope that I will be well soon. The most I complain of is cold weather [and] dysentery; think I will be better in a day or two. I took some medicine[129] this morning.

I have no news new or interesting for you this morning. I have left Waterford and we are now camped in our tents in the woods one mile southwest of Leesburg. Times are rather harder than they have been since the Manassas fight. We are clear out of provisions except flour. The way it happened [is] just before we left Waterford, I sent out four days' rations to our pickets. The pickets were drawn in but left their provisions, so our meals will be short and far between till tomorrow. I lay in my next requisition in the morning. The most of our old men were sent out on picket this morning for forty-eight hours. The picket men see a hard time out these nights. The Yankees show no signs of fight up this way now. The Yankees took two of Capt. Ferry's men at Dranesville. They were, I understand, tight, and when ordered to leave by their sergeant, refused, and the Yankees took them. One of them was Alick Whitten[130] of Bedford; the other was a Dutchman,[131] I don't know his name.

I heard from Centreville day before yesterday. Some say they are expecting a fight, others say not. I don't put any confidence in any report nowadays. Our sick are not much better. Bob Johnson is, I think, a little better. Steve Goggin and Ben Fuqua[132] are at the hospital but very sick. John Graves[133] is here. He is well as usual with the exception of deafness. He is considerably deaf.

I guess you would like to hear something of winter quarters. I haven't heard nothing definite about it yet, but fear there is but little chance to leave this county soon. Fear we will have to stay till January or after, I am afraid.

You are uneasy about me as to clothes. I am doing tolerably well yet. Write me word as soon as you get this whether Pa has had any boots made for me or not. If not, I will have a pair made up at Waterford. Please write soon and give all the news. Tell Ma and all to write. Some of my letters have certainly been misplaced or you would hear from me regularly.

I must close. My love to all and particularly to you and the little babe. Write soon and often. From [your] devoted but unworthy husband,

R. W. Parker

Leesburg Hospital
Dec. the 2, '61
Dear Wife,

I started a letter to you this morning written yesterday through the mail, and when I reached here found cousin John Graves was to leave tomorrow for home, so I could not let the chance slip. We have three here sick: Robert Johnson, Steve Goggin and B. B. Fuqua. All improving, I hope. Our company left Leesburg this morning for Waterford, where I hope we will remain for some time, for I get tired moving about so much. That is a splendid place for us, though a little exposed. It is a great place to get something to eat both for man and horse.

I have nothing interesting for you this morning. The medicine I took has relieved me very much. I feel a great deal better. Hope I will [be] entirely well in a few days. Duck, I guess it would surprise you to tell you I am sitting here by a Yankee writing this note. He was wounded in the fight here the 21 Oct. through the breast. He will be well before long, I think. I have heard of no late move of the enemy. They seem tolerably quiet. Some think they will fight soon, but that is supposition. Some think the enemy are obliged to advance on Centreville and surprise so as to break the blockade on the Potomac.

I am very anxious to hear from our little home and learn what sort of crop they have made and know how Job is getting on by himself. I have not heard yet particularly about winter quarters. Hope I will know soon what we will have to do. I think there will be some provisions made soon, so some of us will have the chance to go home. Oh, that I could be with you and the darling little babe if but for a day or two. Hope I shall see you both soon. I am getting on tolerably well yet as to clothes. Hope I can come to see you before I need any very bad.

I must close, as I expect they are waiting for me at the commissary office. Write soon and often. Tell all to write, Ma particularly. May kind Providence smile and protect and bless you both is the sincere desire of your sincere but unworthy husband,

R. W. Parker

Farewell, dear wife. My love to you and all, part to your ma and pa.

Waterford, Loudoun County, Va.
Dec. the 13, '61
My Dear Wife,

It is now three o'cl. in the morning and I am officer of the camp guard. I received your kind favor of the 10 yesterday which gave me the greatest relief, for I had become quite uneasy about you, for it had been some seventeen days since you wrote, which seemed quite long to me. Duck, please try and write every week. It affords me one of the greatest pleasures of life to hear from you and the little baby boy often.

I was very glad indeed to hear you both were well and sincerely hope you may have good health. Oh, how thankful we should be for good health. I am enjoying excellent health and fattening; weigh more than I have since I came in service. Weighed yesterday 166½ pounds. This is a great country up here. The people generally are so kind. The Quakers are becoming quite kind to us. They send in a good many little [. . .] for the sick.

We have a good many sick in camp. The sickest we have are two servants, one very sick with typhoid pneumonia, the other with the same. Is, I hope, mending. We have quite a number of mump cases, some with a touch of pneumonia with them. Coly is right sick with, I fear, a touch of the fever, but improving some I hope. Our sick at the hospital are some better, I am in hopes, except Mr. Morgan; unless a change for the better soon, he will die.

Stephen Goggin and Ben Fuqua expect to start for home tomorrow on a furlough of thirty days. Robert Johnson expects to start in a few days. His Pa is still with him.

You seem quite uneasy as to my suffering for want of my clothes. I am doing very well as to clothes yet. I bought a woolen shirt a week or two since but have not put it on yet. Have not put my flannel next to my body yet and never used it till this winter, so it keeps me quite comfortable over my cotton. I have an old overcoat. Sam Murrill had two and I took one to take care of for him, which suits very well for a quartermaster. I would soon miss a good one.

As to my boots, I am doing very well. I had my old ones half-soled, so they are as warm as new ones would be. Don't be uneasy as to clothes for me. If I need them bad, I can buy, if those you have don't get here in time. Duck, if you have the chance, make a pocket in my drawers for my money and a watch pocket in my pants.

I must try and give you all the news I have. As to the enemy, they seem quiet in this vicinity. Have fallen back from the direction of Centreville. And if they make an attack, it is expected it will be in the direction of the blockade on the Potomac. General Hill[134] is throwing up fortifications near Leesburg. Some say they are rather looking for an attack there. The report reached here a few days since that the enemy were advancing on Winchester, but I guess it probably was a mistake. I hear no talk now of winter quarters, expect probably we will winter in our tents.

Duck, write soon and often. I hope I can come to see you and the little babe before next May. Take good care of him, do not spoil him. You and he stay some with Pa and Ma. Write me word what sort of crop Job made; how our hogs are; whether they will get fat enough for meat or not; what sort of crop of corn Pa and your Pa made; all the news; how Clem is getting on. Tell her to be a good girl and take good care of our little babe. Duck, write word particularly what sort of killing of hogs Pa and your pa has.

You wished to know whether I was satisfied with the name of our darling babe or not. I think it will suit well as any, a very pretty name. I must close. Give my love to all, to you and the babe. Tell all to write soon. May the Lord bless you both with good health and protect you is the sincere wish of your devoted but unworthy husband,

R. W. Parker

I'll write to Ma and Pa soon. Give my love to all the family, your pa, ma, and family.

Waterford, Loudoun County, Va.
Dec. the 28, '61
Dear Mother and Father,

I received your kind favor a day or two since of the 24 and was much relieved, for I had been very uneasy about home. I can't imagine the reason I don't get more letters. The last I received from Beck was the 8 of this month.

Ma, please write often, and tell Beck too. I'll be uneasy till I hear from Beck and the babe. I started a letter to Beck day before yesterday by George, Lieut. Johnson's servant, who has a wife at Jesse Pullen's. He started home with the sick but all had to come back after getting to the railroad, their furloughs not being right, which disappointed them very much. Our captain a few days since received orders to let several of his men go home at a time, and we were in hopes of getting home soon, but about the time the first furloughs were written the order was countermanded by General Beauregard and issued orders that none except those that volunteered for the war could get furloughs. I wrote to Beck, hoping to get home soon, not to send my clothes for the next winter, but as the orders are changed she can send them if she has a good chance, as I think it doubtful about my coming home till next May, as I don't intend having two halters round my neck at once.

This leaves me well and getting on finely. Through the great blessing of kind Providence, I am enjoying excellent health. We have but few sick in camp, as some have gone home and at the hospital. I hope the sick are improving.

I wish Brother G. was with us now. We have excellent quarters, good warm houses to stay in this cold weather, and plenty to eat and feed our horses on. I think our horses look as well or better than they have since we left home. I sincerely hope we can stay here through the winter, as we have never been to a better place, and people kind as we could wish. [They] send great baskets of provisions ready prepared for eating in camp, and on picket our men have dinners furnished them almost every day. This is a great part of Va.

I have no war news new or interesting. The greatest talk is of the Mason and Slidell Affair. The opinion is now that the Yankees, after saying and doing all they have in regard to keeping them, that they will give them up and make all acknowledgments.

The enemy seems to be very quiet up this way. Have not heard of any late move for some time. I sincerely hope they will not trouble us through the winter, but I fear, if the river freezes over, they will disturb us, for they are people that can't stay on their side and do as they should.

I received a letter from Brother G. not long since. He was well and in fine spirits, but said their rations were rather short. I fear he will see hard times out there. The report has reached here that his regiment has been ordered to Manassas, but I fear untrue.

I must close for this time. Write soon and often, give all the news. Tell Beck to write often also. When all the hogs are killed, send me the weight. My love to you, Pa, Brother, Sister, and Beck and the babe. Kiss him for me; take good care of him.

Ma, I sent forty dollars home by Edward Jones, also forty by Cousin Billie Johnson, but have not heard whether it has ever arrived at home or not. Let me know in your next letter.

From your unworthy son,
R. W. Parker

Waterford, Loudoun County, Va.
Dec. the 31, '61
Dear Companion,

I have received no letters from you yet, but am anxiously awaiting the arrival of one. I hope to hear from you today, as it is the last day of eighteen hundred and sixty one. Tomorrow, if we live to see it, commences the new campaign. Oh, how thankful we should be to our heavenly Father that He has spared our unprofitable lives through another year. Oh, that I could be more thankful. Tomorrow, if we should live to see it, commences the campaign of '62. In the present campaign we have been greatly blessed, and would to God our success, through His protecting guidance, the next may be more so.

Christmas ends today, and I enjoyed it much better than I anticipated. I was at several nice dinners and treated with the greatest kindness. But good dinners is no rarity to me now, for I get them anytime when I go out of camp. A few days since, I was in camp at dinnertime and told some of the boys that I had missed a bid to dinner by staying in camp in the presence of Dr. Bond, the Waterford physician. "Well," he said, "I will give you a pass to a big dinner down in town, if you will accept it," and of course I did, and got an excellent dinner. He saw me just after I had finished my dinner and gave me a bid to dinner the next day at his brother's.

The kindness of the people of Loudoun will never be forgotten by us. This place seems more like home than any since we left home. Our company has the name of being the best and most agreeable company that has ever been stationed here. I think myself we have an excellent comp., with the exception of a few that drink too much.

Waterford, Loudoun County, Va.
January the 1, 1862.

Dear Duck,

I shall now attempt to finish my note tonight, but have nothing fresh for you, though you may think you can take me on this as salt is so scarce, but I am glad to inform you we have plenty. In the first and foremost place, I am well and getting on finely. Get plenty to eat for men and horses. We hear no talk of leaving here and hope we will not till spring. The well men of our company seem to be in high spirits, but have a great deal of hard duty to perform. The sick seem to be improving except Lieut. Johnson and Jo Johnson. Lieut. Johnson started home a few days since, Coly Adams with him, but could not get on the cars, their furloughs not being signed by Beauregard, and had to come back to Leesburg. So I don't think Coly will get home. Lieut. J. is very sick and can't leave now for home under a week.

I must tell you of a little incident that happened near Lovettsville a few days since. It was found out that there was a communication kept up across the river by a lady. So Capt. Graves and a Lieut. White fixed a plan to stop it. So they dressed up Sandy Wilson in ladies clothes, and with several of our company, went down to the river early one morning, near as they could find where the lady went. All of them secreted themselves and sent Sandy with a bundle to make the communication. So he went out in the bank and beckoned to the Yankees to come over. They asked what he wanted. He told them to come over, showing his bundle, so two officers and one private jumped in a boat and over they came. Just as they got to this bank, our men jumped up and demanded, White starting at them, telling them if they fired a gun our men would kill all of them, but one of them drew his pistol and fired. So this caused our men to fire. All of them fell in the boat and our men [. . .] their fire. Soon as this was done, they all rolled out the boat and hung to the boat with one hand and floated down the river calling for help from the other side. Our men fired a few shots at them as they floated down with the tide. Just at this time the balls commenced falling thick round them and our men were obliged to leave the wounded Yankees floating down the river without getting one of them. We think this will stop the communication across at that point.

I wrote to you in my last not to send my clothes, hoping to come home soon, but now I think the chance worse than ever. So if you have a good chance, send them. I am getting on very well yet, not needing them much. Colonel Robert Brother George is here and expects to leave in the morning for home, and Waddy Burton with him on a furlough of ten days. I must close for this time. Why don't I receive letters from you? The last from you was the 8 of last month. Write soon and often. The last news from home, you and our darling babe was sick with bad colds. Please write often. My best love to you and the babe. Kiss him for me. Farewell for this time. My love to all. Tell somebody to write to me soon. From your devoted but unworthy husband,

R. W. Parker

Write soon and often.

1862

The Second Regiment Virginia Cavalry established winter quarters in northern Virginia along the Alexandria Line during the winter of 1861–62. They broke camp to cover Brig. Gen. D. H. Hill's evacuation of Leesburg in early March 1862. While the rest of Brigadier General Stuart's cavalry headed for the Peninsula, the Second were attached to Maj. Gen. Richard Ewell's forces. In April they were ordered to reinforce Maj. Gen. Thomas J. "Stonewall" Jackson in the Shenandoah Valley. They served under Jackson at the Battle of Front Royal then were reassigned to Brig. Gen. George H. Steuart. They finally joined Brig. Gen. Beverly Johnson's Laurel Brigade and brought up Jackson's rear as he led his army out of the Valley toward the Peninsula. They participated in the Peninsula campaign then, in the autumn of 1862, confronted Brig. Gen. John Pope. They guarded the Army of Northern Virginia's rear as it retreated from the Maryland campaign. They returned to central Virginia by the end of October and were then transferred to Brig. Gen. Fitzhugh Lee's Second Brigade. They continued to see action along the Rappahannock River for the remainder of the year.[1]

Waterford, Loudoun County, Va.
January the 5, '62
My Dear Companion,

Your long-looked-for letter of the 30 came duly to hand a day or two since, being the first received since the 8 of last month. I had almost given out receiving anymore from you. I am sorry to inform you I have never received the little ham you sent me; hope it may come to hand yet. Oh, that I could see the natural one. It would be the greatest pleasure imaginable to see you both. Wish you would send me your and his likeness together. I wished to see yours time and again before he was born and now want to see both.

Duck, I was in hopes I could get an overcoat down here with out troubling you, but fear now it is impossible, so I will have to get you and Ma to make me one, if you can get anything to make it of. If you can't, write me word and I can have one made down here. If you make it, have it tolerably long tail with pockets in it, one side pocket—a real troopers coat. You can send my boots and clothes by Burton.

I have no news of interest this morning. We have for the last few days some very cold weather. The ground is white with snow. I have a lively time now getting forage; have, it seems, to go for forage every bad day. Til Scott is getting on finely. Jo Burroughs is out on picket, a little sick; hope he is mending. Mr. Phelps is well, and he and several of the boys are fixing to go in changes to hear the Quakers.

The enemy seem to be quiet up this way, and I hope they will remain so for the next two months, so we may stay in our good quarters during winter and with the kind people of this vicinity, for we were never better treated. Our men are still fortifying Leesburg. They will soon have a splendid fort complete not far from town on the west side, also one on the east. It will soon be one of our strongholds on the Potomac. The sick, I hope, are improving. Have but few sick in camp. Lieut. Johnson and Jo have not started home yet but will start soon. I hope all our sick may go home and remain till they recover, and if I should happen to be sick, that our captain will let me come home, but hope I may have good health, for I prefer good health if I have to stay the twelve months through before going home to sickness. I am thankful to my maker that I can inform you that I am yet enjoying good health and getting finely. Don't be uneasy as to my clothes. They are not ragged yet.

Duck, I received a few lines from one of your relations a few days since and said I must come home soon as possible to see our darling son. Said he was a fine-looking little fellow and greatly doted on. You must take good care of him and not spoil him. Don't have him nursed too much. Kiss him for me and tell him to kiss you for me. I must close. My love to you and our darling boy. My best wishes to all. Write soon and often. My love to Pa, Ma and family. Farewell for this time. Oh, that I may see you soon.

From your devoted but unworthy husband,

R. W. Parker

January the 6, '62

I am well as common this morning. Our company seem to be getting on finely. Had another snow last night about one inch deep. We are having hard winter weather but splendid times. Don't be uneasy about me in any respect, for I am doing well. If you can get anything to make my overcoat, make and send it when you can. Farewell.

My wish is that we may stay here through the winter and that I can come home soon and see you and the baby boy. Kiss him for me. My love to you both. R. W. Parker

Duck, I have a lively time here where I go for grog. I tell the ladies I am a married man, but they don't believe it. The capt. came in from the picket this morning. As I said, I said I was a married man, but they don't believe it.[2]

Waterford, Loudoun County, Va.

Jan. the 10, '62

My Very Dear Companion,

It is with the greatest pleasure I seize my pen this morning to inform you of the reception of your very interesting letters. Yours of the 6 Jan. came to hand yesterday and received yours with our babe boy's hair in it. That was laid aside in the office, not being directed to the care of our captain. Be careful how you direct your letters, Duck. I received a letter from Ma yesterday with some very interesting news and some quite sad. Ma said Brother George had arrived safe at home on a sick furlough. I am sorry to hear he is sick, but glad that he has luck so well as to get home with Mr. Newman with him. It delights me to hear of our sick going home. I was very much surprised to hear of the death of your brother William,[3] but that is a debt we all will have to pay soon or late. Duck, Capt. Pollard has arrived at Leesburg, where his sons are. He came up with them from near Centreville. Two more companies of our regiment have come up, and Col. Radford with them, so Colonel Munford has to leave us. I am very sorry indeed to part with him; he is an excellent man.

I fear Col. Radford will order us back to Leesburg with him from our good quarters, for it's just like him to do so, especially when he finds we have such nice comfortable quarters. We are getting along finely here and wish we could stay here through the winter. Have no one much complaining in camp. Lieut. Johnson and Jo are at the hospital yet, not well enough to leave for home but mending. The Yankees seem to be quiet up this way. Have not disturbed us for some time. You wished to know if any of our Bedford boys were killed in the Dranesville[4] fight. None that I've heard of. The report has reached us that Jackson has had a very successful brush with the Yankees near Romney,[5] but nothing definite.

Don't be uneasy about my needing clothes. I am doing well yet, and if I was about to suffer, I have some money left yet to buy with if necessary. If you can't get me an overcoat on reasonable terms write me word—I think I can perhaps get one down here cheaper and have it made to order. As to getting me a pair of gloves, I can get them handier down here than you can in Bedford. We have had for the last few days some quite disagreeable weather and would like to see my boots come with Burton, but am doing very well yet. Don't send more than two or three pair of socks. You wished to know whether Lil Johnson had [yet] seen his little fellow. No, I guess not, and never a word about unless someone asks him.

I don't know when I ever received a letter that did me more good than your last. The news of you and Robert Moorman getting on so well filled me with joy, to hear he is such a fine, pert boy. Ma wrote me word he was a remarkable pert child and so much doted on and watched by all, I fear all of you will spoil him. Oh, how glad I would be to see how sassy he looks when sucking. Hope I can see you both soon. The Capt. is nearly ready to start. Kiss Moorman for me. My love to you both, also to your pa, ma, Bet, Sarah and all inquiring friends. Farewell this time.

From your ever devoted husband,

R. W. Parker

Write soon and all the news.

Waterford, Loudoun Cty.

Jan. the 15, '62

My Dear Companion,

As I am attending camp guard tonight and feeling rather lonely, thinking of home and the dearest objects on earth to me, which you may well know are you and little Robert Moorman, I shall attempt to spend a few moments in dropping you a few lines. Have nothing fresh this evening. We are still camped here and hope will not leave for the next two months, if the Yankees do not interrupt us.

Colonel Radford wants to move us back to Leesburg, but have heard this evening General Hill objects to it. Sam Murrill paid us a visit this evening for the first [time] for nearly three months. He looks quite well. Col. Radford is trying to get all his regiment up here. I should like for him to succeed, for it would make our duty much lighter. We are still getting on finely, but the weather is quite disagreeable. Had snow yesterday, hail and rain today, bid fair for a big sleet, but has been clearing this evening.

I guess you have heard before this of the marriage of Bar A. Ricard to Miss Mariah Thancock. I was rather surprised to hear of the match. Next comes the war news, though I have none very important. Perhaps you have heard of the skirmish Gen. Jackson had several days since above us on the Potomac. He lost twenty-odd men killed, took twenty-six, five hundred sides [of] leather, five or six hundred overcoats, camps, equipments [. . .]⁶

The Yankees seem quiet along the border here. Hope they will not disturb us during the winter, though it is believed they intend a battle near Leesburg soon. We sent down a flag of truce yesterday to exchange papers but they didn't exchange, which is rather strange, having exchanged some before this time.

Duck, you and Robert Moorman have me completely. You both claimed Christmas gifts on me and I can't study up what to send you. I was up at Hillsborough yesterday on purpose to get some gloves, a pair for Ben Joplin and also for myself. While looking round I saw a pair I thought would suit for my Christmas gift to you and brought them to camp for you and will try and send them by Capt. Wilson or Squire Johnson. I don't know what would suit for Moorman; write me word.

Duck, Ma wrote word that material for overcoats or that overcoats were out of all reason. If you can't get me one on reasonable terms, write me word immediately and I'll have one made here. One made of good homemade jeans looks very well. I have some old clothes [that] when I get my new ones I should like to send home. We have but few sick now, one in camp and three at the hospital. Lieut. Johnson and Jo are there yet. Will start home soon, I guess.

I am still, through the blessing of kind Providence, enjoying good health. I must close, after giving you what news I can think of now, it being after midnight. So goodnight to you and little Robert Moorman. My love to you both. Kiss him for me and tell him to kiss you for me. My love to you, Pa, Ma, and the family.

Write soon. I am anxiously looking for a letter from you; was new the fourth of this month.

My love to all. Farewell. I ever remain your unworthy but devoted companion,

R. W. Parker

What has become of Alick and Ginnie? I have answered all their letters I have received, which was 2.

Jan. the 16. I am well this morning. Have heard nothing new up to this date. Capt. Wilson and Squire Johnson are here this morning.

Camp Waterford, Loudoun Co., Va.

Jan. the 22, '62

My Very Dear Companion,

With the greatest pleasure I shall attempt to transmit you a few lines in answer to your welcome letter by Burton, received the 20, for it was, if I mistake not, the first from you since the 10, which time you may be sure has seemed quite long to me. All the clothes mentioned in your letter by Burton reached me safe and suit me very well indeed. The most that troubles me now is I have so many I fear I'll not be able to carry them and have no way to send them home. But will try and take care of them. I was surprised to see another pair of such nice gloves, and as I had a good pair of yarn ones on hand, I sold them to one of the boys for seventy-five cts. I am very much pleased with all my clothes and particularly the cotton shirts. Several of the boys have wanted them, but I guess they will never get them, for I hate to part with anything you send me from home.

Some three or four of our company came to camp with Lieut. Burton and look fine and fat. I should like very much indeed to come home and stay a while, if it would improve me like it has those that have gone. Improved or not, my greatest earthly desire is to see you and little Moorman, if but for a short time. Months pass off almost like years to me. What would I not give just to be with you both tonight. But if not before, if life lasts, I hope to see you the first of June next, the Lord willing. Were it not for hope, it seems to me I would have to give up in despair. But enough of this, and hope we may meet soon.

Well, Duck, I am still enjoying good health and fattening. I lack but little, being heavy as I was last winter. Hope I may enjoy good health at least till I reach home. I am more than glad to hear of you and little Mo enjoying such good health. Oh, how I wish its continuance.

You seemed to be surprised to hear of Mary Whitten's marrying City. I can't say I was much surprised, for I had heard how some of her older sisters married, and I have heard if the old lady took a notion for her daughters to marry any man, they were sure to do so. I hope that Warner City will have to marry her, for I think he should be made take care of her and his child. I say [. . .] City's while you can. . .

Duck, the most of my thoughts are about you and little Moorman, so you must take the will for the deed. I am obliged to give you what news I do very scattering. We have had some very bad weather for the last two weeks, plenty [of] hail, rain, and snow with sleet. But as good luck has blessed us, we are still in our good quarters and expect to remain here, if the Yankees will be quiet till the last of next month. The people still remain kind to us and we are getting on well as soldiers could wish. The Yankees seem very quiet for the past month and I hope they will remain so for some time yet. The report is here that the enemy intend a general advance soon, but I guess the weather will rather belate them. Good many negroes are running over long the border and carrying their masters' horses with them.[7]

All we lack of having Leesburg well prepared for defense is we haven't enough cannon there yet. Will have soon, if nothing prevents. I received a letter from your cousin Fannie Pullen a few days since. She said her babe was considerably larger than ours but that she didn't know which was the prettiest, but she was sure hers was the best, as it didn't have half so many [to] nurse him. You must be sure not to have ours spoiled. If I could have my wish, I never want him spoiled. Don't nurse him too much. I wish I had something to send him for a Christmas gift, but if get one, I have no way to send it to him, so you must get one for him.

I have given you the most of the points I have and must close, as you will be pained to read what has already been written. Write soon.

Affectionately yours,
R. W. Parker

Camp Waterford, Loudoun County, Va.
Jan. the 22, '62
My Dear Son (Robert Moorman Parker),

No earthly pleasure, I am confident, would please me better than to gratify your wish to pay you and Marmy a visit. You must not let Grandma and all the folks spoil you, for I don't want Marmy to have to whip you. Tell Ma I think you can hardly plant one corn, and had better stay with Ma and take care of her till I come home, and you can then go down with me and Ma and feed the little pigs. You may have two of the prettiest.

Son, next time you must not go to sleep so soon and write a long letter. Well, I must close for this time, lest I weary your little eyes looking over this letter. My love to you. Dear son, be a good boy and mind Ma, Grandpa and ma. Give my love to Ma. Tell her to kiss you every morning and evening for Parpy. My love to Grandpa, Grandma, Aunt Lucy and Aunt Nannie, Uncle Charley and Uncle Jesse. Tell Clem to be a good girl and take good care of you. Farewell, dear son. Be a good babe.

From your affectionate papa,

R. W. Parker

Waterford, Loudoun County, Va.
Monday morning, Jan. 27th, three o'cl, '62
My Dear Companion,

As I am on guard duty this morning, my thought naturally turned homeward to the nearest and dearest objects on earth to me, which you well know are my dear companion and little babe. I shall attempt for a few moments to transmit you a short note—though I have but little encouragement, as your letters are so few and far between. I have not received a line from you since one written the ninth of this month. What is the reason, I can't imagine, but must be through the neglect of the postmasters. Hope such neglect will soon cease and that we may be able to hear from each other often.

I have nothing of interest to communicate. I am well as usual and our company generally is in better health than it has been for several months, though our capt. is a little complaining.

Jan. the 27, evening. I will give you a few of the points this evening, though nothing new has occurred during the day. I have just been in camp but a short time, having been out foraging today, and am quite tired, but will sit up if I can to finish my note to you. I have just received a letter from Aunt May Parker requesting me to answer it immediately. And when do you reckon it was written? The 18 of Nov. '61—over two months since. She said in her letter that the report there was that all Capt. Wilson's company were taken prisoners. I never heard of that report until it came from Bedford. It is surprising how such reports will slant. Aunt Mollie's family were getting [on] tolerably well. Had had the diphtheria there.

I guess you have heard ere this of our defeat in Kentucky; General Zollicoffer and several of his men killed on the battle field.[8] Although we are sad to hear of our defeat once and a while, we can't expect to whip in every battle. The enemy seem quiet up this way and stay pretty close to their side of the river. There is nothing new taking place along this border so far as I know.

Two of the winter months will soon have passed from time to eternity, nevermore to return, and all of us should be more and more humble and ask His protecting hand to overpower us, who has all the power both in heaven and on earth.

Duck, I wrote to you for an overcoat. If you can't get one on reasonable terms, write me word soon. I have suffered but little with cold yet, and it will soon be [. . .] if the weather changes some towards getting warmer. I'll not need one long, and my shawl with the clothes I wear, I never suffer with cold but little.

Jan. the 28, at night. Nothing of interest has taken place up to this time but the arrival of your welcome letter of the 21, which I assure you was the greatest treat I have had for a long time. Every time I hear from you and little Moorman makes me want to see you worse and worse. Wish I could hear from you both every few days. I would give anything in reason just to see you, if but for a few hours. Words can't express the anxiety of my heart to see you. My whole thoughts generally, when I am not busy, is about you.

Duck, you wished to know if the clothes came safe. They did, and I am much pleased and thankful to you for them. As to the overcoat, don't trouble yourself anymore about it. I can get one made here, and if I don't, I will be sure not to suffer. Perhaps you had better send me, if you have not it in use, the other half of my shawl by cousin John Graves, though I am making out finely yet and will if we remain in these quarters, which I hope we will for the next month.

Anyhow, write me word how Alick and Ginnie are getting on. I have not heard from them particularly for several months.

I must close. My love to you [and] Moorman. Kiss him for me. Love to your pa, ma, and all the family. Tell Lucy not to be like Bet, just write one little note to hear from Coly and stop short off.

Don't spoil Moorman. Farewell,

R. W. Parker

Jan. the 29. I am well as usual this morning and getting on finely. Farewell, Robert.

Whit Johnson is at home, nearly well I reckon. Heard from him at Lynchburg on his way home. From your letter, the snow has been deeper in Bedford than here. We have several sleets, have one now.

Waterford, Loudoun County, Va.

Monday morning, February the 5, 1862

My Dear Companion,

Your welcome letter of the 24 came to hand a day or two since, which I assure you was perused with the greatest interest. Was surprised to hear of so many deaths and so much sickness. I fear in the next from home I shall hear of the death of Caroline. What will Miss Catherine do now? I have thought of her many times since I heard of the death of Mr. Creasy. Hope she may get on well. I am very sorry to hear Mr. Pullen is sick. He has had so much sickness in his family within the last few months. I don't suppose he or his family hardly knew what distress was until year '62. I am glad to hear that Pa and Brother G. are improving. Hope they will be well soon. But sorry to hear of Job being unwell, and that Elias Newman's leg is so bad. Hope there is no danger of its causing loss of his life. I am confident if those men had done as they should [and] let someone know they were coming to have stopped the dog, they would have been bit. I don't expect Pit thought he was doing more than his duty to take care of what was round him. If I could just be at home to manage him, I would not take any reasonable sum for him.

You spoke of bad weather in your letter. You will, no doubt, be surprised to hear that the deepest snow we have had here was not, I think, over three inches deep. We have snow, rain, and hail every few days. There has been more raining, hailing, and freezing for the past month, I am confident, than I ever saw in Bedford the same length of time. I have suffered less with cold this winter than I ever did one winter, but am wearing more clothes. I have suffered but little [in] the coldest weather we have had, and only my feet and hands then.

Duck, I was not much surprised to hear of Jimmie's getting married soon, for nothing happens that surprises me much nowadays. You wished me to keep it a secret, which I did till the morning after I received your letter and was asked if Jimmie was not to be married soon. I told them I didn't know, then was asked if nothing was said about it in my letter. I told them that I believed that Jimmie's name was mentioned, I believe, in my letter. I soon found out that two or three of the company had received letters to that effect the same evening. If I mistake not, the letters were to Tom Bernard and Waddy Burton. They have heard he is to be married soon and who to. Duck, what do you reason Mr. Phelps said when they told him Ginnie was to be married soon and who to? He said he didn't believe it because she was a relation of his. As soon as he said it, the boys commenced teasing him, and I am confident he wishes now he had said nothing. Tom Mayhew seems to get on finely with the ladies or he would not have married so soon. I think he is better for marrying than acting the soldier. You mentioned Mr. Nekands coming to this county. He does not expect to come, I have heard, till next summer. You seemed almost afraid to mention the report about Steve Goggin and Cousin Lucy. I have known they loved each other ever since we left home. They have been corresponding ever since they parted in Bedford, and in my opinion, half Steve's sickness was home- and lovesick. Don't let it get out.

I received Aunt Mollie's letter not long since and have answered it. I have never received your letter that had one in it from Bet and Alick, and given up their writing to me. Duck, write me word particularly how Ginnie and Alick are getting on and if there is likely to be a change there soon, if ever. I have been asked several times within the last few weeks if Ginnie didn't have a baby. I had to inform them I had never heard of it.

I have noticed most of the points in your letter and will now try and give you some of the points with us, though have nothing new or interesting. Our company is, I believe, in better health than it has been for several months and in fine spirits. Our captain has been quite unwell but is recovering. Jim Leftwich came down with Burton, went on picket, stayed four days, came to camp sick, and I carried him to the hospital a day or two since. We are still in our good quarters and hope to remain here till next month, if not longer. The people are quite kind to us and we get plenty to eat and for our horses.

The greatest trouble here is among slaveholders. 'Long their borders, a great many [slaves] are running off—not only themselves, but generally take their masters' best horse with them. There is but little expectation of a fight up this way soon. The weather and such are so bad, they could not if they wished to. The report here is that McClellan[9] does not intend to advance till the twelve months volunteers' time is out and advance on raw troops, but I guess he will be disappointed in that. I have heard that there is good many reenlisting for the war in some regiments, but I have heard of but few in our regiment and to the South. I don't know a man, but I guess if everything works right, several from our company will reenlist, I guess, long before this. You have heard of our defeat in Kentucky and our general killed, but we can't expect to whip every time.

Nine o'cl. Monday. It is now snowing very fast and bids fair to be a big snow, and the roads in bad order. It will be almost impossible to get out and get the necessaries of camp.

Duck, I hardly know what to say about little Moorman, he is such a great boy. I could say a great deal to him if I could see him. Oh, it would please me so much to see him sucking and playing with your breast. My greatest earthly desire is to see you and him. I have not words to express my thoughts about you and him. Duck, I want you to say whether I must reenlist for the war or not. If I reenlist I can get a furlough of thirty days and fifty dollars, but fifty dollars would not induce me to volunteer.[10]

Well, I must close, as it is getting late and I have some business to attend to. This leaves me tolerably well, with the exception of a cold. Duck, write soon and often. Tell Ma to write often. Farewell, my dear companion and son. My love to you both. Kiss Moorman for me. My love to you, Pa, Ma, and family and all inquiring friends.

From your devoted but worthy,

Robert

My Dear Little Moorman,

You must be a good babe, and tell Marmy she must not leave you long at a time and left you so hungry. Kiss Marmy for me. Oh, that I could see [you] and Marmy, if only for an hour. Farewell, dear babe.

From your Parpy,

R. W. Parker

Waterford, Loudoun County

Feb. the 14, 1862

My Dear Companion,

With the greatest pleasure I shall try and acknowledge the reception of your very interesting letter mailed [Body camp] Feb. the 7. Also yours the 29 + 31 have come to hand some time since. I have nothing good for you this morning, but quantity of bad news. I guess ere this you have heard of the federal victory at Roanoke Island,[11] also at Fort Henry, Tennessee.[12] But we can't expect to be victorious in every battle, but must take courage and determine to conquer or die.

I am, through the blessing of kind Providence, enjoying good health. Also our company generally and all seem to be in fine spirits. Get plenty of meat and bread, no sugar or coffee,[13] and plenty duty to do. This is just as good as a soldier could wish, with good quarters.

There is considerable preparation-making at this place for the Quaker quarterly meeting, which commences tomorrow and continues till Monday. The people say they generally have a great time. The Quakers are here today hauling away the filth from round the church and fixing up generally. I am anxious to be in church tomorrow and next day, though we may all be disappointed, as the Yankees may come over to see us during the meeting, thinking perhaps we may not be on our guard.

Duck, the theme of reenlisting seems to have a place among your thoughts, and in reply to your wishes, I hardly know what to say. In the first place, I think I had better wait with patience till the expiration of this twelve months, and then perhaps we will know better what to do. If it be really necessary for me to reenlist, I am willing to do so, but would like to see some of the militia come forward to aid us in whipping the enemy. If you have received my last letter, you will hear my sentiments in conclusion. Duck, I want to see you and Moorman, and then we will think more about it.

After so much bad news, of course we expect some good. I heard this evening that General Price[14] has gained a great victory in Missouri over the Federals.[15] I saw in a paper the first of this week the Federals said they had him surrounded and he would have to fight or surrender. I sincerely hope he has succeeded in giving them a good whipping. Duck, what do you think—the Yankees are exchanging prisoners. The two of Capt. Radford's men that were taken prisoners at Dranesville—Alick Whitten and I have forgotten the other name—with several others were exchanged across the Potomac yesterday near Leesburg. They speak of having a hard time with the Federals. A deserter from Maryland stayed with us a night or two since, a very smart man indeed, a member of one of the companies we have in service from that state. He gave us a great many interesting points too tedious to mention. Says provisions are very scarce indeed on the other side of the river. Says that a great portion of Maryland is almost like a barren desert, stripped of everything. We would not have so much confidence in him, but he is identified by a great many Virginians. His name, I think, is Umbaugh.

You wish to know if I reenlist, if there is any chance to come home next June. If I reenlist, I get a furlough for thirty days. If I reenlist, I have a notion going [into] a company of heavy artillery. Have not elected any company yet and hardly know what to do for the best. You spoke in your letter of some who had gone home on furloughs. What a change has taken place. I tell [you] no one at home knows the debased condition of hundreds, and I might say thousands, of our soldiers since they left their lovely homes. Tell me those reports and who they are about. I can keep a secret as good as I ever could. I sent you a few stamps in my last letter.

I must close. Write soon and give all the news. I have not, I think, received a letter from Pa or Ma for a month.

I am grieved to hear of the continued illness of poor little Moorman. Hope he is better ere this. Take good care of him, which I know you will. Kiss him often for this poor unworthy papa far away and who hopes to be with you both soon. Don't spoil him, and may kind Providence protect and deliver you both from all danger is the sincere wish of your devoted but unworthy husband,

Robert

Oh that I could see you both.

Waterford, Loudoun County, Va.
Feb. the 23, '62
My Dear Companion,

It having been some time since I heard from you, I shall attempt to drop you a few lines, though uninteresting they may be. I am, through the blessing of kind Providence, enjoying good health and sincerely hope for its continuance. Have no good news for you this evening but plenty of bad, and no doubt you have heard it ere this, or at least of the greater portion, at least of the Federal victories at Roanoke Island, taking 25 hundred of our men prisoners, and surrendering Fort Henry, and of their decided advantage over our forces at Fort Donelson. The enemy's report of that battle is shocking, if true. There report is that they took the fort with twenty-five thousand of our men prisoners, two thousand horses, and a large quantity of army stores. Our report is, we lost twenty-five hundred killed, wounded, and taken prisoners.[16] I am fearful our loss is great, at any rate. Our count also is, we left of the enemy killed on the battlefield six thousand. They whipped us, we acknowledge, but they sustained great loss. Our forces have fallen to Nashville and expect to defend the city at all hazards if possible.[17] The report reached this point yesterday that the enemy had also taken Savannah, Georgia,[18] but hope this is only a report.

We have rather expected that General Jackson's forces near Winchester would have been attacked before this time, but believe now it will [be] some days first, as some of their forces are returning from up that way, and maybe to attack Leesburg. We would not be surprised [to] have a fight there at any time. It is believed that they will not attack us with twenty thousand men. We have only four thousand here, but will be reinforced if necessary.

The enlisting question is high in this quarter. A good many of our regiment have reenlisted. Last one of our company has enlisted. That is Lil Johnson; he enlisted a day or two since. Gets a furlough for thirty-six days and fifty dollars. Will, if nothing happens, start home in a day or two. Duck, I want you to give me your opinion about my enlisting. Sometimes I hardly know what to do, whether to reenlist now or wait till my time is nigher out. I think perhaps I'd better let the halter that's round my neck now wear a little more before I enlist, as perhaps some change may take place during the next three months.

We have had more wet weather, it seems to me, since first of January than I ever remember seeing, with a great deal of sleet and frequent little snows, and the roads are muddy enough for any use.

I received a letter from Brother G. a few days since, giving me descriptions of things at home. Says they have undergone a considerable change. He said you looked quite well and that Moorman was quite a nice little fellow. Such news as that does me good to read. Hope you both are still doing well; in your last you stated that [you were] rather unwell. I have been rather uneasy about him. I received a letter from Cousin Mat Lipscomb in answer to mine, in which she said I need not say I had the prettiest and sweetest babe she ever saw, for she knew if I was to see hers I would stop bragging, and wound up by saying I must not tell anyone, as it was only one of her little stories. I expressed several mischievous thoughts to her and told her I thought she ought to do her portion raising soldiers to defend our southern homes. She requested me to kiss her sugar pie for her. I replied that the name was enough for me and that I was not use to kissing such creatures in camp.

She stated also in hers that I just ought to hear Uncle Jo Johnson talk about the ladies and marrying. Said from his conversation, Miss Jane Nichols was his intended. I suppose he and Cousin Dick could not agree. After telling me this, requested me to say nothing about it, but I can't keep it from you, so you must not let it get out. She expects to pay you a visit the fourth Saturday in March, as Uncle T. goes to Timberidge. I guess ere this you have heard that Charley Hart has joined Capt. Gordan's company at Gloucester point. I hope every man that thinks enough of his country to defend it will volunteer, and that every coward will be drafted. Present my congratulations to Jimmie if he has taken unto himself a wife, and that he must now volunteer to protect her. Present my best wishes Cousin Lucy (I believe that's her name), and hope they may spend their future days in peace and happiness. Present my best wishes to Alick and Ginnie. Tell them I have received only two letters from them since I've been in service. I heard from Alick and Ginnie a few days since through a letter from him to Til Scott. Scott is well and getting on finely, also Burroughs and Adams.

Having given you all the news, I must bring my uninteresting letter to a close, for I am sure it will puzzle you to read it. Mr. Phelps requests me particularly to present his best wishes to you, your pa, ma and family; also to Pa, Ma, and family. He is looking quite well and, if I mistake not, is several pounds heavier than he ever was before.

My love to you [and] little Moorman—kiss him for me—, also to your pa, ma, and family. Write soon and be particular how you direct them. I have not received a letter from Pa or Ma for a month.

Wish I could hear from you all often. Please write soon and often. May kind Providence protect and keep you, little Moorman, and all is the sincere wish of your unworthy but devoted husband,

R. W. Parker

Perhaps you may wish to know what this sheet was intended for. It was for a forage requisition, and the printer happened to leave one side blank, so I thought it would serve [as] a good sheet of paper and answer my purpose this evening to write on. Farewell,

Robert.

Rapidan Station, Orange County
March the 22, 1862
My Dear Companion,

As we have again pitched tents and expect to remain here a few days, I'll try and drop you a few lines. We left Culpeper CH on the 18 for this place with the baggage, which we reached on the 19—two days' march, a distance of about 13 miles, and the worst road I ever saw, through woods and old fields, in many places where there never was a road before, and raining a good portion of both days and nights. A very disagreeable march indeed.

We are now encamped on the south side of Rapidan River. Near three miles off the above-named station is where the railroad crosses the river. Our encampment is also five miles east of Orange CH and in a hard portion of the country to support an army. We are some thirty miles northwest of Fredericksburg. It is thought the line of defense of the Potomac Army will be from Fredericksburg to Gordonsville and on to Staunton. The principle portion of our army stores are at Gordonsville.

Our regiment is still near Warrenton on the watch for the Yankees. It is reported they have advanced as far as Manassas, but it will be some time before they reach this place, as it will take a tremendous baggage train to bring it on wagons, and if by railroad it will take some time to repair the road. So it will be a month, at any rate, and I hope by that time our army will be reorganized, as the militia are reporting to their different points of destination. I saw quite a number on their way yesterday to Fredericksburg and, poor fellows, they looked so much cast down. I am getting quite anxious to see some of those rampant secessionists of Bedford falling into ranks, who have been so kind to help us with their mouths and not with their hands. We are anxious to see them shoulder their muskets and come forward to the [. . .] of their country. As to the move of any portion of our army save this, I know nothing, but hope they are managing for the best.

I received your very interesting letter of the 10 yesterday, which afforded me much relief to hear you was not sick, for from your last I feared you would be sick, as you complained so much of your head and a bad cold. Hope it may not prove [in] any way serious, and glad to hear little Moorman is well and gaily. Hope I can see you both soon, enjoying good health. I still have the little lock of his hair you sent me, and intend trying to keep it. I have it in the testament. It is a beautiful little lock and fine as silk.

I think if Whit Johnson looks so well, he might come back to his company. I am sorry to have it to say, but some of our men are acting badly, going home and staying nearly all their time, other men doing their duty, and they getting the pay. If they intend staying so long, they ought to be discharged and be drafted with the militia.

You spoke of Fulton Wright wishing to join our company. I wish he could have joined it but don't know yet whether Capt. Graves intends reenlisting yet or not; sometimes he speaks of it. If he would try, he could make up as large company, I think, as any Capt. in the regiment. Why he don't make a company, I can't tell. If he intends reenlisting, he ought to have been receiving recruits for the past month. You mentioned George as being anxious to know whether

I intended reenlisting. I know not what to say. If Capt. Graves does not reenlist and make up a company, I think it very likely, if I reenlist, I will join heavy artillery, but don't know yet what to do for the best.

Duck, I will try and get the indigo for you but think the chance a bad one. I should like to hear from Alick and Ginnie and what he intends doing as to the present military move. I must close. Write soon, and direct your letters to Orange Courthouse, Va.

Yours Devotedly,
Robert

Write soon and often. This leaves me well as usual. Have stood the march splendid, with the exception of a cold.

Farewell, dear little Moorman and Marmy. Kiss Moorman for me. Farewell for this time.

Robert

Culpeper County, Va.
Tuesday, April the 1, 1862
My Dear Companion,

I will try and drop you a few lines, as I have a few moments of leisure. I am with the regiment, now thirteen miles east of Culpeper Courthouse, in the woods encamped like Indians, without tents or anything to eat, and have to live just as we can, on crackers and corn [and] bacon. We get a little bread. I rode yesterday eight miles for my bacon and flour, and happened to the good luck of getting it baked.

I must give you the points in as few words as possible. Our regiment has been scouting about near [. . .] until last Thursday, at which time we had orders that the Yankees were advancing in heavy columns on us and that we must fall back to Fauquier Springs, which we did during that night. The next morning we received orders to reinforce General Stuart[19] at Rappahannock Station, as the Yankees were advancing on him in heavy columns. We pitched off to his position and got there just in time to recross the Rappahannock as the Yankees came in sight, and just as we reached this bank they commenced shelling us, and continued till night, but hurt us none. This next day we expected a big fight, but about sunrise the Yankees moved back and we had no fight. We stayed near there for a day or two and then returned to this place (Oak Shade), thirteen miles east of Culpeper Courthouse, where we expect to remain and picket till the Yankees drive us in.

April the 8, 1862. This leaves me well as usual and at a point I never was before, whether to reenlist or not, as today the question will be asked whether we are going to reenlist or not. I am willing to enlist, but do not want to till I go home. I understand those that do not reenlist today, their names will be returned to the adjutant general's office [and] perhaps be drafted before I go home, but think I shall run the risk anyway. It may be the worst for me, but sometimes there is luck in leisure. Be as it may, I think I will take chances. There is two months of this twelve months to serve yet, and as to the fifty dollars bounty, if I can do with it, I think perhaps I can make out without it.

I understand Capt. Graves is to start home in the evening, and I will try and send this note by him. Perhaps it may go straight and you may hear from me shortly. I received a letter from Cousin Mat Lipscomb yesterday. She was getting on finely. Uncle Tommy was complaining. Aunt Mary's[20] youngest is dead. May be for the best; it is done with the troubles of the wicked world and is at peace, poor little fellow. I have not received a line from you since yours of [. . .] but still hope I may hear from you soon. The mail is so irregular and we move so often, it is hard to get any letters. I received a letter from Uncle John Goggin a few days since. He and Uncle Auville[21] have enlisted for the war, and I don't know how their families and Grandpa's family are to make out without someone to manage for them, but I hope they will be taken care of in this great struggle for our once happy country. My mind is in such a fix that I hardly know what to do or say for the best. There are but few idle moment with me but what my thoughts are homeward to my dear wife and my little Moorman, and wonder if you are well and doing well. Oh that you may be blessed with good health and be comfortably cared for. My love to you and all.

R. W. Parker

Near Gordonsville, Orange Co., Va.
April the 25, 1862
My Dear Beck,

I attempted to drop you a few lines yesterday but had no chance; had to quit before I wrote a line. I will drop you a short note today anyway. I have no good news for you but that I am well and getting on as well as usual, but have, it seems to me, more bad luck in other respects than anybody. I will try and give you a few of the points. We left Oak Shade in Culpeper Co. the 20 for Gordonsville, where we stayed for a day or two, and then to this place, six miles north of Gordonsville at a place called Liberty Mills, where we camped as we went down in service. The bad luck is this: the other day, when our baggage was assigned to Gordensville, I was sent to load on the baggage, which I did, and then was ordered on with the regiment, leaving the baggage in the care of others, and as the road was bad, the teams could not pull the load farther than Orange CH, where it was taken off the wagons and put on the cars. I had a good many of my new clothes in Waddy Burton's trunk, which was misplaced and can't be heard of since. So I am afraid I will lose them clear, but hope I can make out with what I have. As it happened, I got my valise, which had two pairs of pants and a fatigue shirt in it, needle case and several other things which were all safe. Hope yet that I may get them yet, but I must take all fair and say, "For this world is a world of trouble anyway." If I could ever get home I would not mind it so much, but fear my chance is a bad one. Wish I could get someone to take my place till I could see you all for a few days, but fear there is no chance. I guess ere this you heard [of] the plan to hold all between the ages of 18 and 35 in service, so they have me fast anyway. I am a poor unlucky being in some respects. I have not reenlisted yet but think, of course, I am in for the war. I will try and be content and do my duty as a soldier for my beloved country. My greatest wish and anxiety is to see my loved little family, the theme of my earthly thoughts.

The regiment is being reorganized. Some four or five companies have elected officers. Some of the old officers are reelected. Our company has not reorganized yet, but will in a few days. Capt. Graves has reached us. He gave me 4 letters: two from you, one [each] from Alick and Ma. Cousin John Graves and the recruits have not reached us yet. They are at Gordonsville. Hughes came to camp yesterday evening; said he saw little Moorman, was a nice little fellow. Oh that I could see him if but for a moment. You wished to know if we had ever heard from Til Scott. We have never heard a word from him. We started from Gordonsville to reinforce General Jackson, but have stopped here for further orders. I think it is doubtful whether we go there or not. Reports are very conflicting. We get no news of interest now, as we seldom get any papers. The Captain brought me the haversack and contents. I am very thankful to you for it and am a thousand times obliged to your ma for the bread she sent. I think more of it than any bread I have had since in service because it came from her, and the haversack never could have come in better time. I am very anxious to come home and bring the horse I have and get another, but fear there is no chance to do that. Do not think I am dissatisfied here. I am doing well in this branch of service and would have reenlisted, had [it] not been for the hope of getting home when my present term of service expires, but there is no chance for that. I think, by the help of God, I can continue in service as well contented as many of them. I must close, as some of them want their rations, and as it may puzzle you to read what I have already written. Please write soon and often. Give all the news. Give my love to your pa, ma, and family, also to Pa, Ma, and family, to Alick, Ginnie, and family. Tell Alick I will answer his letter soon, and try and give him the news. Am sorry to learn he is so much afflicted. Hope he will be better soon. Tell him to write often, for I really think three letters a year is but few. He has ten times the chance to write I have. Farewell, dear Beck and little Moorman.

My love to your little and my little family. Duck, please take care of little Moorman and have good examples set before him. It does my heart good to learn he is such a good child, and hope he may be a comfort to you in my absence.

Madison Courthouse
May the 17, 1862
My dear Beck,

I received your kind favor by George Martin this morning. Was pleased to hear from you, but sorry to hear you and little Moorman were so unwell. Hope you are both better before this. I have nothing very interesting for you this morning, save that I am well as usual. In the first place, I must try and tell you what a hard march we have had. Our regiment left Swift Run Gap four days since on a scout. The first day we went down the south side of Shenandoah [River] fifteen [miles] to Columbia Bridge. From there we crossed and went down on the north side to Sperryville Bridge, where the Sperryville Turnpike crosses, and down the pike to Luray, the county seat of Page County. Here we took supper, horses fed, and our advanced guard fired into the enemy's rearguard. At this place the enemy took to the left towards New Market and we passed on towards Sperryville by a byroad and stayed in the Blue Ridge Mountains that night. The next morning we crossed the mountains and took breakfast near Sperryville on the south side of the mountains. From there we marched to Washington, the county seat of Rappahannock County, where we rested a while, and from there to Flint Hill, a little village in the same county, where we stayed all night. The next morning we set out for Linders Station on the Manassas Gap Railroad, now in the possession of the enemy. When we got near the station, we halted and sent out men to find out if there were any enemy there. We soon learned some were there, so we soon had orders to charge on the place, which we did, and took fourteen prisoners, a wagon, and, if I mistake not, 8 horses, which were in splendid [ploughs]. There was a considerable quantity of plunder there, but we hadn't time to destroy it, as the Yankees were said to be coming on a train and there was a camp only some two miles distant. We killed one, or was thought to be dying when we left, and wounded another. Before we got to the station, some of our men which were sent out on the pike leading from Front Royal to Flint Hill, the place we left that morning, came in and reported that the enemy were advancing on that road and would reach that place in a few hours after we left, so we were cut off from the road we traveled that morning. So then the question was how to get back to our lines. So there was no other chance but to dodge them by going byroads, which we did, and reached Washington that night five or six miles this side of Flint Hill, and yesterday left the regiment there and came on here with the prisoners last night. The prisoners left here this morning for Gordonsville, and I am to go to our baggage, if I can find it, but hardly know which way to start for them.

So enough of this. I have not heard from or seen [. . .] yet but guess he is at the wagons. Guess my horse is there. I reckon Dolly will suit me very well. Our duty is quite hard on horses now. Our company seems to be getting on finely. Jo Burroughs was sent to Lynchburg Hospital some five days since. He was quite sick, and I fear he will have a hard spell. I am sorry to learn Brother G.'s baggage was burned, but rather 'twas burned than fall in the hands of the enemy. I fear we will fall back farther soon, afraid the army will reach our county soon. It seems to me if I was in the farmers' places in Bedford, I would try and sell the most of my grain that I could spare and long forage. I must close with the promise to write soon. I will write to Pa and Ma soon. I wish I could see you, Moorman, and all soon, but wishing is all hope. I may see you soon but, dear Duck, if we never meet on earth, let us try and be prepared to meet in heaven, when we will be at peace evermore. Farewell. Kiss little Moorman many times for me and tell him to kiss you for me.

Your devoted but unworthy,

Robert

Direct your letters to Gordonsville, care of Capt. Graves, 2nd Va. Cavalry, Col. Munford commanding.

Martinsburg, Berkeley County, Va.

May the 27, 1862

My Dear Companion,

It is with the greatest pleasure I drop you a few lines to inform I am well and getting on finely. We reached this place yesterday morning after a pushing race after the enemy from Front Royal and Strasburg.[22] We routed them and saw them plump into Maryland, and fired on them after they crossed the river. We captured a great many prisoners, arms and [army] both advance, and commissary also with the greater portion of their baggage train.[23] General[s] Jackson and Ewell have completely routed General Banks,[24] and I think those of his division that have reached their horses will be sure to stay there. We also captured three or four trains of cars. Our loss was but small—not over two hundred and fifty killed and wounded. I was not in the chase till after our forces reached Winchester, as I was sent back to the wagons and didn't overtake them till they passed through the town. A great many of our troops got Yankees trophies but I have nothing of much importance, and unless it's something small, I could not carry it. The letter is written on Yankee paper. I never saw Jollord till yesterday to get my horse, and she is nearly broke down. She has given Jollord two tremendous falls, but as good luck had it, didn't injure him badly. She is quite awkward. I don't know where we will move next. No more at present. All our boys are well, none of our regiment are hurt. May the Lord bless you, Moorman, and all,

R. W. P.

[Robert Parker returns to Bedford on furlough.][25]

Rockingham County,[26] Va.

June the 24, '62

My Dear Companion and Parents,

I reached this place this morning, Mr. Parry's, 5 miles north of the Bridge. Stayed at the Bridge[27] last night, got on quite well, and found Dolly yet alive and seemed to be improving some, and think she is worth sending for. I expect to start for Staunton in a few minutes and from there to Charlottesville; intend reaching there, if possible, by Saturday night. Jackson's army is or was at Hanover Courthouse several days since.[28] I heard yesterday morning at Liberty that Capt. Graves was at home and left the regiment at Charlottesville. Everything has quite a different appearance in the Valley to what it did when I passed home. Corn has grown so much, and the farmers are busily harvesting and say wheat is not infused with the rust. The ladies here say they heard cannonading here quite plain yesterday. They are quite interesting and kind ladies. Pa, Dolly is in a good pasture, and whoever you send after her must pay the ladies for their trouble and pasturage. She is at Mr. M. H. Parry's, five miles from the Natural Bridge on the direct road leading to Lexington, and about one mile from Mr. Parry's address, which is Fancy Hill. You pass Fancy Hill as [you] go from the Bridge to Mr. Parry's.

I must close, as it is getting time for me to start. This leaves me tolerably well. My love to all and Moorman. Tell Pa I didn't intend leaving without telling farewell, but it happened I did. Farewell to all.

Your unworthy husband and son,

R. W. Parker

Mr. M. H. Parry, Fancy Hill
Rockbridge County
This is the address.

North Garden, Albemarle County

Monday morning, June 30th, 1862

My Ever Dear Companion,

As I have the opportunity of sending you a note by the train this evening, I cannot let the chance slip. I am now seven miles this side of Charlottesville on the railroad leading to Lynchburg. Reached this place yesterday near twelve o'cl. I started yesterday morning from Charlottesville on to Gordonsville and meet met John F. Graves and Jo Johnson on their way here to the pasture. They informed me that our company went on with Jackson's army as far as Hanover Junction, and was then turned back with Capt. Irvin's Co. to scout back through Culpeper and Madison Counties. So there is no certainty where I may find them, but think I shall start to look for them today or tomorrow, at any rate. I have no news of interest for you this morning, more than I had a

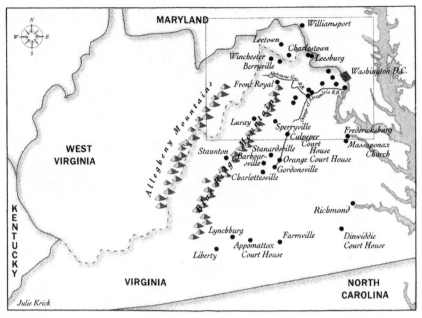

Places referenced in Robert W. Parker's letters, with inset enlarged (page 79). Courtesy of Julie Krick.

long lonesome trip to reach this place. I brought both horses here and got on finely, and think I shall leave one of them here. Found Sam Murrill here and well, with the exception of a sprained foot, which lack something of being well yet but is mending. I have heard nothing more of the battle at Richmond[29] than I guess you have heard ere this, that we were whipping the enemy and driving them back with a heavy loss on both sides, and our troops here taken a good deal of artillery. Major Wheat[30] of the Tigers was killed, and Colonel Seymour[31] of the field officers, both belonging to the same brigade, I think. I had heard that Gen. Jackson was wounded but guess it's untrue, as the papers say nothing about it. No doubt they had a hard fight. I heard the cannon last Friday evening in the Valley, a distance of some hundred and thirty miles, and the cannon are heard, so some say, here this morning. So the battle is still raging. Hope our army may conquer them yet.[32]

Monday morning, 11 o'cl. I have been waiting to hear from my company but can't hear. And James Jones[33] and Jim Lipscomb had just gotten here, and we will leave here this evening or in the morning. I have no more news of interest for you so must close. This leaves me tolerably. Hope I shall be entirely well soon. I don't know where to tell you to direct your letters. Better wait till I find out where we will be stationed yet.

Tell Cousin Tabbie Graves [that] John is well as usual and looks well. The most of the company, I hear, are getting on tolerably well. I wrote to you and Pa and Ma last Friday from Fancy Hill that Dolly was alive and seemed to be

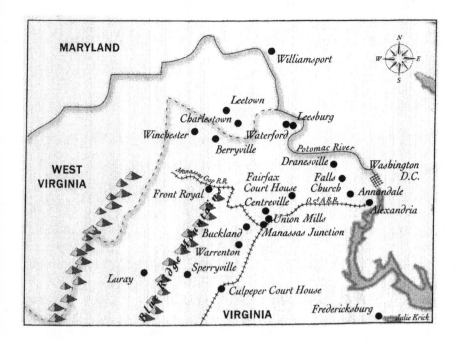

improving some, and I think he had better send for her as soon as possible. She is at M. H. Parry's, five miles on the north side of the Natural Bridge on the road leading to Lexington. Whoever goes after her can ride there in one day and back the next. I must close. My love to you and little Moorman. Tell him to be a good boy, and hug and kiss you for me. May the Lord bless and protect you both is my sincere wish. Don't have Mory spoiled.

Farewell,

R. W. Parker

Culpeper CH

July the 6, 1862

My Dear Companion,

As I have the chance to drop you a few lines this beautiful Sabbath morning, I must do so. Have nothing of interest for you more than I am well as usual. My health has been improving some since I reached the company, which was eight days to the day I left home. I got on finely, had no bad luck, but spent a good deal of money. Brought both horses as far as the pasture and left Nellie with Murrell. No one called for the bay so I am riding yet. He seems to attract attention, and one man was quite anxious to trade with me. Had a nice young horse, but I didn't trade. I intend trying him a little longer and, if he seems to do well, would like to send Nellie back.

Perhaps you would like to know what sort of quarters we have. We are camped two miles east of the Courthouse in a good church and get on finely. Had but little to do since I got here, no Yankees near us and fare tolerably well. We are seeing a good time here while our poor troops are seeing the heaviest sort of a time near our capitol.[34] I have looked over the casualties of our troops up to Friday last and see that many of our neighbor boys are either killed or wounded. Among the killed are Whit [. . .] and Jim Franklin. Among the wounded I see the name of Wm. A. Walker in body and leg, and many others of my acquaintance, Tom Holland[35] and Sam Murrill among them. It seems strange but nevertheless true that most of the boys from our neighborhood have either been killed wounded or died of sickness. We must not murmur, as it has been their lot to fall. The news has reached me that Cousin Jo Parker has died of the wound he received at the fight of the Seven Pines.[36] I guess ere this you have as much of the news from Richmond as I have, so it is useless for me to give the details. We should be more than thankful to almighty God that, through His kind favor, our troops have been able to drive the invader from the front of our capitol. Our loss has been heavy, but nevertheless we, or rather our troops, have slain many of the enemy on the battlefield, and almost succeeded in disorganizing and routing the greatest army the enemy have ever had in the field, and may, I hope, succeed in taking their great leader, General McClellan. That kind Providence and troops have taken their second general in command, General McCall,[37] and a great many prisoners. Enough of this. I have given you the general news. The Yankees down this way all seem to be moving toward Richmond. Nothing more of the war at present.

Tell [. . .] send messages by me. I have tried to deliver them to the best of my [. . .] the best wishes of those sent in return. I must close, having given all the points can think of now. My best wishes to all connections and friends. My love to you and Moorman. Tell him to be a good boy and mind Marmy. Kiss him often for me, and he you for me. Direct your letters to Gordonsville, care of Capt. Graves, 2nd Va. Cavalry, Col. Munford commanding.

Tell Alick Capt. Graves is at home or perhaps on his way here at this time, and I have not been able to see him yet. I have not been able to deliver Mr. Phelps' letter to him, as he was taken sick and Billie Fields and sent to the hospital. I know not where, but at or near Richmond. Perhaps he has reached home ere this. I have not been able yet to learn where Alfred Creasy is, yet you will please inform Tom Creasy, his uncle, the last information I have of [. . .] very sick and on his way home and perhaps has reached it ere this. Farewell for this time. May the Lord bless and protect you all is my sincere wish and prayer.

R. W. Parker

Orange CH
Tuesday morning, July the 15, 1862
My Dear Companion,

As I have a few spare moments, I'll try and drop you a short note, though have nothing of much interest more than we have been compelled by the pressure of our enemies to give up more of our mother state to their brutal army. Last Saturday morning we left Culpeper CH [and] are falling back to Rapidan Station, a distance of twelve miles. We took our time and during the day and skirted backwards and to till night, and at night crossed the river to this side and struck up camp, putting out pickets across the river, and hoped to have a quiet night's rest, but was mistaken. About two o'cl. in the morning of Sunday we were roused up by the firing of our pickets across the river, which was soon followed by a heavy volley, which we were confident was from the enemy. And soon our pickets were run in and reported the enemy three hundred strong on the opposite of the stream, while we had only about forty, and also that there was another forty coming up the rear. So against such 'twas useless for us to combat, so they took possession of the place and about daylight burned the railroad bridge,[38] which was of considerable to us, in case we should move against their front. This was on account of transportation. After they done what damage they could, the report reached us they were crossing the river, so we had to fall back to this place, where we have not been interrupted yet by them, and think we will let them come no farther, as troops are coming to our relief. The report reached us this morning that Jackson and Ewell[39] are advancing this way, so if the enemy do not run back soon, something too will be done soon for them. We have had [none] hurt or lost yet.

There has been a great stir among the citizens made by false alarms. A citizen went to Gordonsville and caused a great stir, and all false. The enemy has never been but a short distance this side the river, and no doubt ere this false reports have reached Bedford. The report has been started by someone that these two companies have been cut all to pieces—false.

I neglected to inform you in my last that I had received your letter written about the time [I] started home. It was here for me when I arrived, and return a good kiss to Moorman for his nice [bayonet], and I intend trying to keep it till I see him, if possible. You may be somewhat amused at my changing from subject to another as I do, but I give you the news just as I think of it. I guess the conscript men think they will be at home soon, as tomorrow will be their day to rest from the duties and hardships of this unholy war. We have 8 or 9 conscripts in this company, all who will leave as soon as arrangements can be made. Tell Alick I have given his letter to Capt. Graves but haven't had the chance to talk with him yet. Guess W. Phelps with his family soon. I have not the chance to see him since we came back, as he was at Richmond. I started his letter to him but it didn't reach him, the man having to turn back before he reached the regiment, and I didn't start it to him when I first came back as I heard he was sent to the hospital, perhaps had come home, and didn't know any better till a few days since. I am sorry to hear of the deaths of his brother John Henry and Mr. Holland. I heard Tom Holland had reached home. I am sorry for poor Emaline McGee, but hundreds are left in like situations. Would like to know if William Walker has reached home.

I must close. We are getting on finely here. All our company that's here are enjoying usual health. My health has improved since we reached camp. My love to all. Tell Ma and Pa I'll try and write them soon. My best love to you and Moorman. Tell him to be a good boy. May you both be blessed with good health is the humble wish of your unworthy husband,

R. W. Parker

Gordonsville
July the 19, '62
My Dear Companion,

As Mr. Phelps gets his discharge today and leaves for home, I'll try and drop you a few lines, though have nothing of interest for you more than I am still in the land of the living and doing tolerably well. Have been quite unwell for the past few days but haven't stopped duty yet. The Yankees made a dash on us at Orange CH and made us fall back four or five miles towards Gordonsville. We took three or four prisoners, kill two, and wounded some. We had one wounded and I understand since has died. Yesterday we were reinforced by our regiment and some other forces, and marched on them and run them back across Rapidan and took near thirty of their cavalry. A portion of General Ewell's command are at Orange now, and I rather expect we will march towards Culpeper soon, perhaps this evening or tomorrow.

Well, I know nothing more of interest down this way for you, so must touch on some other subject. I am quite anxious to hear from you, Moorman, and all at home. This is the fifth letter since I left you and haven't heard a word from you since I left. Write soon and often.

Your unworthy husband,
R. W. Parker

July 20
My Dear Beck,

I received yours of the 16 this morning. Never was more relieved by a letter. I have been so anxious to hear from you and Moorman. I am afraid I will have to keep Nelly here, as my secession horse is lame. Afraid he is [. . .] I had been thinking of sending Nelly home, but will have to delay for a while. I must close for a while. Hope you will write soon and often. This leaves me rather unwell. My bowels are in rather a bad fix, but hope they will be well soon.

Farewell, dear companion, son, and relations and friends,

R. W. Parker

July the 27, 1862

My Dear Beck,

I received your kind favor of the 15 the 26, and was more than glad to hear you and Moorman were getting on well. We hope you will soon be entirely well. This leaves me well though considerably complaining with my throat, but hope I'll be well soon [. . .] Tell Charley if they got him under the Conscript Act to come to this company. If not, he can come to see me anyhow. Tell Brother Alick he may come down and take my place for a few weeks, and I will come home to see you all and improve my health. He can see some of [. . .]

I am sorry to hear of the death of Will Walker. It seems that nearly all are at loss. The great number of our neighbor boys have lost their lives in one way or another in the past 8 or 10 months. Wish I could be at [. . .] 'Tis no use to wish. Hope you may have a pleasant time. Glad to hear Pa has Dolly at home, for I will want her some of the times. Mr. Lee leaves for home this morning, has put in a substitute. I reckon Fanny will rejoice to have him at home again. I hate to part with him, for he is a sturdy man and good soldier and will be much missed by the company. Our company (that portion that's here) seem to be getting on finely, and if I had good health there is nothing too hard in camp for me. You was mistaken as to Lieut. Johnson's being at home. He has not been home since he was sent on sick furlough. Jimmie Helms, I think, has been discharged and gone home. Ben Joplin seems to be getting on finely. I have not seen his brother Jo for several days.

There is no news of much interest as to the move of the enemy down this way. They have been sending out small scouting parties, but to little effect. I must close, as Mr. Lee is nearly ready to start. Tell Mory to be a good boy and do as Marmy says. My love to all.

R. W. Parker

Write soon and often.

Camp near Barboursville, Orange Co.

Aug. the 17, 1862

My Dear Parents,

As I have the chance, I'll this evening try and answer your kind letter by Coly Adams, which came to hand a few days since. Was glad to hear you all were doing well as could be expected. Sorry to hear Febe mends so slow.

Hope all will be well soon. This leaves me tolerably well, and the most of our company seem to be enjoying themselves finely. All tolerably at camp except Josiah Martin.[40] He has, it is thought, the rheumatism, but is on foot. Will start, I think, for the hospital perhaps this evening. Tom Bernard has not returned to camp yet, has a very bad toe. Billie Fields has returned to camp but looks quite thin yet, but is improving fast. John Lipscomb is still at the hospital. Have not heard from him for some time, but was mending the last time we heard from him. Have not many sick at this time.

I'll try and give you a few points as to the movements of the enemy. They still occupy Madison Courthouse, Culpeper, and a large portion of this county, Orange. They have been doing a great deal of mischief in almost every way. Also taking up our loyal citizens and burning their property and taking all their servants. You mentioned the horse I rode home and that Billie Ballard would write me word how to dispose of him. I have written to Capt. Tutwiler and also to Ballard. Capt. Tutwiler wrote a note to Col. Munford concerning the horse, which was forward to me. As soon as I received the note, I went to the Col. and informed him I had the horse still in my charge. He ordered me to turn him over to the quartermaster here and forward his receipt to the quartermaster at Lexington, which I have done. So I have complied with all orders given me and the horse is now in the hands of the quartermaster.

I must close, as 'tis nearly time to drill, and have given you all the news. Hope you had a nice time at the association.

Aug. the 9, 1862. This leaves me tolerably well. There is nothing of much interest taking place yet, but would be surprised.

Aug. the 11, 1862. This leaves me on foot. We have had another fight.[41] 'Tis reported our troops killed ten to one. This hardly seems sensible. I understand we are reinforcing and the Yankees also. We are expecting another fight equal to almost any or at least to there is [a frenzy of] preparation-making. We lost one general killed, I think General Winder.[42] I must close. Farewell, dear parents. Remember [me] far away. My love to all,

R. W. Parker

I have their Nelly and she can't stand heat at all, as expected—pants like Shep by riding her a short distance. I want you to fatten Dolly, and if nothing happens I want to get her soon as possible, if I don't trade Nelly off.

Aug. the 18, 1862
My Dear Companion,

As I have the chance, I'll try and drop you a few lines, though have nothing of importance for you. This leaves me in tolerable health. My stomach is not entirely well yet, but I think is improving. I have the worst boil on my face near the left corner of my mouth. It has ris[en] twice, and this morning I had it split with a knife. I think it will be well soon. I wish I could give you all the news, but haven't time, so will have [to] furnish you with a part. As to our recruits, several have come in, perhaps twelve or fifteen, and some four have been discharged: Uncle Auville Goggin, Ammon Phelps, man by the name of Payne, and one other, Ethereel Walker. Ethereel says he likes the camp far much better than he expected. He seems to want to stay in service with us. He is quite anxious to see the army, and if I had anything to say in the matter, I would like for him to stay with us and see the army, if no longer. He seems quite anxious to stay and I would not be surprised, if he was to stay, if it didn't make a man of him. I heard Charley is to come soon to service. If he does, I would like for him to come to this company. It has been a lucky company so far, but don't know how long it will remain so, but hope for its continuance. We are quite anxious to get our company up to eighty men.

Since my last to you, we have fallen back to the west side of the Rapidan, and the Yankees followed us up to that stream and have fallen back, I know not how far. And I have learned that our army have commenced another advance in three columns,[43] but don't know anything as to the truth of the reports. I learned from a man confined by the enemy during last fight in Culpeper that they had over twelve hundred wounded, and I know they had a great many killed. I look for a big fight soon and sincerely hope we may be successful through the help of almighty God. It is believed the reason the Yankees didn't attack us was, they wish to move from place to place so as to keep our troops moving about till the Yankees can get their fresh troops in the field before the next fight comes off.[44]

Enough of the army. I received a letter from Ma yesterday which reached me with bad news, as did your last. It seems that the fever is taking fast hold of the family [and] will go through it before it can be stopped. I fear the family will see hard times, as they, or at least the most of them, knows but little about sickness. I am sorry to learn that your and Moorman's health is declining. Hope it will soon begin to improve some. Don't you nor Mory eat too much fruit, and take good care of yourselves. Oh that I could be at home to attend as best I could to your wants, for nothing would afford me more pleasure than to be with my dear companion and dear little Mory, and wait on you in sickness, and would do all in my power at any time to come and see you if it would do any good, for it is getting to the place that it's hardly worthwhile to attempt to get home if one's companion or parents were believed to be at the point of death. There was a man in our company who only asked for four or five days to see his wife, who was thought to be almost beyond hope, and the leave of absence was not granted; and as to a sick man's getting home now, that is almost impossible, unless he is able to dodge the guard and run the blockade, as they are carried, as I am informed, by the doctors now.

[Duck] Ethereel says he don't want any one to know that he has discharged, so don't you say anything about it, as it is his business and not mine. The colonel has not signed his discharge yet, and if he don't, he can't get home on the discharge with out his signature.

I fear this note will pain you to read it, but I have to scribble it off in a hurry when I have the chance.

Don't divulge any secrets in this. Read this note before you tell any of the news. Capt. Graves and Uncle Auville left camp this morning for home. The capt. is quite sick. Uncle A. is free from the C.S.A. service.

I guess Mr. Phelps has given us a great name. I am not at all surprised to hear he has such good opinion of Lieut. B. and Ad Wade, [45] for they are both the greatest ladies men in camp. If they are the sort of ladies to suit them, one might guess what sort they are.

Duck, tell me in your next what you think has caused your declining health, if you are like you were spring before last.[46] Don't keep back anything. Please tell me why your parents want you to wean Mory. Poor little fellow, he is too little to wean.

Farewell for this time. Love to you and little Mory. With many kisses,

R. W. Parker

Chimborazo Hospital,[47] Richmond, Va.[48]

My Dear Companion,

As I feel it my duty to write you every chance, I try and drop you a few lines, though I am lying flat on my back. I hardly know what to say of my sickness. I have suffered but little from severe pain. I am considerably troubled with fever and my mouth seems dry nearly all the time. I am not eating [. . .] and sincerely hope I will get [. . .] hospital, get up and down when I wish, and after all my affliction I have a boil at a very inconvenient place to sit on. I am not at the first hospital I went to. I stayed there a day or two, and Read Lebo heard of me and came to see me, as he was ward master, I got a transfer to his ward, where I expect to remain for some time. Oh, what a delight it would be to me to see you, Ma, Pa, or any of my acquaintances here, for there seems to be but [little] prospect of my leaving here soon if ever.

I get as much to eat here as I want, and as good as any the sick get here. This is a mighty [ugly] place, nobody about here but men. No lady's kind word to sooth the burning brow of the poor soldier. I must close, as I have given you all. Write soon as you get this and give me all the news.

Direct your letters to Chimborazo hospital, Richmond.

My best love to you and Mory with many kisses. My love to all. Tell all to come and see me.

[Robert Parker returns to Bedford on sick furlough.][49]

1863

The Second Regiment Virginia Cavalry, as part of Brig. Gen. Fitzhugh Lee's brigade, was stationed near Fredericksburg in early 1863. They defeated several Union regiments at Kelly's Ford on March 17, 1863. As Maj. Gen. Joseph Hooker prepared to attack the Army of Northern Virginia in April, Lee's brigade pressed across the Rappahannock to halt the Union advance. They fought at Chancellorsville, the Wilderness, and the Gettysburg campaign, during which they protected the army's rear during its retreat. When Gen. Robert E. Lee ordered the Army of Northern Virginia across the Rapidan River to find and battle Maj. Gen. George Meade's Union forces in the autumn of 1863, the Confederate cavalry under General Stuart led the way. Then they went into winter quarters near Charlottesville along the Rappahannock River. They were detached from Stuart on December 14 and sent to the Shenandoah Valley to reinforce General John D. Imboden. Upon their return to Charlottesville, Fitzhugh Lee disbanded several regiments for the winter.[1]

Spotsylvania County, near Massaponax Church
Jan. the 9, 1863
My Dear Companion,

I'll try and drop you a few lines this morning for the first time since I parted with you. I reached the company yesterday evening, found them in fine spirits and looking well. Also in rather an easy place, doing but little duty.

I made the whole trip without meeting with any of my company, but had a tolerably fair trip, costing me about $5.00. I fared well all the way. Had a chill last the night before I reached camp and expected one last night, but slept quite comfortable and begin to feel like I use to in camp. There is no news of interest in camp. Wade Roberts and Poindexter's trial come off today. Their punishment was, I heard, to cut wood one day—light punishment.

I found some of my clothes: one pair of pants, checked cotton shirt, two pair of socks, flannel belt, paper and envelopes. My shawl is also at camp and valise in tolerably good order. The boys have gotten their new uniforms and they are tolerably good ones, pants and uniform costing $18 dollars. I brought everything safe to camp and had good luck. I think I'll come off without any trial. Happened to get in good time. This leaves me tolerably this morning. I am quite anxious to hear from you, Moorman, and all, especially the sick. Kiss Mory often for me. My love to you, Mory and all. Farewell for the present. Direct your letters to Guinea Station, Caroline County, Va., soon as you get this and often. I haven't opened my snack yet.

All quiet near Fredericksburg.[2] Farewell. Love to all,

R. W. P.

Massaponax Church, Spotsylvania County
Jan. the 18, 1863
My Dear Companion,

I'll try and drop you a few lines this morning, though I have nothing of interest to communicate. There seems to be a [feint] near Fredericksburg, as all the artillery has been ordered there. Two thousand artillerists camped near us last night on there way there. I heard the enemy only entered a feint at Fredericksburg to attract our attention and moved on some other front, North Carolina perhaps, as some of our troops has been sent there. We have great confidence in Gen. Lee and believe they will meet them forcefully at every point. I have heard of no move of interest with either army recently, and we are so [blessed] that we get the daily mail and papers every day. We are still acting as couriers for the court-martials, and hope we may continue through the winter with it, as we are now detached from our brigade for that purpose, and the court will not get through for months to come, as they have a great many cases on hand. Our company is generally in good health and fine spirits. Bob Johnson is complaining, nothing serious I hope. I heard from a letter from Jimmie Robertson that Henry Ballard has reached Liberty very sick. Have not heard from Tom Martin for some time, hope they are improving. I saw George Parker[3] a few days since. He was well but said Will was quite unwell and had gone to a private house. Have not heard from Uncle Pleasant[4] since I left him. He is over in the Valley. I saw Sam Turner last evening. He was well and looked finely. I have seen a good many of my old acquaintances since I came to camp. Jimmie Robertson and Board are exchanged and will look for them to camp soon. You must try and send me a letter by Jimmie. I would like for you to buy me a good sheepskin from Peter and send it the first chance.

I am quite anxious to hear from you, Mory and all. I have no more news of interest for you. I have not heard a word from any of you since I left and wish you to write soon and often.

This leaves me tolerably. I have not been on duty but twice since I left home. I think I will pass this time without being court-martialed. I have to go out sometimes now and impress [. . .] for the company, something I hate to do.

Direct you letters to Guinea Station. My love to you, Mory and all. Kiss Mory often for me. Farewell for this time.

R. W. Parker

Massaponax Church, Spotsylvania County
Jan. the 19, 1863
My Dear Wife,

I'll again attempt to drop you a few lines, though have nothing of interest for you. I wrote you a short letter yesterday morning but happened to the misfortune of losing it,[5] though it was of not much force, no secrets whatever in it. This leaves me tolerably well with the exception of a bad cold, and hope I'll soon be relieved of it. The most of our camp is tolerably well with the exception of colds. The company seems to be in fine spirits. There is no news of interest down here. We are expecting an engagement at any time. Heard this evening some had crossed the river in town. I fear 'tis only a feint and the general attack will be in North Carolina.

The capt. received a note from Cousin Joel Preston[6] stating the wishes to join our company. I am sure he will have no trouble in coming to our company, and hope many others join us soon. I have seen a good many old acquaintances since I reached camp. Saw Sam Turner a day or two since; he looked fine. We are camped near Billie Snow's regiment but have not been to see him yet. I saw George Parker a few days since. He was well, but said Will was quite sick and had gone to a private house. We have plenty of smallpox down this way, several cases in a quarter of a mile of our camp. We are still detached from our regiment as couriers for the court-martial and hope we will stay with it through the winter, as 'tis rather an easy place.

I want you to buy me a sheepskin from your uncle Peter and send it by the first chance. This is the third letter to you since I parted. Hope you will write soon and often. Direct your letters to Guinea Station, care Capt. Graves.

My love to you, Mory and all. Kiss him often. Farewell for this time.

Yours devotedly,
R. W. Parker

Cavalry Camp near Culpeper CH
March 4th, 1863[7]
Dear Beck,

I'll try and drop you a few lines, though have nothing of interest to communicate. We reached camp yesterday evening safe and had tolerably good luck. The worst news in camp is we get nothing to feed our horses on but a little wheat, and not half enough of that.[8] I would give you a history of our trip but I expect Charley[9] has said enough for that.

Waddie Burton has some money for me, if he has not sent it to you. Stephen Goggin and John Garrett has been sent to the hospital, thought Steve had the fever. The company is in tolerably good health. Bob Dinwiddie[10] and Les are both complaining. I got Charley in my old mess with Lieut. Johnson and I shifted to another mess. Duck, look and see if I didn't [. . .]

Sam Murrill and Steven Goggin wrote to me and perhaps you have gotten them before this.

Duck, write to me how your health is. If you get sick, write to me all the particulars. Don't hold anything back for fear of making me uneasy, for I always want to know particularly how you and Mory are. Wish I could hear you pray everyday. Duck, I am always obliged to tell you everything that bears any weight on my mind. Duck, there is a man in our company from Bedford. I am sorry to say the way he is going on is distressing to anyone who knows his situation. I am sure you will say nothing about him so his friends will get it from me. 'Tis Henry Ballard.[11] 'Twould be, it seems to me, almost enough to kill his wife to know how he is going on. His failures are drinking and gambling, poor fellow. I fear unless he changes soon, he will [be] a goner. I heard an officer in our regiment say yesterday evening that he got drunk every time [he] can get the liquor. I fear he spends his wages as fast as he gets them. He was drunk last evening. Don't say anything about it where his friends can hear of it.

Duck write me word if you have been sick much since I left.

Mr. R. W. Parker

Politeness of Mr. Snow

Duck, envelopes are worth $200 a package, paper saw at $50 for quire.

Cavalry Camp near Culpeper CH

My Dear Companion,

I'll drop you a few lines this evening, though have nothing of interest to communicate. This leaves Charley and I well as common. He seems well satisfied, all to getting nothing hardly to feed his horse on. All our company seem tolerably well this evening. Whit Vance arrived in camp last evening and wanted to know why I left him. I made known my reasons in few words. Jim Lee and McCabe[12] near camp also yesterday.

We have no news as to any engagement down this way soon. Some of our cavalry made a dash to Fairfax Courthouse a few nights since and caught a brigadier general, one capt., three lieut., and some thirty privates.[13] A good haul for us. It seems that our enemies are quiet throughout the Confederacy.

This time last spring we were in active operations, but the mud is so deep we can't do but little anyway.

Duck, I wrote to you on [business] by John P. Graves. Write me word if you got the letter, and if you did, see what you can do soon as you can [commence], although if you can't it will make no difference. If you conclude to send me a box soon, put it on the train for Gordonsville and take a receipt for it and forward the receipt for it to me. I send in this two rings, one for you and one for Nannie. If Nannie's do[es] not suit her, I will make her another. Write soon and often. I have not received a line from you.

Direct your letters to Culpeper Courthouse, care of Capt. Graves, 2nd Va. Cavalry. My love to all and particularly to you and Mory. Farewell.

Yours ever,

R. W. Parker

Culpeper CH, Va.
March the [8], 1863
Dear Beck,

As I came up to camp and have this chance, I'll try and answer your letter, and will try and answer Ma soon. I received a letter from you a few days since and also one yesterday, containing the receipt for the box. Will send to Gordonsville today for it.

Charley is quite unwell this morning. I think 'tis nothing more than foul stomach and cold. Hope he will be better soon. Duck, words can hardly express my feeling this morning as to Mory's constitution. Fear he will have a hard spell, if he even recovers, but still hope he will recover soon.

I know little else to write, and what I did know seems squandered now. There is no news of much interest down here anyway. Everything seems quiet down this way. You ere this have heard of the death of [. . .] Goggin. Poor fellow had to go at last, it seems. We have bad luck of late.

The balance of our company seem tolerably well. Most of them out on picket. I come in from picket yesterday and will have to go back, perhaps this morning. I started on a scout to Loudoun yesterday from picket, but it happened so we didn't meet our party [as we] came back to camp. I think it happened very well, for the roads are so bad and the weather so disagreeable. It seems that it rains or snows nearly every other day. Duck my mind is in such confusion, I can't write and will close with the promise of answering with a long letter soon. This leaves me tolerably well. Farewell for the present, with the sincere wish for your and Mory's health. My love to you, Mory and all. P.S. Do not be uneasy about Charley. If he gets worse I will write immediately, if nothing prevents.

Robert W. Parker

Cavalry camp near Culpeper Court House
March the 9, 1863
Dear Beck,

As John Graves starts home tomorrow, I'll try and give you a few of the points, though have none of interest. This leaves me well as usual. Charley is also well as common. The most of the camp seems well as common, some little complaint among them.

No news as to any fight soon. There is a camp rumor that we leave this place soon for the Valley. Hope 'tis true, for I am confident we can't get to a harder place and there is some hopes for a better one, for our horses are starving here, having nothing to feed on but a little wheat, and not half enough of that.

Your uncle James Joplin was in camp yesterday, seemed well. He came down to see Will and Jo. I shook hands with him but he didn't find out who I was. Will and Jo are well as common. George Parker is also well. Will has reached Pa's ere this on his way home. Payne and Leftwich have both received furloughs for home. Bob Dinwiddie was sent to Charlottesville hospital a day or two since with [pleurisy].

Duck, I want you to send me some butter by Will Parker on his return to camp, if you can buy it any where in the neighborhood. If you can get it, be sure to make Will bring it, if no more than a pound. I want you also to buy me a good silver watch. Get one of Jimmie's, if you can at a reasonable price. It don't make any differ[ence] as to being fine, so [as] it keeps good time and is a hunterman's case,[14] for if it is not this sort I will soon break out the crystal.

Whit Vance has not reached camp yet. We are looking for him everyday. I have given you the general news and must close for the present with the promise to write soon. I have not received a line from you yet. Hope I'll get one soon, as I am quite anxious to hear from you and Mory. Kiss him often for me. Don't let him be spoilt, and learn him to obey you at the start, for you haven't me with you now to speak to him, as you also say. Train him in the way he should go and he will not depart from it. Tell Nannie I'll try and send her ring soon. Present my best wishes to Bet and tell her Coly is looking well, better than common, for he has just shaven. My love to you, Pa, Ma, family, and all enquiring friends, and take all the balance for you and Mory. Excuse bad writing.
Farewell,
R. Parker

Charley was on camp guard last night for a first.

Cavalry camp near Culpeper CH
Sunday morning, March 18, 1863
Dear Beck,

As I have the chance, I'll try and drop you a few lines in answer to your kind favor which came to hand a day or two since, and you can't imagine how it relieved me, for I had been very uneasy as to your welfare, and rejoiced to hear you both were in good health. I shall now attempt to give you all the points, though have none of much interest.

The two Vances have reached camp all right. You wished to know where we stayed: The first night at Mr. Wilman's—stayed there two nights and a day. Charley seemed to stand the trip very well. Seems to like camp quite well and says his leg is well. Should have liked to have seen those letters to me. Maybe all for the best. I presented your best wishes to him and gave his in return.

I have not felt the pain in my breast since I came to camp. I didn't discover I had the wrong sheepskin until the night after I left your Pa's. Am very sorry I made the mistake. You must pay your Pa for it. I was very careless in doing such a trick and will try and do better for the future. I am glad to hear your lambs are getting on so finely. Tell Mory he must suck mine and let Tabby suck his.

I was in hopes Burton would leave the money with you, but it makes no difference, as I have bought a six-shooter and will take that money to pay for it. Waddie has returned to camp and paid me part of the money. It makes no difference as to sending me my part, as mine suits camp very well yet. I am sorry to hear you have suffered so much with your toe. Hope 'tis well.

You wished to know as to the letters you wrote when I came home sick. Yes, Steve got it and burnt ones when he saw who it was from.

You must excuse this note, for I guess 'twill pain you to read it. Am glad to hear you get on so well spinning, but think you might spin more moderate so as to sleep some at nights.[15] As I have answered all your questions, I'll endeavor to give you some of the camp news. We have nothing of importance in camp, and what we have is mostly bad. I am tolerably well, but the most of our mess is sick. Steven Goggin in Lynchburg quite sick with fever. Bob Dinwiddie in Charlottesville sick. He has not left for home. Cousin Joel is in camp quite sick, also Les Dinwiddie.[16] He is completely laid up, don't know what is the matter with him. His forehead is the worst swollen I ever saw and he has almost suffered death with a pain in his head. So there is only three in one mess able for duty. Several of others of the company are sick.

There is no news of an attack down this way. Hope it will be some time before we have an engagement, for the roads are too bad to do anything yet. It seems the enemy are quite slow in moving this spring, but they are making such great preparation they are sure of success, but hope they may be disappointed yet.

Charley seems to be getting on fine and in good spirits and well satisfied. I must close, as I have given you all the news. You must write soon and long letters. Kiss Mory for me and make him obey you and be a smart boy. Give my love to all inquiring friend and the remainder to you and Mory. Coly [says] howdy to all. Tell Bet it was sent for her benefit. Farewell for this time.

Yours devotedly,
R. W. Parker

Charley will also send a letter.

We expect to leave camp in the morning for picket. Hope we will have a good time.

Hope your and Mory good health may continue. Let Mory stay with Pa and Ma all you can. Duck, I just stopped to read a letter from Mr. Kinnett. He expects to stay down there another year. Says he has not seen Pa yet, but thinks Pa and I will do the best we can for him, which is very true. Says he took a few days' planting, having all his fallowing done. Mr. Kinnett seems to think it did Jobe and Elvy a great deal of good for me to write to them. I will try and write again to them. I must close for the present, will try and drop you a few more lines if I hear any news before I close the envelope. You must write soon and often, and give me all the news. My love to you and Mory and all. Tell Mory to be a good boy and mind Marmy and all. Farewell. May the Lord bless you both and keep you as under the hollow of His hand, is the sincere wish of your devoted but unworthy,

Robert

Camp near Culpeper CH
March the 19
Dear Companion,

As the battle of the 17 is over and I am yet spared, I will try and drop you a few lines giving you some of the points.[17] The battle commenced before sunup at the river, at a place called Kellyville. It commenced with about 30 sharpshooters on our side and rifle pits, and we kept back four brigades of the infantry and cavalry for one hour and a half before we left our pits. You will understand we were dismounted, and when they did cross they took twenty-six of our men prisoners before they could reach their horses. There was only five of our company at that post and two out of five taken prisoner: John Newman and Alfred Creasy. I had the good luck of reaching my horse a few seconds before they got to it. We killed about twenty-five of the enemy while crossing the river, besides numbers wounded. We fell back a short distance, and the fight was renewed and continued for several hours. Our loss in the latter part of the fight in wounded was heavy. Had but few killed. Among the killed in our regiment was William Burroughs;[18] Jim Leftwich[19] is thought to be mortally wounded. I hope not more than six or 8 from our regiment will die from wounds.[20] Charley is mad as usual. He was on picket when the fight commenced, and in going to the rear, his horse threw him and run off, so he lost his horse for several hours. I found his horse, and today he got everything back safe and has gone back on picket. He didn't get at all part [. . .]

Cavalry Camp near Culpeper CH
March the 25, 1863
My Dear Companion,

According to promise, I'll try and write to you often, though I haven't received but one letter from you since we parted. If I mistake not, I have averaged two letters a week to you since I arrived in camp, and why I don't get letters from no one, I can't exactly comprehend, unless they have never been written to me. I have written several letters to Pa and Ma but have received none, and if I don't receive one this evening I shall begin to despair, as we are looking for Will Parker in today by the train.

I have no news to communicate more than I am well as common, except a touch of sore throat. Nothing serious, I hope. Charley is well as common, I guess, as he just passed our tent on his way to the spring with a boiler and his clothes in one hand and an axe and chunk of pine in the other—preparatory for washing his clothes, as I suppose. He seem in fine spirits and as lively as ever. The boys say they have an excellent joke on him. The day of the fight, as he started to the battlefield, something happened that his horse threw him and ran off, and he didn't get her for a day or two. So as the battle was raging and he could not find his horse, he came back to Culpeper and took the train for Rapidan Station, where our baggage was ordered. He did perfectly right, for as he could not find his horse, it was the best to go with the baggage. The boys tell him he jumped off his horse and left it and took to the cars because he thought they would get on the fastest, but they do this just to have a laugh. He has gotten his horse with all the equipment. They have their fun at him, but he has some as good jokes on some of them as one need to want, for I think they did worse than he.

I guess ere this you have more of the particulars of the fight of the 17 than I could give, so 'twould be useless for me to say anything more about it. Everything seems quiet down this way now, but we look for a fight as soon as the weather is fit, for I am confident we will have a lively time this campaign. There is a camp rumor that we are to move soon, but where is not known. Some say Fauquier, some say Loudoun, though none know certainly. As to my part, I am not very particular. Sam Murrill, Jim Lee and two others are now out on an independent scout to Loudoun. We rather expect them in about the first of next month, if the Yankees don't catch them.

I heard from Stephen Goggin by a letter from Uncle Tommie. He was quite low. Also received a letter from Leslie Dinwiddie in our mess last night. He is at the Charlottesville hospital very sick. Bob Dinwiddie is also at Lynchburg hospital, if he has not gone home. Hope they may all get home. I stated in my last that John Vance and Alfred Creasy were taken prisoners in the last fight.

March the 27. Will Parker has returned and no letter from you. I received a short note from Ma, the first and only scratch of a pen I have received from home since I left. Ma's feelings seem to be hurt that I had not written to more of the family since I left or inquired after their welfare. I am sure I have written two if not three letters to them, but if the letters never get to their destination, I can't prevent it. I am sure there is no one in camp more anxious to hear from their parents and relations than I.

There is no news of interest in camp. I understand the order as to our move has been changed and we are to continue here. There a good many horse details out now and expected in soon. Coly Adams, Gills and several others of our company are among them. There seems to be a premium on men that keeps the poorest horses, as they get to go home the oftenest. As to myself, I like to go home as well as anybody, but hate to have to get a horse as often, but fear I'll have to get one soon and don't know where to look for one.

The company are generally well, though some little complaint. If you have any chance to send a box, send it by express and [get] a receipt for it. Forward the receipt to us. Such things as butter, dried fruit and such like are very acceptable in camp.

I am sorry Will Parker didn't bring our butter.

Heard through Ma's note you and Mory was well. Hope your good health may continue. Write soon and often. My love to all.

Farewell.

R. W. Parker

This is the day set apart for fasting and praying. Hope strict attention will be paid to it throughout the Confederacy. Don't tell what I have written about Charley. He is well.

Cavalry Camp near Culpeper CH
March the 29, 1863
Dear Beck,

As Charley has written a letter to your ma, I'll also include a short note in his, though guess he has given all the news. There is nothing fresh in camp. All of our company who are here are generally well. John Graves arrived in camp safe last evening with a letter from you, which was one of the greatest treats I have had since I parted with you, being the second since I came to camp. G. Leftwich also came with him and informed us they left [...] in Bedford down with the smallpox. And Leftwich has a chance also to take them, but hope he will not break out with them, for if he does our company will be in a bad fix.

Capt. Graves has not been promoted yet and I hope will not be, for I should hate very much indeed to lose him as Capt. He is still on the division court-martial at Culpeper CH. Les Dinwiddie is still at Charlottesville hospital, quite sick with bilious fever. His wife came down yesterday to see him. Bob Dinwiddie has gone home and is improving. Poor Steve I fear will never recover.

S. L. Murrill, Lee and others have not returned from their scout yet. We shall begin to look for them tomorrow, but they may never return until they go through a course of Yankee life, but hope they are smart enough to take good care of themselves. Everything seems quiet down this way. The pickets haven't been disturbed since the last fight, but fear they will try us again next week, as twill be our time to go out on picket, and they are generally apt to make a show when our company is on picket. And it seems that we also have bad weather when out. But we have so far had good luck. There seems to be but little moving with the army now anywhere, but as soon as the roads get dry I look for lively time, especially with the cavalry.

I should like to see Jim now and tease him a few about Papa. Tell Jim I am glad he has proven himself smarter than he once thought he would be. I mean he stands more bowlegged now than ever. Present my best wishes to Jim and his lady, and tell her if she never thought enough of me come and see me, I wish her great luck.

You wished to know what your ring was made of. If I tell you, you must not throw it away, for I am sure you will be surprised to know what it was made of. The material of which it was made was the bottom of a cow's heel. It was quite easy to make, and would have looked quite nice if I had have had some emory paper to polish it with. I'll try and make Nannie one soon, if I have the chance. I am sorry Will didn't bring my butter, but if he could not bring it, of course he is excusable. I hope Uncle Tommy will succeed in getting a watch for me, as I need it badly, for but few like to lend theirs, though I succeed in getting one whenever I want it.

I am sorry you and Mory are in such bad health, especially Mory, for I am sure he gives you so much trouble with his throat so badly swollen. I sincerely hope you both will be well soon and enjoy the best of health. Tell Mory he must suck my titty and let Tabby suck his. He must not let his little sheepy starve, for he can do better without milk now than the little lambs. Tell him to [be] a smart boy and obey Grandpa and Ma and all.

Beck, you must not fail to write often. If you hear the regiment has moved, direct you letters to the same office till I write you word to change direction, for they will follow us up. All letters to the 2nd Va. Cavalry will follow them up. I must close, having given all the news.

March the 19, '63. My love to you, Mory, and all. Farewell.

If you have a chance to send a box, direct it to Culpeper Courthouse, R. W. Parker, 2nd Va. Cavalry, care of Capt. W. F. Graves, and so on. Take a receipt for it at Liberty and forward it to me. We generally have to send to Gordonsville for boxes for the regiment. This leaves me well as common.

Yours devotedly,

R. W. Parker

Camp near Culpeper

Apr. 5, 1863

My Dear Companion,

As Mr. Gills expects to start for home in the morning, I'll try and drop you a few lines, though have nothing of interest to give, save the return of those of our regiment taken prisoners at Kelley's Mill [Ford]. They look very well, and Creasy and Vance expect to start for home tomorrow. A good many of our camp have left for home on horse details, among them Jesse Pullens, Adams, Sandy Wilson, and Gills. They have twenty days furlough. I guess ere this you have feared of the death of our messmate and fellow soldier Leslie Dinwiddie. His wife reached him the evening before he died. He knew her. As soon as he saw her he seemed willing to die. He begged her not to shed tears for him, said, "The Lord's will be done," and that he was done with this war. I fear without a change soon he shall die like cousin Steven, but hope for his recovery soon.

Duck, if you can possibly do so, send that butter by some of the boys, if you can't get them to bring anything else. If you succeed in getting me a watch, send it by the first chance. If you happen to see Uncle Tommy soon, tell him Steven had one of my blankets. Uncle T. wrote me word he saw two pair socks marked in my name. I left them with him when I went home the last time and also one of my blankets. I'll say here that Sam Murrill, Lee and others who went north, they have returned safe. They met with nine of the enemy and seemed to have learnt but little as to the enemy. All seems quiet down this way, but we don't know how soon a storm maybe will be kicked up. I must close for fear of wearying you with my numerous and lengthy notes. I have never received but two letters from you yet, and I might come to the conclusion that so many of mine may tax you. Give my love to Pa, Ma, and family, and tell them I should like to hear from them, and that I would like to hear from them, as I have never received but one short note from them since I left them. Looking for letters and getting none. I have tried to average two a week. Please write soon and often. I almost get out of heart sometimes. All of you have double the chance to write I have.

My love to you and Mory, and to your Pa, Ma and family. May you all be blessed with good health and have the kind protection of Providence is the sincere wish of Robert.

Farewell for this time.

Yours devotedly,

Robert

April 11th, '63
Dear Wife,

As I received a letter from you last evening, I'll try and answer yours. Have nothing of interest for you. This leaves me well as usual. Charley is better this morning. Think he will be well soon. We are to move this morning to Loudoun or Fauquier, as our horses will starve here. We are to leave at half past eight. The enemy seem to be, from all reports, falling back. It is said Hooker fell back ten miles some three nights since. We have had two or three fine days at last. If it is such weather long, active preparations will take place soon. I don't think I need any clothes yet. Have as many as I can take care of now. Want to send my overcoat home soon, if nothing happens, also my flannel. I am glad to hear Mory is better. I would like hear him say "titty." Nothing would please me more than hear him talk. You must continue to direct your letters to Culpeper till I write you word where to direct them.

I would like to give you a long letter. Have not had the chance, as we are busy fixing to leave. Please write soon and often. Give my love [to] Pa, Ma, and family. Tell them I will answer their letters soon. Give my love to you[r], Pa, Ma and all the family, also a large portion for you and Mory.

Farewell,
Robert

Excuse this note.
Mr. Robert W. Parker

April the 21, 1863
Duck,

As Mr. Gills didn't stand this morning, I'll add a few more lines to my short note. I am a little unwell, but nothing serious, I hope. Duck, I want you to send me a few scraps of cloth like my pants I brought from home, as they will need repairing about the seat soon. Send them by Mr. Gills or John Franklin. Tell Pa not to sell any of his horses except the colts. I fear I shall need one soon. Duck, I have an idea of going to heavy artillery at Richmond, as horses are costing so much.[21] I can get an exchange very easy, I think. I wish to know what you think about it. Charley is well this evening. Tell Lucy and Bet to drop me a few lines. I'll answer any letters to me. My love to you, Mory, and all.

Farewell,
R. W. Parker

Beck, present my wishes to your pa and tell him I have sent his pistols home by Jesse Pollard.[22] I would have turned them over to Charley, but he said he didn't want them. Tell him I am sorry one of them is injured. Suppose it was done by a horse wallowing on it. I wish to pay for the repairing of it. I am greatly indebted to him for the loan of them and would liked to have kept them, but have purchased a six-shooter. Charley is well as usual and seems in fine spirits and seems to get on finely with the company. Tell your ma I think it would be useless to send the *Advocate* to Charley, as we get four copies per week in our company, and if a single copy was sent, perhaps he would not get one copy in ten, and he has the chance to look over them as soon as they reach us. We get tolerable good rations now of beef, bacon, and flour, and but short rations for horses. Goodbye.

Devotedly yours,
Robert

No letter from you yet.

Cavalry Camp near Culpeper CH
April the 24, 1863

As we are again in camp, I'll try and give you a few of the points, though have nothing of interest. We have thus far escaped another battle so far, but for the past week have been expecting one almost any day, but hope 'twill be some time now, as the enemy have gone back across the Rappahannock, though they may come across and give us battle any day.[23] There seems to be one general move down this way now. They are quite backward this spring to what I expected, but the weather and roads are so bad that 'tis almost impossible for an army to move. We have had rains almost every day for 8 or 10 days, and yesterday and today were dreadful rainy days, and our camp is nothing more nor less than [a] mudhole, in many places ankle deep. Hope will have good weather some of these [days]. The most of our furloughed boys came [to] camp day before yesterday. Coly started [the] next morning after reaching camp, and also Jim Lipscomb on a scout to Loudoun. I have not seen them yet, as I was on picket and didn't get in till last night. I think Coly brought everything safe [to] camp. Duck, your pa's pistols are at Mrs. [. . .] Jesse Pollard left them there as he went [. . .] I received a letter a few days since enclosed in Charley's. Was much relieved to hear you and Mory are getting on so well, but sorry to hear you was so uneasy about my being sick. I haven't been very sick since I left home. Charley has been quite sick but is well as common now. Has fleshened up considerably for the past week. He would amuse to see him walking about under his new hat. It is rather too large for him but suits splendid for camp. I received a letter from Aunt Mary this morning. She is tolerably well but some sickness in her family. Uncle Davy is quite unwell, also Sissy [. . .] I am obliged to you for the soap and pieces. I'll try soon and have all damages repaired to the rear of my pants. We are getting on finely, if we could get plenty for our horses [. . .]

Cavalry Camp near Culpeper CH
Apr 28th, 1863
My Dear Beck,

I'll try and answer your kind and interesting letter by Mr. Gills and was
[. . .]

May the 5 1863
My Dear Beck,

With the greatest pleasure I drop you a few lines to inform you I and
Charley are well and through the kindness Providence our lives are still spared
but don't know how soon we may fall.[24] Farewell. My love to you [and] Mory.

R. W. Parker

Camp on Plank Road, 12 miles from Orange CH
Dear Beck,

As I have the chance, I'll try and drop you a few lines, though have nothing of interest for you. This leaves me tolerably well. There is but little complaint in our company, not a man sick much in camp. We seem to enjoy good health, but horses are starving, if not for the fine grass in the county. The report is now that we are to go down to Culpeper again and picket on the Rappahannock. Some say we will make a forward move on the enemy soon, that they are concentrating all their forces in Va. If so, we will have to fight another great battle soon, and if so, I hope by the will of almighty God we may whip them well. You have heard ere this of the death of General Jackson. Hope his old corps will never falter for want of their old leader, but remember how he has led them and press forward in honor of his death.

The enemy are still on the north side of the Rappahannock, keeping up pickets at every ford. They have a great cavalry force and I don't think 'twill be long before we try their strength. I hope we will soon be able to attack them successfully. Charley has gone on detail [as] his horse is lame. [. . .] put any in yet, but my horse is getting quite lean. Think I will have to have another horse soon. Hope I may reach home soon. No one loves to get home better than I. 'Tis always the greatest pleasure to be with you and Mory and all my friends and connections. You and Mory must write soon. Would like to hear from you all. You must write soon and often. I have not heard you for some three weeks. My love to you, Mory, and all. Farewell.

From your unworthy,
Robert

Cavalry Camp near Culpeper CH
May the 17, 1863
My Dear Beck,

Your kind favor of the 30 Apr. came to hand this evening after laying over so long in the Culpeper mail, which we didn't get till this evening. Sincerely wish I could have gotten it sooner, but we have been moving about so much we have hardly part of the time had the chance to read them, had we received them. This note is the first I have received from you since we left this camp, but thanks be to heaven I heard from you and Mory this evening through Alick Pollard, and that you both were on foot. Was greatly disappointed at not receiving a note from you, but have to look over such things. I am sorry to inform you that my hopes of getting home soon are somewhat blended, as orders have been received to grant no more horse details after the 14 of this month, and I failed to get one in before, so I can't tell what the result will be, but guess the order will be changed soon, as we will be obliged to have horses to keep up this branch of service.

Duck, you wish me to get a substitute. I would gladly put in one if I could, but fear the chance is bad even if I could get one, and I am not able to buy one at the prices now, but would be glad to put one in even if I had to borrow the money. I would be perfectly willing to pay 2,000, twenty-five hundred and even more if I could get out of this war, even if it didn't last six months longer.[25] The officers of this regiment have tried to make a law among themselves to take no more substitutes, but one was fired on them a day or two since. I'll try and find out all I can soon and write to you again soon. Tell me your particular reason for writing me to put one in.[26] Duck, how do you know Pa and your pa would let me have the money? Wish you could wean Mory. Oh, how I want to see you both.

Am glad you bought paper and envelopes. Perhaps you had better keep them, as I can get some down here.

Am glad to hear Mary Scot has such good luck; guess John would be glad to get home now. Will Tompkins is dead. Tom Bernard has not been to camp yet. Guess he will not report to this camp anymore. Tell Mory Parpy will bring him some candy when he comes home.

Will try and give you some of the points. Everything is quiet down this way, but don't know how soon we will have to fight the Yankees again, but hope 'twill be sometime first, but we have a considerable cavalry force down here and may make a move soon. Charley is well and is looking for a furlough to get him a horse.

Direct your letters to Culpeper CH.

Sorry to hear Ben Hilton made his escape. Hope they will catch him. Duck, my horse is nearly played out, and if they don't give me a detail I hardly know what to do. Waddie Burton wants me to send for a horse, but don't think

I shall do so. If I can't have the privileges of other men, I'll stay in rank a while longer with Nelly. Duck, please don't delay writing to me. I am always anxious to hear from you. My love to you and Mory and all friends.

Say nothing about my writing you so as it will get out publicly. If I attempt it, I want to put it through. Your unworthy husband,
Robert

My love to Ma and Pa. Tell them to write soon. Farewell,
Robert.

Headquarters, 2nd Va. Cavalry, Culpeper CH
May the 26, '63
My Dear Beck,
I now acknowledge the receipt of your letter by H. C. Ballard, which came to hand yesterday. I had almost come to the conclusion that you had forsaken me, as I had not received a line [. . .]

Our thoughts are turned westward to the welfare of Vicksburg.[27] Hope our arms may achieve a glorious victory. Nothing new has turned up down this way for sometime. Our company lost but little or no clothing in the last raid by Stoneman. James and John Pollard have returned to camp, also Adams. I fear the chance for me to get home soon is rather a bad one, owing to previous orders issued, and my horse looks as well as it did a month since. And as to the substitute, I fear 'twould be almost impossible to get one in, as late orders have been issued as to substituting. It requires the su[bstitute] to be able bodied as the man who hired him [. . .]

It is English cloth. I could, if I know, draw him a pair of pants, but guess he does not want any. The coat has no metal buttons on it, so if he wants such he had better bring nine with him to put on it. We have a chance to draw any clothing we wish. You need not be uneasy as to my clothes. My coat hasn't a break in it. I am doing quite well as to clothes, have as many as I can take care of. [. . .]

Culpeper Courthouse
May 31, 1863
Dear Charley,
As I promised to drop you a few lines, I'll now try and do, though have nothing of interest for you. This leaves me well as usual. The company seems to be doing as well as when you left us. There is nothing new down this way. We are still at the camp you left us at, but there is some talk of moving tomorrow to a fresh camp not far off. I guess I hope we will not move far till you come back, as I will have more plunder than I can take care of well, but will do the best I can at any rate.

I drew you a jacket a few days since, I think a good one, so if you want it you had better leave your coat at home. If not, I will take it or let someone have it when you get back. You need not dread coming back, as we get plenty to eat now: half-pound bacon, plenty flour, salt, rice, sugar, and have plenty of eggs. Can have them cooked any way you like them. They are as cheap as you could wish. These times are somewhat dull in camp now, as 'tis quite dry and hot. We also have a young crew in camp that's always ready to challenge everybody as they pass. I should like to have been present to see you meet all at home, from what Adie Pollard [said] of their meeting him and thinking he was you. He spoke as though he tried to get them to believe 'twas not you, but they seemed not to believe him, and he could hardly keep some of them from kissing him. Lucy and Nannie, for instance, said if your ma had come running out, he would have had to retreated, but he finally got them to believe they was mistaken. You must try and get some stamps, envelopes, and paper as you come down, for we are nearly out. I must close. My love to your pa, ma, Beck, Mory, Lucy, Mary, Jesse, and little for you and all inquiring friends.

Farewell,

R. W. Parker

Tell Lute I heard Mr. Allwood was trying to get married over in Orange. He was a few days since. I have not forgotten Nannie's ring. Tell all friends, relations, and the neighborhood sincerely that I am now ready and prepared to read all letters written to me and will take the greatest pleasure in doing so.

Tell Beck to write soon. I have not time to write to her this evening, as the mail is about starting.

Tell Brother Alick to send me some of Pa's best tobacco. Bring me some tobacco and pipe stem and a piece of tallow to grease my boots.

Camp 2nd Va., near Culpeper CH
June the 3, 1863
My Dear Beck,

As George expects to start for home in the morning, I'll try and drop you a few. Have nothing worth writing but will give you the best I have. This leaves me well as common. Some sickness in camp, nothing serious, I hope. Duck, I am all anxiety to hear from you, as you was quite unwell in your last and promised to write again soon, but I have not received a line for several days. Fear you are quite ill. If you can't write, get someone to write for you, for I would like to hear from you very much now and Mory. I requested Charley to tell you not to put yourself to any further trouble as to a watch for me. Capt. Graves, if I mistake not, said Pa had one for me and wanted him to bring it down for me, but guess 'twas a mistake, as Ma didn't say anything about it in hers. I heard through a letter from Aunt Mary not long since to Bob Snow that Uncle Davy was quite ill. Would be good to hear from him.

I shall look for a letter from you this evening, as I have been getting one generally as soon as I start one to you. My love to you, dear Beck and Mory. Please write often.

Farewell,

Robert

No more has taken since my last to you of interest, but we are expecting one at any time. Would not be surprised any moment to hear the bugle sound for a move. We are much relieved to hear the besiegers have fallen back from Vicksburg. Hope they will conclude they are slightly whipped.[28] I see in the last Yankee news they acknowledge a repulse.

We have a very interesting meeting going on in the regiment in charge of Mr. Perrick of the north side of Bedford. He takes Mr. Berry's place for a short time, as his lady is expected to stay pretty close to home for some time and he wishes to be there. I intend sending a little money to you by George, as I have some more than I wish to keep in camp, but it takes a good part of our wages to buy paper and envelopes. Paper is worth from $4 to 4½ per quire, envelopes from $2 to 2½ per package, and everything else in proportion.

I'll try and send you fifty dollars by George. Excuse this uninteresting note. My love to you, Mory, and all.

R. W. Parker

Write soon and often. Be sure to write one, Duck.

2nd Va. Cavalry Culpeper CH
June 9th, Sixty-three
Dear Beck,

As I proposed in my note this morning I would receive a letter this evening, sure enough, to my great pleasure and surprise, this comes to hand, and afforded me much relief. Never received a letter that did me more good, but am grieved to think your illness is still protracted, and that our little Mory is yet so puny, but live in hope you both will be better soon.

There is nothing new in camp except that a move soon is evident. Hope it may be a victory [and] easy one. Duck, your envelope came in the best time, for I shall send off the last to you in the morning. Got five dollars worth of stamps this morning and will try and send you two dollars worth and also fifty or [sixty] by George.

Duck, don't think I had any hard feelings when I wrote that little word, "forsaken." It was only an expression of the moment. I am frequently doing or saying something to grieve me afterwards and above all things earthly with me is to save your feelings and render you as happy as possible. My dear companion, who I love beyond all others on earth, please forgive me all errors I have committed since we were united in holy matrimony, for it is my greatest desire on earth [to] treat you as I should.

I must close, as it is getting dark. My love to you and Mory. My prayers to God is daily for His protection over you both. Farewell, my dear companion,

R. W. Parker

Oak Shade, Culpeper County
June the 10, 1863
Dear Beck,

Your kind favor came to hand night before last. Was glad to hear you and Mory were improving. Would have answered your letter yesterday, but had not the chance. Charley reached camp safe Monday night, is well as common and in fine spirits. Got here just in time to get into a fight. None of the men who went with him have come in yet. We had quite a close little battle yesterday evening.[29] The Yankee cavalry crossed the Rappahannock in the morning, but one brigade didn't get into the fight till evening.[30] We succeeded in driving them across the river last night about dark. Don't know what our loss was on the right, but we lost several in our brigade and some in our regiment and our company. Our squadron are all sharpshooters now. We lost in our company James K. P. Preston[31] killed, son of John Preston who lately joined our camp. 'Twas the first fight he ever was in. Also Ben Turner[32] wounded, not serious, I hope. Tom Johnson was slightly wounded but very slight. Lieut. Johnson got his horse wounded. Bob Dearing had his horse killed and Tom Saunders horse badly wounded, was the casualties of our company. Company C that was with us got three men wounded, all slight, I hope, and several horses wounded and killed. Comp. A had 2 badly wounded and several horses wounded. Co. B had one man killed—young Langhorne—and one wounded. Some other casualties in the regiment, but have given you all I have heard of that was killed. Would like to give you the whole particulars of the fight, but don't know but little further than our regiment. The enemy's loss was thought to be heavier than ours. I think there is a grand move some way but don't know what. Our troops have been maneuvering about here for several days. General R. E. Lee was at Culpeper a day or two since, and a good portion of our army are in that vicinity.[33]

Duck, tell your ma I would like get home to roll her bees, but fear the chance is a bad one for the present. I think Charley's horse suits him finely and seems to take fighting quite gentle. She was valued at $800—just what he gave for her. I am much obliged to you for the goobers and pipestem and all the little trick you sent me. I am very thankful for Mory's tin cup. Tell him I will try and keep it for his sake. Tell him he must be a good boy and [. . .] Charley thinks he is a great little fellow. I must close. Will try and answer Ma's and Ginnie's letters soon. Write soon. Direct your letters to Culpeper CH. My love to Bet, you, Mory, your pa, ma, and all the family.

Farewell for this time. All remember me. [. . .] My love to Pa, Ma and family. Farewell. May the Lord protect and bless you [is] my sincere desire.

From your unworthy but devoted,

Robert

Kiss Mory for me.

Lindon Station, Fauquier Co., Va.
June the 16, 1863
My Dear Beck,

As we have been marching today and have stopped for a few minutes, I'll drop you a few lines, though have nothing very interesting for you more than I and Charley are well. A part of our reg. are fighting on the Manassas Cross Railroad and down towards Culpeper.[34] Our regiment has had no engagement since my last to you, but would not be surprised to see the Yankees at any moment. I think our regiment is on the way to the Valley. We are now resting in five miles of Front Royal and expect we will get there or in that vicinity. We have cheering news from Winchester.[35] Some say we have captured Milroy's whole garrison, consisting of several thousand. Our forces have whipped them is sure, but we have not heard the casualties of our army yet. General Ewell is over there with Jackson's 2nd corps, and our sincere wish is that we have given them a good [losing]. The latest report from Culpeper is that the enemy are across the river and lying under the shelter of their guns on the opposite side of the river. Guess they will have a fight there soon, not withstanding the fighting around us. All interest is in this way as to the critical situation of Vicksburg. Fear its fall but hope for the better. Also Port Hudson[36] is in a critical situation. God forbid they shall fall. Good news from Winchester: taken from five to six thousand prison[er]s, all their wagon train, commissary stores, and nearly all their artillery. I must close. Don't be uneasy about me. I hope I will be protected by the all-powerful hand. My love to you, Mory, your pa, ma and family. Charley's love to all. Farewell to all and Bet,

R. W. Parker

Write soon and direct your letters to Culpeper CH. We go every other day for them.

Near Berryville, Clark County, Valley of Va.

June the 21, 1863

Dear Beck,

As I have the chance to drop you a few lines, I'll try and do so. This leaves me well as common except a bad boil on my left wrist which is quite painful. But didn't leave the regiment till today. Am now with the baggage train and will leave for the regiment as soon as my arm is fit for duty. Charley is well as common and with the regiment. He happened to the good luck of not being in the fight of the 17 at Aldie, Loudoun County.[37] He lost his horse but had the good luck of finding her. The 3rd day after he found her. We had the hardest fight on the 17 I ever was in. The only loss in our company was Jack L. Preston severely in hip, Ad Wade saber cut in head. I hope Jack will get well but fear not. We killed and wounded a great Yankees and lost but few men in our regiment. Only one man died as yet. Our cavalry had a fight nearly every day and we don't know what moment we will be called into a fight, and expect a general fight in a day or two, as General Hooker is advancing [on] our army. General Ewell has cleared the Valley of the Yankees and is now said to be at Sharpsburg, Maryland,[38] meeting with no opposition over that way, but guess the Yankees will give him a fight soon.

The news from Vicksburg is quite cheering to us.[39] I saw Read Lebo a day or two since, also Billie Snow. Both getting on finely. Saw Uncle T. C. Goggin this evening. He is well and sends his love to all. His horse has broken down. I must close as it is getting dark. My love to you, Mory and all. Show this to all. Farewell for this time,

R. W. Parker

Direct your letters to Culpeper Court House, Fitz Lee's Brigade,[40] 2nd Va. Cavalry, and they will come to me. George Martin has not returned yet. Farewell, R. W. Parker.

Camp near Berryville, Clark County, Va.

June the 23, 1863

My Dear Beck,

I will drop you a few lines, though have nothing of interest for you, as I gave you the news in a note day before yesterday. This leaves me well as common except boils, which are quite painful to me, but hope I will be well soon, for the wagons are a disagreeable place to me. George reached here yesterday evening, broke down, but brought my letters safe, which relieved me very much. I have been quite anxious to hear from you for some time, as the last from you you was quite unwell. Hope you and Mory will have good health. Wish I could see you both, but fear 'twill be some time first. Some of our cavalry are fishing nearly every [day] [. . .]

Our regiment have not been engaged for several days and was last night at Hillsborough, Loudoun. I heard just now that our forces were expecting a fight at or near Charlestown, some fifteen miles from here. Charley is with the regiment and well yesterday. I will write every chance to you while times are so changeable, but they are delayed sometime at different places. You must not think hard of me for not writing you a whole sheet, as you can read the one to Pa and Ma, and I write to you two or three times to their once. I will [write] to Ginnie soon if nothing happens. Don't be uneasy. Hope we will come out all right. I must close. My love to you, Mory and all. Write soon. Direct your [letters] to Capt. W. F. Graves, 2nd Va. Cavalry, Lee's Brigade, and it will be sure to come safe.

Farewell,
R. W. Parker

Culpeper CH
July [6th], 1863[41]
Dear Beck,

As I have the chance, I'll try and drop you a few lines, though have no news of interest. I reached this place this morning after a fatiguing march of three days from Leetown in Jefferson Co. 'Twas rather a force march, as the Yankees had all the gaps of the Blue Ridge that we had crossed through going to the Valley, and our force tried to whip them out of [Chester] Gap. I don't know where our army is moving to, but think towards Fredericksburg, as 'tis reported the Yankees are moving towards Richmond. Our brigade, I heard, had a fight yesterday with them and routed them,[42] but have not learned the particulars, as I was not with it, as Charley and I have gone out to get our horses shod and have not found the brigade yet, and don't know where it is now, but will go soon to look for it. Expect it will come up this way today. I am thankful to learn from Jimmie Robertson that Cousin Joel Preston is so [well] that he could go about on his crutch and is at Gordonsville in a hospital, if he has not gone to Lynchburg or home.

I wrote to you in regard to some clothes. Try and have them ready, and if you don't have a good chance to send those pieces I named, I hope to get home soon, if life lasts, as my horse is about played out and they have commenced to condemn them again, and I certainly think I ought to have one soon. I was at the shop the other day where the horses were condemned. I hope you will write soon as you get this, as I have not heard from or received a letter from you since the 8 of this month. Wish I could hear from you everyday, but of late I have to be satisfied with hearing from you once a month. I wrote to you a few days ago by Burton's Jim. I have not received a line from Pa's for I can't tell when. Hope I will hear from them soon. Hope they are well. I must close as I have given you all the news I can think of now. My love to Pa, Ma and family, also to your pa, ma and family. Oh, how I wish I could see you and Mory. Don't seem to me I ever wanted to see you both as bad in my life. Please write soon and often. Farewell. May you both ever be protected by the kind hand of Providence.

Your unworthy husband,

R. W. Parker

Washington County, MD

July the 11, 1863

Dear Beck,

Though this note may never reach you, there is nothing like trying to get one to you. Of course you have been in great suspense as to my being dead or alive. I am thankful to Almighty God that I am still spared and in usual health. Charley is also well as common, or as well as we could be from hard fighting. We have been fighting regularly for three days.[43] The first day had five men wounded from our squadron; second day none hurt; had one killed in our squadron yesterday. Lost no man killed in our company since I wrote to you. Creed Hubbard[44] is slightly wounded. Our [whole] army is near here, and when we cross we will cross at Williamsport.

The river has been up so we could not cross none of our men, only in ferry boats,[45] and but few except wounded. Our loss at Gettysburg, Pennsylvania was quite heavy.[46] Tom Holland killed, many of our neighbor boys.

I must close. Farewell. This leaves me well. Remember me. Send my love to all. Our troops are now forming a line of battle in sight of us. We are expecting a big fight. Wish I could give you all the particulars.

All remember me. Kiss Mory for me. Farewell,

R. W. Parker

Reserve picket camp near Brandy Station, Culpeper County, Va.

July the 28 and 9, '63

Dear Parents,

As we are reserve picket and have nothing to do till the outside picket is interrupted (which I hope will not be today), I'll attempt to drop you a few scattered thoughts. The greater portion of our regiment are on picket on the Rappahannock, and our squadron, as they are sharpshooters, are held as reserve a little in rear to reinforce if an attack is made, which is expected hourly, as the Yankees are on the opposite bank of the river in considerable force. Cavalry, infantry, artillery, and baggage trains all in sight, and at the railroad bridge they run the cars up every day to the far end, and our men stand on this and are not suffered to fire on them till they attempt to cross. They also splash in the river and talk to each other. But hostilities will commence as soon as they reach this bank. Although they are so numerous at this point and picket up and down the river, 'tis believed by many to be a feint, and that they are concentrating their forces at some other point lower down, perhaps Fredericksburg, and may not cross here at all.[47]

I have no interesting news for you as to our success anywhere now. It seems to me 'tis one of the darkest hours of our Confederacy, but He who rules on high can only tell, to whom we should ever look for protection. We are getting on tolerably well down here, considering our shortness of rations, but we can live on it. Also the rations for horses is nothing but grazing.

You have heard ere this that we had [lost] the most of our clothes, so we are getting quite dirty and ragged. I lost a pair of pants and clothes, and the pants I have are getting the worse of wear, so I fear I shall get quite ragged before I get any, though we expect to draw from the government a suit at any time, and hope they will be in a few day[s], and if so I won't need them before I get some, if I have luck. My boots is also almost gone. I have not seen Uncle Pleasant for nearly a month nor heard from him. He was quite well when I saw him and [. . .] had to leave his horse in that rain of [. . .] in the Valley last spring. I have not heard a line from any of you since about the first of June. Can't imagine what can be the reason. The last I received from Beck was the [8] July. Am quite anxious to hear from you all. I commenced a letter to you some week since but had not the chance to finish it, but sent it anyhow. If you get this and can read it, I hope you will answer it soon, as I am quite anxious to hear from you all. I heard through Beck['s] letter that the corn on the bottoms was ruined, and from somebody else that the wheat has sprouted in the shock. We have had a great deal of rain with us. Had a very hard storm and rain yesterday evening, and bids fair to rain today. Henry Ballard is quite unwell. The remainder of our company are as usual. Charley is well as common and here with us. He says Alick must write to him. Farewell. [. . .]

R. W. Parker

Camp near Fredericksburg
Aug. the 7, 1863
Dear Beck,

As I have the chance, I will answer your most interesting note of the 30, received a day or two since. Was more than glad to hear from you and Mory but quite sorry to hear Mory has hurt his leg so bad. Hope he is well ere this. I can't imagine why I don't hear from Pa's. I have not received a line from them for some two months. Something must be the matter. There is nothing of interest down this way. We left Culpeper the evening of the 30 and came near this place. That night I expected to have a lively time by having to march all night, but to my great surprise have had no disturbance since we came here. The enemy have appeared on the opposite side of the river, but not in much force. A portion of our infantry are here now. Would not be surprised if we have another fight here soon.

The enemy are reported to be on the south side of the Rappahannock. Had a fight there last Saturday.[48] Guess you have heard the result ere this. We got the best of them, I learn.

Duck, I still hope to get home soon, but fear I can't get Nelly home, as she has hurt her ankle so she can hardly walk, and I fear she can't hold out home. If I get my detail, I shall try and get her to the pasture near Charlottesville. If you have not started my clothes, keep them a while longer, as I want to get these home. George nor Whit has not arrived at camp yet. We are looking for them everyday. Charley is well and writing to Alick. Guess he will get home soon if he gets his detail. This leaves me well as common. Farewell. Write soon. My love to you, Mory and all.

May kind Providence ever protect my son.

Yours devotedly,

R. W. Parker

On the upper Rappahannock

Our brigade was not engaged in the last fight at Culpeper. We happened to miss that. The report is they are moving, and if so, we will be sure to be on the move soon, but know not to what point. The health of our company [. . .]

Be more cautious the more cautious how you cool off when you get so warm. Hope Mory will get well soon and that his leg may take its natural shape again. Hope you both may be well soon, and when I have the good luck to see you you may be in good health, and if I am never allowed that privilege, that you both may ever be kept as under the hallow of the hand who made you. Tell Mory to be a smart boy and obey Marmy, and will try and bring him some candy when I come home. Write soon to Robert. Farewell.

Camp 2nd Va. Cavalry near Fredericksburg

Aug. 15th, 1863

Dear Beck,

I have delayed answering your letter of the 7, owing to being unwell, but will try and give you some of the points this morning. We have nothing new in camp. We are doing but little anyways at this time, eating and grazing our horses. We are camped within one mile of the city, but have not visited yet, but think I shall pay my best regards to it this evening. I am quite anxious to take a view of the ruins. There is no enemy in view on the opposite side of the river, but learn they are quite numerous. Generally very good at this time. Something near twenty of our company are due here this evening from home, but they may take the advantage of the president's late proclamation and stay a few days longer. I still hope there is a chance for me to get home soon. Think our details will come soon, as those at or on the way get in. I don't know why Lieut. Burton should have said I would be at home the time he did, when he knew I had no details in and was out on picket when he left camp. As to my clothes, if you have not started them, do not send them yet. If I am obliged to have clothes, I will try and get some to last till I can get to go home. I am sorry to hear of the death of little Jimmie, also to hear you suffer so with cold. [. . .]

Camp near Fredericksburg
Aug. the 21, 1863
Dear Louisa,[49]

I take this opportunity to drop you a few uninteresting [lines], for we have nothing of importance down this way. We are still in camp doing nothing but [grazing] and lying in camp. There is no late move of the enemy in this vicinity, except they have pickets on the opposite side of the river. I spoke to one of them and asked if he had a paper he would exchange. He answered me very abruptly no, so I had no further use for him and gave him to understand I didn't care.

There was a considerable accident happened down in the city yesterday. Two of Company B Wise Troop had a difficulty with a Texan, and the Texan killed one of them and wounded the other. The man killed was Tiny, the one wounded was Tucker,[50] both from Lynchburg. Horrid affairs. The row was at a house of ill fame. Oh, that our men would turn from such wicked deeds. The health of our company is very good at this time, and the most of those on detail have come in, but hear nothing of our details, but am still hoping they will come in yet. Today is fast day with us and all military orders are suspended as far as practicable.

This leaves Charley and I well as common. I am getting quite anxious to hear from you and Mory again soon. Oh that this unholy war would close and let us return to our homes in peace. I must close. Write soon. My love to you, Mory and all. Write soon.
Farewell,
Robert

I received your letter directed to Winchester a few days since. It was quite interesting though old. Farewell, Robert.

[Robert Parker returned to Bedford on horse detail.[51]]

Camp Second Va. Cavalry, Fredericksburg
Sept. the 13, '63
My Dear Companion,

According to promise, I'll try and drop you a few lines, though have nothing of interest to give you. I reached camp soon Friday morning in usual health and found all stirring in camp. I didn't catch up with Adams at all, and a portion of my trip was quite lonesome.

Duck, I am sorry I have put you to so much trouble about my handkerchief. I had so many things in my pockets I didn't find it at the time, but have found it since. Am sorry you sent your pa's, but will try and take care of it. I didn't know you knew I had missed it. I told them at Roberts's I had missed it and don't recollect of missing it till I got there.

Duck, I guess there is not money out of place. I know I took seventy dollars. If you remembered, I took fifty dollars when we exchanged those notes, and then you told me to be sure to take enough money with me, and then took twenty dollars more, making $70, and then got a dollar or two more that I recollect of, and might have got more. I don't think it any more than your duty to anything I do. I wish I could be with you to take dinner and supper too with you, for I want to see you and Mory almost as bad as I did before I went home, but feel rather satisfied. Wish I could get home in the course of a month or two. Poor little Mory—how I wish I could be with you both. Charley also reached camp yesterday, well as usual and in fine spirits. Duck, tell Pa to try and get Nelly fat and take good care of her.

I think your pa had better break that colt for Charley, or get him somewhat use to the saddle and we can soon break him here. Flora look[s] tolerably well, but the saddle rubbing on her back hurt it some. Hope it will soon be well.

Charley says they took him as soon as he got off the cars and put him in the soldiers home in Richmond till the train started—nothing more then they do all soldiers passing that way. I suppose 'tis to keep them from straggling.

There is nothing new down this way. Longstreet's corps has left us for some point unknown to us—some say to Charlestown, some to Tennessee[52]—but none know. The Yankees are still on the opposite side of the river.

I must close. Write soon and all the news. Duck, let us ever look unto Him who rules on high for protection. Let us put our trust in Him, and if we never meet on earth, oh may we met in heaven. Duck, remember me. Tell Mory to [be] a good boy and mind Marmy. My love to you, Mory and all the family.
Yours devotedly,
Robert W. Parker

Sept. the 14, '63. All well this morning as usual, with orders to prepare and keep on hand three days' rations, as we learn the enemy are moving to some point and we are to be ready to meet them.

I am sorry to inform you that our little Fitz has been promoted to major general and Brigadier Wickham[53] takes his place. Farewell.

Your unworthy but ever devoted,

R. W. Parker

Kiss Mory for me.

P.S. Let me hear from you soon and often. Let Ma and Pa know you hear from me. My love to all, Robert.

Camp 2nd Va Cavalry, Orange County, Va.

Sept. the 17, 1863

Dear Beck,

I'll try and drop you a few lines, though have nothing of interest to give you, more than this leaves me in usual health. Also Charley is as usual. We have moved camp since I wrote to you last. We are now twelve miles east of Orange Courthouse, so as to reinforce there, or Fredericksburg rather, as we are expecting a fight at any time. I learnt yesterday that the Yankee force had advance[d] into Culpeper and their front is near our lines on the Rapidan River.[54]

The latest from General Stuart's command, or that portion which was stationed in Culpeper, is that a few days since were badly whipped, losing five hundred sharpshooters, three pieces artillery, and forty men killed on the field. I can't vouch for the truth of this report and hope 'tis not so bad on us.

There is occasional cannonading along the lines. I look for a general fight soon. The Yankee pickets are still along the Rappahannock near Fredericksburg. There is a report in camp General Fitz Lee's command is going to Western Va. Hope 'tis so, but guess we will not leave till something is done down here. The general health of our company is tolerably good. Sam Wade is complaining. Lieut. Johnson and Tom Faris left yesterday morning for the hospital, Johnson with bronchitis and Faris with [. . .]. We are getting plenty to eat now for man, but horse food is as scarce as ever. Get a little corn every few days and grazing quite short. Duck, Ginnie was valued at $950. I forgot to tell you—we had a fine mess of stewed tomatoes for breakfast. We are living high for soldiers. I must close. Farewell. My love to you, Mory and all. I have not heard from you yet.

Devotedly,

Robert

Camp Second Va. Calvary, Orange County

Sept. 28th, '63

Dear Beck,

I received your welcome letter yesterday evening and will try and drop you a few lines, though have nothing fresh for you. Am sorry to hear of so much sickness in your pa's family. Hope no more bad luck may befall it. I am sorrowful indeed to hear of your illness. Hope you will be well soon. Glad to hear Mory has recovered from his spell, and live in hopes that the same hand that has protected you this far may still spare your life and restore your health. Let us ever look to Him for protection, for His kind hand is ever ready to help in time of need, if we will only ask Him with the right spirit.

I wrote a few lines to you yesterday morning and give you the points of our last little cavalry fight.[55] Our loss was but small, and so was the Yankees'. We have heard some very favorable news from northern Georgia, if it is but true,[56] and hope 'tis true. We are in our old camp twelve miles below the courthouse. Hope we may have a few days' rest now. I must close, as I have given you all the news. You must write soon and often, as I will be quite uneasy about you till I hear you're well. I have some camphor gum for you if I could get it to you, and hope I may have the chance soon. Write soon and often. May the blessings of heaven ever be with you is the sincere wish of Robert. Farewell to all.

It does me good to hear of the good meetings you all had at Ephesus. Wish I could have been there. Hope it may be a saver of life unto life to those who have made a profession of religion and a blessing to the neighborhood. Robert.

A few more days of sorrow and the Lord will call us home.

Mr. Robert W. Parker

Camp 2nd Va Cavalry, Orange County
Sept. the 29, '63
Dear Beck,

Your kind favor came to hand a day or two since, which relieved me very much to learn you was better and that Mory was no worse. Hope you both may soon enjoy good health. Sorry to hear the diphtheria is spreading in your pa's family. Hope 'twill not prove very serious. This leaves me a little unwell, nothing serious. Hope to be well soon. There is no news of interest down this way. All seems to be quiet along our lines, but would not be surprised to have a fight at any time. Our camp is in usual health. I must close, as we are to have inspection of arms this morning. Guess Charley has given all the news, and [I] written this to let you know I had not forgotten you with the promise to write again soon. I must go and catch my horse for the review. My love to you, Mory and all. Farewell.

Your devoted but unworthy husband,
Robert

P.S. Write soon and often and all the news.

Duck, I gave Sister the particulars of a murder in our company which happened day before yesterday of one of the members of our company. If you wish to hear them, send for the letter.

Robert

Va. Cavalry, Courthouse
Oct. the 3, 1863
[. . .] I'll try and drop you a few lines to inform you I am in usual health and Charley also. There is no fresh news in camp. We have moved camp several miles now near Orange Springs, twelve miles from the Courthouse. Our horses are faring better than they did at the old camp, but none too well now. [. . .] I sent the camphor gum to Liberty yesterday with a letter to you and asked him to leave it at [D.] Bell's, James Kasery's, or the post office. Hope you will be sure to get it. I could not get a vial to put it in. There is no late move of the enemy reached this camp.

Dear Mory,
I wish I could see you and hear that sweet little voice and hear you ask for pookey and for many other things. You ask so sweet for Marmy. You must be a smart and sweet little boy and obey Marmy. Hug and kiss Marmy for me. I must bid you goodnight. Dear son, you and Marmy must write to me often and give me all the news. Farewell, dear Marmy and son. My love to you, Marmy and all.

Devotedly yours,
Robert

Near Summerville Ford, Rapidan, Orange County
Oct. the 9, 1863
My Dear Beck,
I'll drop you a few lines in answer to yours of the 30 Sept., though have nothing of much interest for you. [. . .] Our brigade moved this morning from our old camp to this place and we have stopped to rest for a while.

I am sorry to hear through yours of the 30 that Mory is still so puny and [. . .] hurt himself so bad. Hope he will soon recover. I am glad to hear through your ma's of the 4 that you and Mory are still on foot and that Mory seems some better, and also that there are no new case of diphtheria in the family. Oh how I wish I could be with you and take the trouble of Mory off your hands and do the best I could for my family, but far from it. I fear I will have no chance to visit you soon, but if I do I will be sure to come. [. . .]

I am glad to think that such a [good] impression has been made on his [mind]. Duck, you see that, though young as he is, great impressions can be made on [his] mind, and I hope that good examples may be set before him at all times. [. . .]

Remember me, though unworthy as I am, and if I ever return home to you both, it will be through His protecting power. Then let us ever look to Him who can help in every time of need. Duck, tell Mory he must learn some little prayer to say every night before he goes to sleep. I remember the one my mother learnt me to this day.[57] Tell him to be a good boy and mind Marmy, and I will bring him something when I come home. I see but little chance for me to come home soon, but will do all I can towards it.

I sent the camphor gum to Liberty by [. . .] and told him to leave it at [. . .] the post office. Hope you have gotten it ere this. I guess I have gotten all your letters due there up to the time. How did you hear I had to walk the beat when I reached camp? I heard no talk of it, or but little, much more to perform it. I and was surprised to learn you had heard it. Tell Lute I think her soon writing is a long time coming. I must close, with the promise to write soon. You must excuse this [. . .]. Buy ink. My love to you, Mory and all.

Farewell,
Robert

Camp 2nd Va. Cavalry Co., Near Gainesville, Prince William [County]
Oct. 18, 1863
My Dear Beck,

As we have stopped to rest and feed (I hope for a few hours), I'll attempt to drop you a few lines in answer to your[s] of the 9, received the 16 at old Manassas Junction. We have had a time of trials and troubles since I wrote to you last. We have experienced some trying scenes in the various battlefields since we left Orange County, mixed with the dead and shrieks of the dying and wounded. On the 10 we crossed the Rapidan River at Raccoon Ford, and came in contact with the enemy soon after in position, and before we took our position they killed and wounded a number of our regiment, besides numbers from our brigades and divisions.[58] In the enemy's first assault, we lost from our regiment our adjutant Tayloe killed,[59] Capt. Irvine's leg shot off,[60] surgeon of our regiment shot through who has since died, Jo Nelson,[61] our major slightly wounded, and numerous others who were wounded or had their horses killed or wounded.

The loss of our company was Sergeant J. P. McCabe, had his leg shot off at the knee, his horse killed, and Lil Board's horse killed on his right. Board was not hurt only by his horse falling on his leg. John E. Jones slightly wounded and his horse slightly wounded. S. L. Murrill horse slightly wounded on this field. But by the help of almighty God we soon got them started for the Rappahannock and a running fight ensued to Brandy Station in Culpeper, leaving their dead and wounded on the field a distance of 8 or ten miles. At Brandy they made a stand, being largely reinforced [by] another command coming down [to] Culpeper CH, and here one of the hardest fight of cavalry and artillery I have ever witnessed,[62] but our loss here I think was comparatively small, and by night that day we had them down in supporting distance of their infantry on the banks of the Rappahannock, and as good luck would have it, we were not interrupted during the night and had a good night's rest for soldiers. The next day, the 11, we were sent to the front between Brandy Station and the Rappahannock and kept up a line of skirmishers till an hour or two by sun in view of their skirmishers, when they commenced advancing and made us fall back to within 2 miles of Culpeper CH, where we made a stand, and as they advanced our artillery soon let them know, and then our sharpshooters that we were ready for them. A brisk fight ensued, which soon sent them back. We lost none from our company that day, only Sam Murrill had his horse killed. Since that time we have had no hard fighting except on the evening of the 15, on Bull Run below Manassas.[63] Here we come in contact with their infantry. We held our position till we were ordered back to camp. On the evening of the 16 we formed in line of battle between Manassas and Bull Run, but the Yankees didn't come up to meet us and have done nothing but scout since.

I have given you a few points under my own observation of our troop so far. The infantry so far, I think, have done but little fighting. Meade the Yankee General fell back too fast for them.[64] The Yankee force is at Centreville, and ours I know not where, but guess somewhere west of us. We have taken a good many prisoners. Thus ends our run up to this time, so will have to wind up with something else. This leaves me tolerably well, Charley also.

Our horses are very much fagged. Mine I think has the distemper, and I fear will give out. She is falling off very fast. I am glad to hear you and Mory are improving and that you have got the camphor and letters I have sent you. Duck, tell Lelian I saw her pa. He sent his love to her and all, and said he would write soon. I must close, as we are about starting. My love to you, Mory and all. Send this to Pa.

Farewell,

Robert

Oct. the 19, 1863. Culpeper. This leaves me tolerably well. I was very sick yesterday and was sent to the rear. Our army has fallen back across the Rappa-hannock River.[65] Will write you in a day or two.

Robert

Buckland, Fauquier Co., Va.

My Dear Companion and Parents,

Through the kind guidance and protection of our heavenly Father, my life is still, but very unwell and I might say sick, but can help myself yet. Won't know how the Dr. will dispose of me till morning, whether back to a hospital or follow our wagon trains. Oh how I would like to be at home during my sickness, but fear no chance. We have had a big fight and but few save the badly wounded are looked after, and the slight wounded and sick are but little noticed. Our regiment, with some help, made a great and gallant charge on the Yankee cavalry and routed them.[66] The Second's loss was, if I mistake not, was four killed on the field and quite a number wounded. Our company's loss was small: four wounded, all I hope slight. [. . .] arm and head, G. Roberts an arm—both the above saber cuts; G. Leftwich touched by ball on knee slight; Fred [Huriss] on head slight; and Bob Johnson misfiring. The infantry fight was desperate. We whipped them and took a good many prisoners

Duck, I want Sam to have a pair of good boots. Alick['s] measure will do. For me, pair of pants and overcoat. My close-bodied coat is considerably rent.

Must close. Hope this will find you all well, and I may be enjoying good health also.

I heard this morning that a portion [of the] army is at Fairfax Courthouse and below, and the enemy at Centreville.

Give what I hear.

The blessing of heaven on you all. Love to all. Duck, you and Mory each other often.

From

R. W. Parker

I have received no mail from you on this march, as the railroad is not completed down this way.

Camp 2nd Va Calvary, Culpeper County
Oct. the 21, 1863
Dear Parents, Brother, Sister, and Cousins,

With the greatest pleasure do I try to drop you a few lines this morning in answer to yours of the 11 + 9, which gave me the greatest pleasure to read, and more than all to hear my relations and friend at home and around have had such a refreshing season. Hope the revival may not stop when the protracted meetings does, but that may continue for days to come. And one of my desires is that while you all are enjoying such great blessings, you would not forget your unworthy son, brother, and cousin, far from you, exposed to the deadly missiles of the enemy, disease, death, and the privations of camp—for I can assure you, my dear parents, if ever one should be thankful to almighty God, I am one, for His kind protection through the trials we have been for the past ten or twelve days, and I am thankful to almighty God that I have felt that He has protected me. Different times in within the past few days while confronting the foe on the field of battle, it seemed as if He was directing the balls either side of me, and none has so far as I know touched my clothes.

I will now try and give you some of the news. All our army, or the most part of it, is now on the west side of the Rappahannock. We followed the enemy to Bull Run and fought them across the stream for a hour or two. The loss in our cavalry I think is light. The enemy cavalry lost much heavier than ours in killed, wounded, and prisoners, and nearly have taken some two thousand prisoners, three pieces artillery, and a good many horses, but our horses are nearly worn down. Ginnie is about broke down, but fear I can't send or bring her home soon. I want Nelly to be fattened as soon as possible, if I should have the chance to come home. Charley is well as usual. We have lost only two men wounded from our company. Sergeant McCabe lost his leg.

I must close. Mr. Franklin got here with the regiment last night. My love to all. Write soon and often.

I saw Uncle Pleasant a few days since. He was well and in fine spirits. Said he would write soon.

Robert W. Parker

Your unworthy son, brother, and cousin. Tell Lelian her pa says she must learn fast.

Camp 2nd Va Cavalry, Culpeper County, Va.
Oct. the 22, '63
Dear Parents,

As I missed sending my note of yesterday, I'll drop you a few lines this morning. This leaves me well as usual, though I have been laid up for a few days, more or less, with something like neuralgia. My head is nearly easy this morning. We are camped about six miles east of the courthouse. Have quite cool weather now. We have had some quite hard rain within the past week, and fear from the present prospects 'twill rain again in a day or two. I want you to get Nelly in good order soon, as Ginnie is getting quite thin.

This leaves Charley well as common. Send this letter to Beck. Give my love to Beck and my Mory. Tell Mory he must stay with you some and be a smart boy. Am glad to hear Billie Snow has gotten home. Hope he will soon recover. I will write soon again to you all and Beck. My love to all.

Your devoted but unworthy son,
R. W. Parker

Camp 2nd Va. Cavalry, near Culpeper CH
Oct 30th, 1863
My Dear Rebecca,

I'll try and answer your kind favor of the 16 and 26, though have nothing new for you. This leaves me in usual health, and sincerely hope it may find you and Mory enjoying much better health than when you last wrote. It filled my heart with sorrow at the reception of your note received this morning to learn you was so unwell, and that poor little Mory was so afflicted. I sincerely hope that you and the doctor both may be disappointed in that he may soon be, by the help of almighty God, soon restored to good health, but His will be done, not mine. Oh that we were more humble and were worthy to be called the children of God. Let us try to be humble followers of Him who died for us. No one knows the feeling of my poor heart. I can't tell when I ever had such feelings, nor when I ever felt my unworthiness as I have this morning. It would be one of the greatest pleasures that earth could give to be with you and do all I could to comfort and take care of you, and share in the pleasure of nursing little Mory, but fear it will be some time first, but live in hopes that I may see you both soon.

Duck, try and get Mr. Gills to bring my overcoat to camp with him, also my gloves. Would not trouble you so much if I could draw one. I sent a pair of pants and shirt by him, also a knife to Mory. I have since that drawed a jacket and another shirt, which I will send as soon as I have the chance. As to the shirts, you can use them for anything you wish, as I drew them just for the cloth. They cost me 2½ dollars each, much cheaper than you can. By the cloth, I wish to save you all the trouble I can and will draw all the clothes I can. I want you to alter the pockets of the pants, if they reach you. Put them in like these I have on. The jacket I have drawed I think is an excellent one, and cost me twelve dollars.

This leaves Charley tolerably well. He has been unwell but is improving. Our horses both look badly. Mine has had the distemper very bad, think she [is] getting some better. There is nothing fresh in camp. All in usual health. We are still camped near the Rappahannock River. The enemy, not far from the other side, show but little motions for fight. Duck, tell Pa to try and have Nelly in as good order as possible, as I don't know when I will have to come home for her. Give my love to Pa, Ma, and all the family, also to your pa, ma, and family, but the greatest portion to you and Mory. Write soon and often, as I will be quite uneasy about you and Mory.

Tell Lelian Goggin that her pa was well when last I heard from him, and sent his love to you all. We are faring tolerably well now on beef and flour. We have no right to grumble. I must close. May the Lord bless and save you, Mory, and all is the sincere wish of

Robert

Camp 2nd Va. Cavalry near Culpeper CH
Nov. the 1, 1863
My Ever Beloved Beck,

Your welcome note of the 30 came to hand today and I'll try and answer, though have nothing fresh for you. This leaves me tolerably well, except I have spells of diarrhea, which are quite severe at times, and hope to be well soon. I am confined to camp now, as I am acting orderly sergeant. There was a considerable stir in camp this morning. Received orders to detail 175 men for some purpose, but know not what. Guess was for a scout, and just as they were ready to start, our regiment received another detail for fifty men, so the last detail took Charley, but hope he will be in tonight, as he took neither baggage with him. So the most of our regiment are out at this time.

I will now try and answer your note. It grieves me to hear Mory is no better, but still live in hopes he will take a change soon for the better. Poor little fellow, I know he must suffer a great deal. Wish I could help you nurse him. Duck, if Mr. Pullen will let you have leather at the price you stated, you had better get a pretty good supply, not under the quantity you named. Tell Mory he must keep that knife and not cut himself with it and be a good boy. Duck, the pants and shirt you spoke of belong to me. If you think the pants are large enough, fix the pockets for me. As to the shirt, I drew that just for the clothes for you, and have another for you to use up if you wish. The bleached cloth Charley sent, it came out of a Yankee's pocket and that is the Yankee's blood on it. The poor Yankee was killed at Stevensburg,[67] the last cavalry fight we had near Brandy Station in Culpeper. I am doing very well without my blanket or flannel yet. I drew these pants to save you the trouble of having them to make. Won't need any coat if I have luck. Drew a very good jacket a few days since that I wish to get home for next summer, if I live. Charley also drew a jacket and pair of pants, and his pants and coat are good yet. Will try and tell him what your ma said when he gets back. You need not make me any coat this winter. Present my best wishes to Bet and tell her I thought she was secesh but think she is union.

I received a letter yesterday from Ma and answered immediately and will send this this evening. Please write soon and often, for I will be uneasy about you and Mory. My best love to you, Mory, and all the family. Farewell. My sincere desire is that you and Mory may ever be protected by the hand of kind Providence.

Robert

2nd Camp near Orange Courthouse
Nov. the 11, 1863
Dear Wife,

As we are still for a short time, I'll try and drop you a few lines, though have nothing of interest for you. This leaves me and Charley well as usual. I guess ere this you have heard of the fallback of our army across the Rapidan.[68]

All our infantry have gone across the Rapidan but our division of cavalry that is between the Robertson and Rapidan. You have also ere this heard of our loss on the Rappahannock, said to [be 1,600]. They were on the east side on picket, also near artillery lines. I fear little John Welch was taken, as the most of his brigade was captured. It was a very unexpected fallback to most of us, but hope 'tis all for the better. There was no casualties in our cavalry, so far as I know, in the fallback.

It is said our army [may be sent] to some other point, but I know not where. Mr. Gills has not arrived yet. Look for him tonight. Hope he will bring me a letter if nothing else, for I am quite anxious to hear from you and Mory. John Graves, Jimmie Robertson and others have arrived yesterday and today. I am quite anxious to send a shirt and my new jacket to you the first chance, as I have more than I can carry and fear I may lose them. I am sorry to inform you that my horse is so nigh played out that I don't expect to go in ranks much longer. She has something like distemper or something worse, but have no idea when I can come home. I don't know how I shall manage to carry my flannel when the weather gets so I will need it. Wish I could get me a pair of old saddlebags to carry mine and Charley's in, as a pair would do for both of us. Wish Charley and I could get something good to eat from our homes. Duck, tell Pa and Ma to try and get Nelly fat by the time I come home. I don't know what time it will be, may be shortly, and there is a great deal said about soldiers bringing poor horses back to camp. Hope this note may reach you and Mory in good health. I will stop writing for tonight and finish in the morning, the Lord willing.

Nov. the 12. Mr. Gills has just arrived in camp brought me a letter from you and Sister. Why you have not received my letters, I can't tell. Think I wrote you 3 or 4 letters last week, or at least since you received the one you mentioned. Glad to hear you are well and that poor little Mory is better. Hope he will soon recover and be as lively and playful as ever. I received my overcoat by Mr. Gills, also my gloves. Charley will take it till he gets his. I am anxious to send you my jacket and another shirt. Guess ere this you have gotten my letters. You must write soon and often. This [leaves] me rather indisposed. Farewell.

Your devoted but unworthy husband,
Robert W. Parker

Duck, don't send my blanket or flannel till I send you word.

Camp 2nd Va. Cavalry
Nov. 24th, 1863
Dear Parents,

I'll try and drop you a few lines, though have nothing fresh for you. This leaves me in usual health. Nothing new in camp. One of my reasons for writing at this time is to know why some don't write to me. I can't account for it, unless it is you keep putting it off from time to time and thus neglect it, for I have not received a line from you all since Gills came down, and if I mistake not, I have answered it long since. I used to get one a week but now they are few and far between. I received a letter from the Dr.'s of the 18 a few days since, which relieved my mind very much and was glad to hear they are getting on so well, and hope if nothing happens to see them before long.

Pa, I want you, if you can, to have Nelly fat by the time I get home. I am sorry to inform you that Ginnie has been condemned and I fear getting her home, but will try and send her soon if I have any chance, even before I have the chance to come. She has something like distemper for near a month and is greatly reduced. Are getting but little to feed on, but think we will get more as soon as the tax in kind begins to come in.[69] The board is getting very strict receiving horses. Pa, I want you to write me word what you think of my buying a young horse at a reduced price and keep him till next spring to ride, for horses will be horses next spring if we live to see the time. I am well aware that the expenses wintering a horse would be heavy cost—some $200 or three hundred dollars, and say 300 or 400 to pay for one now would be quite heavy. Write me word what you and Ma think of it. I have not bought one but want your opinion. I have not heard from Uncle P. for some time nor had the chance to send the letter to him except by mail. I must close. Write soon and often. My love to you and all.

Camp 2nd Va. Cavalry, Madison County, Va.
Dec. the 7, 1863
Dear Beck,

I'll try and drop you a few lines, though have nothing fresh or interesting for you. I received your kind favor of the 1 a day or two since. Had almost despaired getting one from you anytime soon. Was glad to know you was able to write to me again, and that the robe was such a good one, and that both of them were doing so well, and live in hope that your good health may continue, but sorry to learn Clem was laid up with her throat. Hope she will be well soon. It seems your pa's family has been sorely afflicted for the past few months. Hope Burton will soon be able to be moved. Where is Lieut. Urwin? I have not heard him mentioned for sometime.

Duck, you spoke of Wade's marrying the 22. I have not heard when it was to be. He is now on a scout to Loudoun. I fear if he does not look sharp he will not be there to marry, for the last news we had from him the Yankees were after the party he was with. Coly has gotten back and has heard all the points from home. He seems to care but little for it anyway. I think Alick Gray was rather the hardest up of anyone I know.

I wish you could get the leather and Sam could make the shoes for Clem. I started a pair here this morning, but they will not suit for Clem's winter shoes. If they will suit Pa, I would like to swap them to him for a pair for Clem. I hope we can make out without borrowing leather from your pa. I shall need a pair of boots soon. Hope Uncle Peter will get out my leather as soon as he can. Charley['s] horse keeps up yet but is quite thin. Don't think she will hold up much longer. I started Ginnie home this morning but fear she will hardly make the trip. I started her in the care of Mr. John W. Morgan. Hope they may both reach home safe. I started by him a halter, my saber, and four boxes of partial cartages. If they reach home, take care of them. John Graves sent a shirt in one of the pockets. Some of Pa's family will send that to his wife. Duck, write me word if the things by [Mallow] has reached home yet.

There is nothing new from the camp. All quiet down this way and the Yankees are said to be falling back east of the Rappahannock, but can't vouch for the truth of the report,[70] but wish 'tis so. We are getting good rations for men, and if my horse gets home safe, short rations for horses won't hurt me for sometime. You need not look for me till you see me, for I have no idea when I will get home.

The company is in usual health at this time and all as usual. Your acquaintances and relations are in usual health. This leaves me and Charley in usual health. I must close. Please write soon and often and all the news. My love to you, the little boys,[71] and all the family. Tell Mory to be a good boy and take good care of little brother, and I will try and bring him something. Kiss them often for me. Farewell for this time. Your devoted but unworthy,

Robert

Duck, I have heard a good deal about what is to take place at your pa's lately, but will say nothing about it in this, as 'tis too late to do any good now. Let no one see this. R. P.

[Robert Parker returned to Bedford, probably on horse detail.]

1864

By the spring of 1864, the Second Regiment Virginia Cavalry had returned to service under the command of Brig. Gen. Williams C. Wickham. In May, Brig. Gen. Fitzhugh Lee's division broke camp and headed for Todd's Tavern to gather intelligence on the movements of Gen. Ulysses S. Grant and Maj. Gen. George Meade. With Maj. Gen. J. E. B. Stuart's death at Yellow Tavern, the Second came under the command of Brig. Gen. Wade Hampton. Under Hampton's leadership, they fought in the Overland campaign, including the battles of the Wilderness, Spotsylvania Court House, and Cold Harbor. They countered Gen. Philip H. Sheridan's raids on Confederate railroads in June 1864 then held the center of the cavalry lines near besieged Petersburg. In late summer and autumn the Second joined Fitzhugh Lee in his move against Philip H. Sheridan in the Shenandoah Valley campaign of 1864. They endured a difficult winter near New Market under Gen. Jubal Early.[1]

Camp 2nd Va. Cavalry, Middlebrook, Augusta CH
Jan. 9th, 186[4]
Dear Beck,

I hasten to drop you a line to inform you that I reached camp safe and found all getting on as well as could be expected. I had quite a hard time getting to the command, as to weather and roads, but fared well both myself and horse, but I am sorry to inform you he has the scratching on every foot so bad he can't hardly walk. I will give you a short account of my trip. I stayed the first night with your uncle [and] aunt's, in second with your uncle Sam's, the third at Poindexter's in Amherst, the 4 at Mr. [Mantaply's] in Amherst, the 5 with those old maids where I stayed going home and won't charge a cent anywhere. I had good luck and bad mixed. The worst is my horse having the scratches.

Uncle Pleasant Goggin started from Pa's Friday morning and got here about the same time I did and stayed with us last night, and also Mr. Lamier of his company. A good many of our company have gone home without leave, I think about 17 in all. We had 12 at role call this morning. Some companies have not more than half that number. Beck, I want you [to] tell Alick to bring my canteen with him when he comes. Tell him if he brings it to keep it with him of a night. If he does not, it will be stolen from him. We are getting but little for our horses and I fear no chance for disbanding. We have plenty of cold weather and snow here.

I must close for this time with the promise to write soon again and send you all the [news].

May the hand of kind Providence ever protect you.

Devotedly yours until death,

R. W. P.

My love to you, the children, and all. Farewell.

R. W. Parker

Camp 2nd Va. Cav., near Barboursville, Albemarle Co.
Jan. the 19, 1864
My Dear Beck,

As we have marched only ten miles and will stop for the day, I will try and drop you a few lines. This [is] the prettiest day we have had since winter commenced, and finds me enjoying tolerably good health but in low spirits, for I fear my horse will starve in a month or two, as I see no chance to get anything for them. We have had a very hard time since we left the camp I wrote to you from, Middlebrook in the Valley, marching everyday except one since we started from there to this place, and fared very hard indeed, getting no rations part of the time. I reached the regiment the 8 of this month, four days after my time was past, but the officers thought I got in before time and I did not tell them any better, so I am all right anyway and fared splendidly all the way, and traveled about from fifteen to twenty miles a day. I had good luck and bad luck too. My horse took the scratches about the second day after I left home and has had them very bad, but hope he is getting better now. And the third night, being the night after I left your uncle Tom's, the little negroes where I stayed I suppose stole every sweetcake out of my haversack, but as it happened they took nothing else. Uncle J. M. Goggin left Pa's on Friday and stayed all night with me in camp the night I got there. Duck, the disbanding fever has all blown over and we will go into regular camp tomorrow near Gordonsville and picket on the Rapidan River. I hope we will be still in camp the balance of the winter and get a snack from home now and then. John Krautz[2] promised one if he came back on the train, which I am sure he will do. If Alick don't bring my canteen and bag of smoking tobacco, get him to bring them to me. He will be due in camp about the 29 of this month. We have only 6 men in our camp for duty now and two non-commissioned officers. I am acting orderly sergeant for the company. It has gotten quite small. We have 18 men absent without leave, and I think they will be sure to be court-martialed, and nearly all the balance of the company absent sick and after fresh horses, though a good many of them are due here tomorrow, Alick among the rest, but I don't look for them for several days yet. I must close, having given you all the news. I looked all through Charlottesville for Alick yesterday but did not get to see him. Guess he had not gotten there. Direct your letters to Gordonsville.

We are detached now from Rosser,[3] and I am glad of it and wish to join Wickham's Brig. My love to all, you, and the children.

Devotedly yours,
Robert

Remember your promise and write twice a week.

Duck,

Since I wrote a letter to you today, George Martin tells me he is going home tomorrow, so I will try and drop you a few more lines. I will send your ten dollars' worth of postage stamps by him and wish I had something to send you and the boys, but 'tis out of my power at his time. Be sure to send my day book by George, if you can. I want it almost every day. You may send my tobacco by him, if he can bring it, and any little thing he can bring that you want to send. Try and let me know by him whether Alick thinks there is any chance to get me a watch or any on the subject. If so lucky, send it by George. I have written to Aunt Ann this evening, also commenced a letter to Bet, but don't know whether I will have any chance to finish it today or not. I will close. Farewell.

Devotedly yours,
Robert P.

Camp 2nd [Va.] Cavalry near Orange CH
Feb. the 22, 1864
Dear Wife,

As it is getting time again, I will try and drop you a few lines, though have nothing worth giving you. This leaves me in usual health with the exception of a slight cold. Our company seem to be in usual health at this time and in fine spirits. We get enough to make out with, though short. We make out better than I expected when we came down. The enemy seem to be quiet along our line, and but little news anyway but reenlisting—that is running high now.[4] I tried at Orange CH for [veils] but could get no sort. I received your letter a few days since, also a note from Charley. I think he might write oftener or longer notes, but guess his mind is so full of other stuff he don't think of writing to camp.

I guess the 17-year boys are somewhat stirred up on the war question, while it seems to have but little impact on the regulars.[5] They have become, it seems, satisfied to their fate. Nelly has been sick for several days but is some better I hope today. She has fallen off a great deal. It seems I was born for bad luck with horses, but am thankful for the luck I have. Duck, I should like to give you some advice as to what to do with what little money we have, but do not. Some think it the best to keep it and give three of the old for two of the new.[6]

I wrote to Brother Alick to get me a watch, and if he could not, to get someone to get it for me, or anyone that would do the favor for me to pay a good one if possible, and give from one $150 to $200, if can't get one for less, but it will be useless to give all I have for one. I have had two offered to me. [...] ones at that, one at 200 and the other 300, and now is the time to get [out] in buying such things. Duck, I had two good apples given, one just now. I wish you and the boys had them. 'Twould do me more good for you to have them than to eat them myself.

I wish I could see you and the boys very bad and wish I could hear from you everyday. Hope Mory is better before this. Poor little fellow, he has seen hard times. I have given all the news. You must write soon. My love to you, Mory, and Georgie. Kiss them for me. My best wishes to all. Tell all to write soon. Farewell for this time.

Yours devotedly but unworthy,

Robert W. Parker

Camp 2nd Va Calvary
Feb. the 22, '64
Dear Beck,

I will try and answer your letter this morning received yesterday evening, also a letter from Ma. You wrote as to what to do with it. I hardly know what to say to you about it. If you have a hundred dollar bill, take a four percent bond for it. If not, hold to and try and exchange three of the old for 2 of the new after the first of April, as the hundred dollars notes, in addition the 33 1/3 percent, an additional tax will put on theirs of ten percent per month, and on less size notes this percent will not be put on them. I sent yesterday the bill and an explanation to Pa, which is the best I have seen. Send and get it and look over it. I have bought me a watch and want you to send me one hundred and twenty dollars by George or Charley or the first good chance you [have] so I get it by the middle of March and sooner if you can.

Duck, hold on to your two-, one-, and half-dollars bills and Bedford County money, as the currency bill does not include them. Dr. City will certainly refuse to the present money for his pay. Hope it will be settled as soon as possible. I'm sorry to hear Mory continues so poorly. Hope he will soon be well. I think the Lieut. must be in earnest. Tell Lucy to write me word how to direct a letter to him.

My love to you and the children. Kiss them often for me. Best wishes to all. Farewell.

Devoted[ly] yours,

R. W. Parker

Write soon and often.

Duck, there is no discount on postage stamps. Take care of what you have till after the currency takes a chance, and I will send you some more the first chance I have. I sent a letter by George and $10 worth of stamps.

Robert

Camp 2nd Va. Cavalry
Feb. the 23, '64
Dear Beck,

As I confided yesterday evening that I had given you all the news, but as bad luck will have it, more happened last night. One of the best soldiers in our company, R. J. Dearing,[7] on his way on guard with his pistol and saber in hand, hurt himself in some brush and fell down, causing his pistol to go off, and shot himself through the hand through the center, breaking the bone of the middle between the first joint and the joint below. H will be sent home this morning. Duck, tell Pa, if he thinks proper, to fix in a light box, a[ny]thing. George will bring it if it is sent to Liberty. This leaves me well. Farewell. My love to you, the children and all.

Robert

Send you ten dollars of stamps on with George.

Camp 2nd Va. Cavalry
March the 2, '64
Dear Beck,

I drop you a few lines to inform you I am yet alive and well as one could be under existing circumstances. We have had quite a hard time since last Sunday, marching to intercept those Yankees that went from near Charlottesville last Monday,[8] and yesterday was the trying time with us. On their way near Charlottesville, they stopped at Stanardsville, the county seat of Green County. We [were] expecting them to go back to Madison. That night went around to get ahead of them, which we did, and lay in ambush on the road they had to travel, but they did not come that night, being last Monday. So Tuesday morning we started to Stanardsville and were met by the enemy, some three thousand strong. Gave them fight, but was flanked so heavily that we had to fall back. The force on our side consisted principally of the 2nd Va. Cavalry. Our losses has not ascertained yet, as some may come in yet. None from our company. Quince Dickinson[9] and several other of Co. A. The only one of our regiment wounded bad that I have heard of and since reported dead is Lieut. William Parker, shot through the bowels. We reached camp some two hours ago and have just received orders to be ready with two days' rations to move at a minute's warning in the direction of Fredericksburg. The Yankees have crossed cavalry and infantry, and the cavalry have reached the central road and turn[ed] up a good deal of it. I think our army seems to be moving. I fear the enemy have touched in a tender place, with all of the principal part of our cavalry and infantry back in the rear. I hope General Lee will turn up right for them yet. The Yankee[s] didn't get farther [than] the Rivanna River, five miles from Charlottesville.

I wrote a letter to Pa a few days since but failed to send it, and tore it up when I started in the fight. I have written to you to send me $120 and hope to get it soon, but fear you may not receive the letter in time. I also wrote to Pa to send it but failed to send it. You or he either will send it as soon as possible, as I want to pay it out before the new currency comes in. The money is for Sam Nichols, $100 dollars of it which I borrowed from him. I had hoped on reaching camp I would get a letter from you but failed, as we looked for George yesterday and day before but he didn't come.

Our horses are reducing as fast as they can, as we have had nothing for them to eat for three day[s]. The news has just reached us the enemy are going in the direction of Lynchburg, but hope the report is false.[10] All in usual health.

I must close, having given you the news. Send this to Pa and Ma. My love to you, Georgie, Mory and all. Farewell. Write soon and often.

Devotedly,
Robert

Camp 2nd Va. Cav., near Orange CH
March the 11, '64
Dear Beck,

As Charley has written to some of you, I will send a few lines in the same envelope to you. This leaves me well as usual. Nothing fresh in camp. We had quite a hard day's rain yesterday and has, I hope, stopped all rainy moments for the next few weeks. It was thought a move was on hand yesterday with the enemy, as they come to one of the picket's post and fired on them, killing a horse. No other casualties that I have heard of yet. A good many of the raiders have been killed, wounded, or captured. Over three hundred prisoners have been sent to Richmond.[11] Hope they will not undertake it again soon. Duck, it seems our boxes had a good impression, as we drew yesterday full rations of flour, pickles, beef and [bacon].

Duck, I heard by George [that] Alick had bought me a watch. If he has and will be troubled to get rid of it, you had better pay him for it. If the man will not take it back, the one I have keeps good time and I think is a good watch, cost $200 dollars. I must tell you what we had for breakfast. Had nice fried home sausage, wheat bread, could have had coffee and butter if we had wished. We are living just as good a soldier could wish, unless he could be at home, which is impossible, we all know, but live in hope of a better time. Hope you and the children are all well. I must close for this time. You will please write soon and often. My love to you, the children, your pa, ma, and family.

Ever devotedly yours until death,

R. W. Parker

Camp 2nd Va. Cavalry, near Orange CH
March the 13, '64
My Ever Kind Wife,

As the most of our company are out on picket and all is quiet in camp, I'll attempt to answer your kind favor of the 7, which came to hand yesterday. I was more than delighted to hear from you and the children, and began to think long of the time between letters. I hope your anxiety and suspense ere this has been removed by the reception of my letters, that through kind Providence I am yet spared from the deadly missiles of the enemy. I wrote to you on my return from the fight in Greene [Co.] and as soon as we returned from the last expected fight in Spotsylvania. It is my wish to prevent your uneasiness as far as possible at all times, and would to Him who rules on high that I could prevent it at all times, but 'tis out of my power. 'Tis true this war causes a great deal of trouble and anxiety with those who have friends and relations engaged in it, but it can't well be helped now, and as a good old soldier once said, "We must trust in God and keep our powder dry,"[12] which is very essential in this our struggle for liberty and rights, for 'tis Him who rules on high that can fix the destinies of a nation, and in Him alone we should put all our trust. It has ever be[en] my sincere wish and prayer to God that my life might be spared through this cruel war and spend the remainder of my life with my beloved little family at home. Oh that I could be with my family and fulfill the responsibilities. I endure them, but 'tis out of my power now. But a few months at longest since we made our vow before the law of Him who rules on high have we enjoyed the happiness I anticipated with the companion of my bosom and the beloved children which it has pleased God to give me. But through His kind Providence it may all be for the best. Let me ever be resigned to His will.

You mentioned hearing that all of Capt. Dickinson's[13] men had escaped but C. D. Nelms.[14] May be true, but I hardly think so. I will be sure to try and keep them from getting me if possible. You seem to be uneasy about Nellie's getting away with me. I will try and not get in their way if she is too weak to carry me. She gets nearly as much corn as she will eat but not enough long feed. We have plenty to eat since the box came to hand, and have a good deal of its contents yet, which we use with our rations and live as good as soldiers could wish. Have a good mess of peas and bacon nearly every day, have several messes of them yet, and half the ham, some butter, sausage, dried fruit, and I think if nothing happens we will be sure to enjoy all the luxuries of that box, and since the above was written, I was called on to eat a splendid rice pudding with plenty of sugar. We also have coffee when we wish—'tis old constitution, or the real coffee. I am rejoiced to hear you have settled with City and will call on him again when we are obliged to do so, and hope Mory's health will improve and that he will soon become healthy. Glad to hear Georgie is getting on so well, and sincerely hope his good health and temper may continue. Am proud to hear he thinks so much of your pa. Wish I could see both of them, you, and all the family. I guess there is quite a stir with the conscripts, and many of them will soon know their future lot. Bet seems to be quite uneasy as to [Hersey's] future resting. There is no news of interest in camp. All quiet along the Rapidan. There were 9 Yankee prisoners sent here yesterday evening, some more of Mosby's work. He is a great trouble to them. Charley has gone with the company on picket. I must close with the promise to write again soon. Farewell.

Robert

This leaves me in usual health and in camp when the company is out.

Camp 2nd Va.
March the 27, '64
Dear Beck,

As Charley has written to his ma, I will drop you a few lines, though I gave you all the news a few days since. This [finds] Charley and [I] both in usual health and both on guard, as it happened to be Sunday for the first time for some time.

Our company are all in usual health except John Jeter, recruit who joined our company not long since. He, I fear, has the fever. Was taken last night, has not been up or out of his tent today that I know of. As to news as to any change of the enemy, I have none. There seems to be but little stirring in any way. I fear ere this time next month that our troops will be moving for some point or fighting along our present lines. The best I have now is that Robert Mattox[15] received a box with a good many little goodies in it and we have had plenty since its arrival. Every little is a help. I wrote a letter for George Martin this morning to Mr. Pullens to send him a box, and I said in it to tell Pa to send me a piece of meat in George's box. Let Mr. Pullens know to direct it to Capt. Graves or to me.

I wish I could give you a few points that might interest you, but have nothing, so I will close soon. You must write soon and often. Remember me to Mory and Georgie especially. I wish I could see them. Some of our company are getting furloughs. Ad Wade has one of thirty day[s]. Guess his new wife will be glad to see him. He is a fellow for luck. One furlough for every fifty men for duty in a company and one for every hundred men, so two from our goes soon from our company, but guess I will not get one anytime soon, but hope I may see you all soon, but if my health keeps good and my horse keeps up, it may be some time first, so you must not look for me, for you know I will get there as soon as possible. Remember me though far away, exposed to all the trials of this unholy war. Accept my love, also Georgie, Mory, and your pa, ma, and family.

Ever devotedly yours until death,
Robert W. Parker

Camp 2nd Va. Cavalry, near Hamilton's Crossing
May the 2, 1864
Dear Beck,

Your kind and interesting note written at your Uncle Thom's came to hand a few hours ago, and I hasten to acknowledge its reception. I was more than pleased to learn you had left home once to see your relations and friends on the north side of Bedford, and hope you will visit them all before returning home, and try and see all and stay some time with them. It would have afforded me great pleasure to have accompanied you and the children to see them, but they are well aware of the fact that 'twas out of my power, and has been so ever since we were married, and hope they will not think hard of me for it, and will try and do better in the future if I should be so lucky as to survive this cruel war. You wished to know when I expected to come home. I am sorry to say 'tis out of my power to inform you, but don't think I can come under a month, if then. I have not had my horse condemned yet and don't know when I can have it done, and then 'twill be some time before my papers would get around. So I hope you will remain at your uncle's and relations' for two week[s], if no longer, and if I should happen to get home sooner than I expect, I will write to you or let you know some way. As you have made a start, I hope you can stay long enough to remain a few days with each of them.

There is no late move, so far as I know, along our lines, except the Yankees have made their appearance on the Rappahannock above Fredericksburg in the last few days. Guess 'tis nothing more than a reconnaissance in force.[16] 'Tis reported that Burnside is making a junction with Grant at Culpeper CH[17] with all possible speed, and I guess as soon as that is complete we will have a fight soon after. We would not be surprised to hear the din of battle any day and hope we are prepared for it.

May the 3. I would have finished this note yesterday, but we had a very hard storm late in the evening which stopped me from writing. No news of interest this morning. All quiet along our lines. 'Tis reported we leave here in a few days for Orange CH. Wish we had have stayed there, for I am not fond of moving so far for nothing. This leaves Charley and I in usual health, except my throat is a little sore this morning. I must close, as the horn will be up soon. Charley joins me in love to you, Uncle T., and Aunt Sarah, also to the family and your friends generally. Farewell.

Yours devotedly,
Robert

P.S. Tell Mory I will come to see him as soon as I can, and he must be a smart boy. I mailed a letter for you yesterday morning.
Robert

Camp 2nd Va., near Spotsylvania CH
May the 9, '64
Dear Beck,

I will drop you a few [lines] for the first since the fight commenced. It has been terrible and will continue so for a day or two to come. Our regiment was in the fight[18] the 6 and 7 and suffered [. . .]. A good many of our company were wounded both days. On the 7 Charley was slightly wounded on the side of the jaw and neck and has gone to the rear. I have not been able to see him, but the men who have seen him, Peter Rucker for one, says 'tis by no means dangerous. I sent a [. . .] John O. Morgan to the railroad to telegraph to your pa and give him all the particulars. Lil Johnson was killed, Creed Hubbard was mortally wounded and left with the enemy. Sam Murrill, Crantz, Jesse Board, and several others, Billie Fields was mortally wounded and thought to be dying this morning. I must close, as the regiment is moving off. Through the blessing of our heavenly Father, I am yet safe and well. We have whipped the enemy at every point. General Longstreet [. . .]

Farewell for this time,
Robert W. Parker

Camp 2nd Va. Cavalry, 8 miles from Richmond
May the 14, 1864
Dear Beck,

As it does always afford me the greatest pleasure to drop you a few lines, I will try and do so today. I know my letters to you for the past two weeks have been few and far between, but you must pardon me for this, for I haven't the chance to write. We have been fighting the Yankees almost incessantly for ten days together.[19] We didn't fight any yesterday or today for the first [time] since our move commenced. I will try and give you some idea of our loss in regiment.

Lost 18 killed dead in our company.[20] One killed (Sid). Two mortally wounded: Hubbard, left with the enemy; Fields, he was brought out but is dead perhaps. The wounded were: Board in hand; Fariss on finger, slight;[21] George Johnson on finger; Krautz flesh wound through thigh; J. Vance in foot, slightly; Whit Vance head, slightly; Murrill through leg, badly; Charley in jaw, slightly; Capt. Graves, slight but in command now; John T. Morgan, slight, now with the regiment; [James] Hughes in breast, slight;[22] Sergeant Jones captured. There are a few others but I have forgotten who. Ad Wade was wounded in back, all slight; John Franklin through the arm;[23] Sam Nichols killed. Of Co. A: Hugh Nelson badly wounded; Capt. Pollard badly; Capt. Septue badly; and many others too tedious to mention.

Our armies are still confronting the enemy before Fredericksburg and fighting almost everyday. General Beauregard is still fighting below Richmond.[24] The battle is raging now and the cannonading has been almost incessant there today.[25] The raiding party we have been after have fallen backward, only, I fear, to get a fresh supply of rations and ammunition. I am sorry to say they were too strong for the force we had after them, though we killed a good many and captured some two or three hundred, but sorry to say we lost some four hundred killed and wounded in our brigade, but the most of our men are in fine spirits, and a man that won't fight now ain't worthy [of] the name of a man. Our cavalry have confronted both infantry and cavalry frequently five to one. Our men have stood up to the struggle beyond all expectation. Would to God we may finally be successful, for I think this is the last struggle. The greatest fear I have of them are their raiding parties. I must close. I have not heard from you since you were at your uncle Tom's. Henry Ballard came in today and said Charley was at Lynchburg. Hope he has gotten [home] before this.

Remember me to the children and my friends and relations and tell them not to forget me, a poor rebel soldier far from them struggling [for] liberty. My love to you and all. Kiss the children for me.

I hope to see you all soon through the blessing of God, who has protected me thus far in the past battles.

This leaves me well. My horse has given out or near so, but I can go afoot and sharpshoot.

Robert

I will send Charley's horse home the first chance.

Camp 2nd Va. Cavalry
May the 15, 64
Dear Beck,

A word to you today. Nothing new. This leaves me well as common and all of the company that's here is in usual health. I have heard of no fighting below Drury's Bluff[26] this morning. Would like to hear from you and Pa's, for I have not heard from you for some time.

Robert

I heard by Martin Fuqua that four of Pa's family was very sick but didn't hear who they were. Oh, how I wish I could hear from you all. Please write soon. Oh, that this battle may soon end and we may be yet at home. May the Lord bless and protect you all.

Robert

Camp 2nd Va., near Dinwiddie CH
July the 28, '64
Dear Beck,

As Will Carter is going to start home, I will drop you a few lines. This leaves me in usual health. No news of interest down this way, and I fear bad news from Georgia, for I fear Atlanta will be sure to fall.[27] The usual quietude prevails along our lines before Petersburg.[28] The enemy are throwing troops across to the north side of the James, supposed to number 30,000, and General Grant is reported to be busy tunneling, and our troops also.[29]

I have not received a line from you since John Graves came down, and but one letter by mail since I left home.[30] What can be the reason, if 'twas not that I expect to come home in a month or two. I would write to you to send my watch, as there is none in the company, but guess we will commence active operations in a few days and maybe won't need it. I sent a letter to you by Jimmie Robertson. Hope you have it ere this. I got a letter from Brother Alick yesterday. He was in usual health but said a good many of the company were sick and some gone home. Hope he can get home soon. I must close, as Will is nearly ready to start. My love to you, the children, and all. Write soon.

Devotedly yours,
Robert

Camp near Dinwiddie CH, 2nd Va Cavalry
Aug. 3rd, 1864
Dear Beck,

'Tis with the greatest pleasure I take this opportunity to inform you of the receipt of your kind and interesting letter [. . .] which came to hand a few minutes ago. Was pleased to hear that you and the children were getting on so well. Hope your good health may continue, but sorry to hear that prospects are so gloomy as to the crop. Hope a good crop of corn may be made yet, and hope ere this you have had a share of what we are getting now: a share of rain. For a plenty of rains with the hot weather we have now would make the corn come up considerably. I am rejoiced to hear Mory and Georgie are both well, for it seems [. . .] both happen to be enjoying good health. Wish I could see them enjoy themselves eating. I think it would please me almost as well [. . .]. And I hope to get home some of these times and hope Georgie will be walking by that time. I hope ere this Granpa and Granma are better, also Uncle Davie.

I guess if the reserves have to stay a month or two and get into a few hardships they will have a better idea of the war. Mr. [. . .] came to Petersburg and then to Richmond, but 'twas my misfortune not to see him. Tom Sanders saw him at Petersburg and said he spoke of coming to Richmond the next morning, so the next evening I went to Richmond, but happened not to see him. I went up to Belle Isle[31] and saw Brother Alick. He said he had seen him, I think that morning. I would like to have seen him so much, and if he walked from Chaffin's Farm[32] to Richmond, he came along near our camp. I have received no letter from Mr. [. . .] yet. Hope he may reach home safe. Tell Charley not to be so chicken-hearted, but have the ball taken out.

No unusual stir along our lines since Grant sprang his mine on Saturday last.[33] His loss was double as heavy as ours, besides prisoners.[34] At last 'tis reported so some Yankee prisoners taken recently by Grant. Over three thousand killed and wounded. Our loss is just down at six hundred, but fear 'twas heavier. It seems that there is greater uneasiness as to the welfare of Atlanta[35] thru Richmond or Petersburg. Today's paper states General Stoneman, 75 commissioned officers and 500 prisoners were captured in the last few days in Georgia.[36] And cavalry are as quiet as usual, with rather short rations for man and horses. Wish I could get home in watermelon time. This leaves me in usual health and the company also [. . .].

Camp 2nd Va. Cavalry near Winchester, Frederick Co., Va.
Aug the 18, '64
Dear Beck,

Having stopped for a short time in camp, I will try to drop you a few lines, though have nothing of interest for you. This leaves me well as usual, but several of the company are sick, among them Capt. Graves and Lieut. Johnson. Guess he will leave for hospital tomorrow. I will give you a short detail of our trip from Front Royal,[37] and while there we remained quiet there till the evening of the 16, when our brigade was ordered out to drive the Yankees from a position they held.[38] The points was carried by our brigade and some infantry. Our regiment didn't lose a man in the fight, but several were lost in the brigade. The greatest loss on our side was with the infantry. They, 'tis reported, 150 men, the greater portion captured. On the 17 in the morning, while a portion of our company were skirmishing with the enemy, we had two men wounded, Alick Pollard and G. Leftwich, Alick near the elbow and Leftwich in the hand. Both gone home soon after this. The Yankees fell back below this place within the above fight.[39] I was not engaged, was on picket and saw a good portion of the fight.

18th. Had a little skirmish with the enemy, our regiment not engaged. The Yankees have all fallen back below this place several miles, but are in considerable force. I have no idea what we will do now, whether follow them or hold our position, but guess tomorrow will stand. We have made a junction with General Early, though not with him now. The most part of his command has moved off today. Their whereabouts I can't say, but don't think 'tis at all back. I am sorry to say our horses, I fear, or at least a good many of them, will not be able to go with us much longer. All we get for them now is grazing and they can't hold out a great while on that alone. The rations for men are good enough and tolerably plentiful. I am sorry to say that the enemy in their fall back from Strasburg burnt all the grains the people had with few exceptions. I have seen one crop of wheat spared from the flames from Front Royal to this place, and saw a good many burning as I came down. They said that they did not intend to leave anything for the rebels to eat. Some of them say they can't whip us and that they will burn up all the grain and starve us out. We had a pretty shower of rain yesterday and some today. I must close. I have not gotten a letter from you since before I left Richmond.

Devotedly yours,
Robert

My love to you, the children, and all. Farewell, Robert.

Aug. the 20, '64. This leaves me on foot, all [wet in the] pouring rain. Farewell. Please excuse this scrawl and write often.

Camp 2nd Va. Cavalry, near Charlestown, Jefferson Co., Va.
Aug. the 29, 1864
Dear Beck,

I'll attempt to drop you a few lines, though have nothing of interest to give you. We reached this place yesterday morning after driving the Yankees the 21 from four miles above Berryville. They were in heavy force and fell back very deliberately, clearing off their dead and wounded with them. Their loss was supposed to be much heavier than ours though, and loss was small considering the time engaged. The loss in our regiment was, I think, 2 killed and five wounded, among them Major Breckinridge slight,[40] four of Co. A, one of Co. C, one of Co. K, one of Co. D, one from Co. B and K killed. And the infantry was engaged on our left at the same time, though have not heard the result, and were also engaged yesterday.[41] The body of our infantry is on our left, but I know not where.

We are faring tolerably well as to rations. Get good fat beef and flour, also plenty of good apples by sporting for them. The people over here are as kind as ever to us and would do a good deal for us, but the Yankees here engaged them almost of all they had.

Received your kind and interesting letter of the 6 of this month. Was relieved to hear from you and the children and all generally, but sorry to hear the children were so unwell. Hope you are all well ere this. I also I received a letter from Brother A. last evening. He was getting on as usual. This leaves me in usual health, but my horse is almost played out, but have no idea when I can get him home. I must close. You will please write to me soon and often.

Farewell. Devotedly yours,

R. W. Parker

The Battle of Berryville[42] was the hottest fight I ever was in, but I hope we didn't get any of the men who were taken prisoners wounded. We took possession of the battlefield. Enemy left some their dead on the field and we followed them back across the river. I must close, as it is supper.

Camp 2nd Va. Cav.[43]

Novem. the 31, '64

Dear Beck,

I'll attempt to answer your kind and interesting letter received yesterday evening, but hardly know to commence, as there is no news in camp of any importance whatever. We are doing but little now except drilling once a day for an hour. The enemy seems to be quiet also, or at least all is quiet along our lines, and the streams are so flush that a move can't be made now. Every preparation is making for the opening of the present campaign.

I am glad to hear you have let Mory stay at Pa's some, for it pleases all of them so much for him to be there, as there is no little fellow in the white family. Duck, am sorry to hear you had such bad luck with your little pigs. Hope you may have good luck with the remainder of them. I fared very well during the snow, and the first night slept very comfortable in my little tent under it. As to our coming home, 'tis all a notion, for there is no chance for that now and that report is dead in camp. I have written to you not long since. [. . .]

I am sorry to learn from the tenor of your letter that you are so low-spirited as to the present campaign. Cheer up, for 'twill do no good. I know that there is no one that thinks more of his family than I do, and no companion thinks more of each other than I think of mine, but I am confident you see a great deal more trouble about my welfare than I do for myself, though I am exposed to the enemy at anytime. One reason is you have more time to think of the danger than I do, and [the] other is that I try not to think so much about it, for 'twill do no good. And the good book says, "Sufficient for the day is the evil thereof,"[44] and we have trouble enough not to take it on interest. I generally try each day to do my duty and leave the rest to Him who rules on high, and if I should fall, I think 'twill be in a good and just cause. I wrote to George Johnson yesterday, trying to get him to [. . .] for me, and somewhat hope he will, if he has not agreed to do so for someone else. If he should, I hope to get a furlough [. . .]. Say nothing unless you see him, unless you think proper. I guess, unless my letter reaches him soon, some of the Johnsons will get him. I will close, hoping to get a letter from you soon. Kiss the children for me. Write often. My best love to you, the children, and your pa, ma, and family. Devotedly yours,

    Robert

Bethel Wilson[45] and Charley W. Kidwell[46] leave our company Saturday for our navy.

[RWP returned to Bedford County on a furlough for several weeks in December 1864 and January 1865.]

1865

The Second Regiment Virginia Cavalry left the Shenandoah Valley to rejoin the Army of Northern Virginia in the spring of 1865, when General Sheridan also left the valley. They fought in the Appomattox campaign in the spring of 1865 under the command of Col. Thomas Munford. On the morning of April 9, the Second encountered and fought several bodies of Union cavalry near Appomattox Court House before truce flags were flown.[1] Several men of the Second reported Sergeant Parker as the last man killed during the Civil War.

Camp 2nd Va. Cav., near Barboursville, Orange Co., Va.
Jan. the 20, '65
Dear Beck,

I have been waiting for an opportunity to drop you a few lines and guess I will not have a better one soon, so I will try and give you a short note. This leaves me in usual health, but more despondent than I ever was in my life, prospects are so gloomy here. We are sometimes with rations and sometimes without, our horses, I might say, and tell you the truth, starving. I have not drawn an ear of corn since I have been at this camp, and but little of anything else. The news also from Richmond and down south is also discouraging.[2] And my watch stopped last night and won't run a tick, and I miss it so much. And another thing that keeps me down: in the month, I have not heard or gotten a line from any of you since I left. Hearing from you and the children often is one of my greatest comforts in camp. I wish I could give you an interesting note, but 'tis out of my power. Our company, or what's here, is in usual health, though we have but 14 present. None of those who left without leave have returned yet, and a good many gone after horses are over time. I have been looking for Alick Buck for the past day or two, but he has not arrived in camp yet.

I guess ere this you have heard that Co. A has been detached from the regiment to procure rations in Bedford. Wish it had been our company, but we are unlucky. And as to disbanding, that's out of the question, and some who have been furloughed by General Rosser has been ordered back to their commands by General Fitz Lee.

I will try and give you a sort of list of the clothes I sent to A. A. Belle's by Sargt. Lee. I sent a cap wrapped up in my shirts and draws to Mory; also two shirts; two pair of draws; two pair of socks, cotton; two pair of blue pants, the largest pair mine, the other pair Bob Johnson; and a pair of shoes with my name on them, are mine. You will also take the jacket and take care of it for me. The old black hat in my shoes is Bob Johnson's. Please take care of it for him or have it done for him. The shoes with black [clasps] are Sargt. Lee's. The rest of the things in the sack are Bob Johnson's and George Johnson's. Besides the things I sent home, I drew a good little tent and a good blanket, which I have with me. You can do as you think with the shirts, but I think the draws are large enough for me, and I wish to save you all the trouble I can, so I drew everything I could. All that were present in the company made a pretty good draw for clothing. The cotton socks I thought would last me a while next summer. I hope the clothes have gotten to Pa's ere this.

I forgot to tell you: the people of Albemarle aimed to give our brigade a big dinner, and it made quite a big show altogether, but when divided out to the men 'twas rather a small meal. I got aplenty, being one of the committee to receive it and divide it all in our company. Got 4 or 5 apples a piece, and meat and bread in proportion.

Duck, as John Krautz will come back to the command on the train, I want you tell Ma to send me several little tricks. I want a piece of soap, a little piece of tallow, also some thread and a little snack, if he can bring it. And if Alick don't bring my coat, get John Krautz to bring it. He promised to bring any little thing he could for me. I must close for this time. This leaves me in usual health. My love to you, the children, and all. Remember your promise to write to me twice a week. Farewell for this time.

Devotedly yours until death,

R. W. Parker

Jan. the 21. All on foot here this morning. My love to all. Robert

Lynchburg
March 10th, 1865
Dear Beck,

I shall attempt to drop you a line the second time since I have been here. When I last wrote I was with Ned's command, but now am with Brother Alick's company, Sixtieth Va. Infantry. And if Hortin's Division leaves here and can't get on to my command, I will join the city battalion or local forces of this place. I have wished for my horse many times since I have been here, but hope I am doing for the best.[3] If I knew my horse had not left here, I would try and get it. If John Graves comes here and don't find me, he will carry it to camp. My bundle was so heavy, I left the sack of rations with your uncle Sam Walker, and if I don't get it he will bring it back home. I have not been able yet [to] get any reliable information as to where the Yankees are, but they have not been sighted here [within] 20 miles of this place, and are said to be going down the river, reported 30 miles down the river this morning—but all this is rumors. I suppose the generals know where they are, but we can't find out. All our troops are in fine spirits and I think they will do their duty. I don't know how to tell you where or how to direct your letters to me, but hope to be able to inform you in a day or two. This leaves Alick and I well as usual. You must not be uneasy about me, for I will try and take care of myself. I have stayed in a house both nights since I came down here. Farewell for this time.

Devotedly yours,
R. W. Parker

Lynchburg
March 11th, 1865
Dear Beck,

I will attempt to drop you a few lines for the third time since I have been here, but fear you have not received any of them yet. I have nothing of interest for you more than I am well as common and getting on finely. Have not had to stay out-of-doors of a night since I left home and have met with the greatest kindness everywhere. Have stayed with Ned's command every night except one since I came to this place. I stayed with Brother Alick's company part of the time. Left that this morning and joined the local forces of this place, and we were disbanded this evening to go to our commands, and I expect to leave in the morning for the [High] Bridge or Farmville, as I heard this morning that our dismounted command was there, and I will stop there till I hear from my horse. The mounted part of our command I heard was at [Cumberland] CH today, but I fear 'twas a report not well founded.

As to the Yankees' whereabouts, there is no direct information, but they have left this quarter and gone down on the north side of the river towards Richmond,[4] and I think will cross the central road between Gordonsville and Richmond or take up that road and destroy it for the balance of the war. I believe some were anxious for them to cross to the south of the river, which they may yet, but hope necessary preparations have been made for them. I expect to leave in the morning for my command, and you will write to me and direct to Richmond, as I am anxious to hear from you all. I think Brother Alick's command will be sent to western Virginia in a day or two. I paid Lieut.

Confederate Cemetery at Appomattox. The grave believed to be Parker's is marked by the fourth headstone from the right. Photograph by Catherine M. Wright.

[Tompkin] a visit last night. He was getting on finely and expects to come to Bedford soon. I have given you all the news and must close for the present. You will please write soon and all the news. My love to you and all. Farewell.

Devoted,

Robert

Kiss Georgie and Mory for me and tell them to be smart boys.

I will drop John Graves a line tonight. Send this down to Pa's.

LETTERS FROM
FAMILY AND FRIENDS

[Martha Goggin to Robert Parker]
Flint Hill
March 24th, '61
Devoted Cousin,

It is with no small degree of pleasure I seat myself to answer your very interesting letter which I received not long since. And I assure you cousin that it was perused with the greatest imaginable pleasure. I have no news worth writing to you at present. I reckon if I could see you I would hear some though. Cousin I saw A. L. W. last Sunday. He was as fast as a cricket [and] he said he was coming up again before very long. He told me you was fixing to get married.[1] Cousin I hope if it [is] really so you will not fail to extend your tickets up this way; if you don't I will not invite you to my wedding. I did not go to preaching last Sunday at [Rovin?] Church, I suppose there was a great many people there. Sallie Goggin and Sue Linwith was there. Sue came home with Sallie and that evening we went home with her and did not get home until Tuesday morning. Went to Cousin George Lipscomb's Monday night. Sue is as gaily as ever and equally as pretty. You said you heard that her and Mr. John Lipscomb was going to marry. I don't think they will marry at all, that is all false I think. I reckon you have heard of Miss Bettie C.'s marriage and I expect you was greatly grieved about it, was you not? Cousin you must come up and tell me all about that beautiful picture that you have. Bring it and show it to me and how it is not as pretty as the one I have. If it is it must be something uncommon. I did not tell you Sue sent her best respects and a ten cent piece to you, and said you must charge the ten cents to Alexander Walker. You must give him my respects and a 5 cent piece and tell him to charge it to George Parker. Give my love to all your Pa's family and all others that inquire for me, if there be any such individuals.

Well Cousin, I presume you are getting very tired reading this, so I will close by asking you to look over all mistakes and write soon please. Do not wait as long as you did before. Receive my best wishes for your future happiness and great success for your undertakings.

Hoping I soon shall see you. I remain
Your affectionate cousin,
Mattie F. Goggin[2]

Please do not let anyone see this.
Mat

[Frances Parker to Robert Parker]
Bedford
June 9, '61
My Dear Son,

I woke this morning about 3 o'clock [and] the first of my thoughts were upon my absent child, the state of our once highly favored country, and our present distressed situation. I felt that I could not remain in bed but I must arise, get on my knees, and try with all the sincerity of my poor treacherous heart to implore direction and protection from Him who has all power in heaven and on earth. I feel that this great calamity is permitted to be on account of the great disobedience, ungratefulness, [and] unthankfulness of us as a nation, and if we are engaged as we should be in the right kind of a spirit, call on God clothed as it were in sack cloth and ashes. He is able to avert this great calamity and restore peace when we are sufficiently humbled. . . . I have often wished you had read the bible more and recollected more of His inscrutable providences. I wish you would write me what the state of your mind is. I have hoped for years past you had experienced a change of heart and had tried to put your trust in a stronger power than this poor uncertain world and its perishing objects.[3] You see from your daily experience there is nothing certain here; that we are all tending to the grave and to the judgment is certain, whether at home or abroad, on the land [or] on the sea. But the Christian has the promise of [. . .]. My grace is sufficient for thee, fear not. My child, can you by faith lay hold on the precious promises of our blessed Savior, who died to redeem us and arose again and ever lives to intercede for those who put their trust in Him? Our lives at best are short and uncertain here; the important part is to secure that rest that remains to all the people of God. Oh, try to be engaged; don't let your precious time go to waste. Don't be ashamed to let your companions in arm know that you believe there is a God who has power to create and power to save or destroy. Come out and be on the Lord's side. Let all your example and precept go in that way—it might be that you would save some friend a great evil by being decided. You will not have so many temptations to wrong courses if you at all times perseveringly determine to let your light shine as a believer. I must close. My prayers attend your welfare. All join me in love to you all. Farewell for the present.

Your Mother

Try to get a furlough and come home before you leave Lynchburg,[4] if you can.

[Frances Parker to Robert Parker]
Bedford
July 12, '61
My Dear Rbt.,

I once more seat myself to tell you we are all, through the mercy of our kind benefactor, continued on the stage of action, blessed with many blessings and privileges which we have not merited. I have been unwell several days and have the headache this morning. Several of the family have been troubled a good deal lately with indisposed bowels. Our neighbors are generally well as far as I know. The oat harvest is on hand; oats are unusually low. I never saw a finer crop of corn at this season than we have, the best everybody say they have seen. George says yours is more even, but does not average as large. In fine order, nearly all laid by. Your Pa sent word for them to commence cleaning up for wheat every chance they wanted. Best to save the oats (they said); say theirs are better than up here. They saved right smart chance of hay. Billy Rucker and Minnie Newman stayed there with [G?] that night. I reckon they had soldiers lodging our straw bed for your men. The garden looked very well, fine looking beets. June apples [are] ripe, brought some up for us and Beck. She talked of going down this week, but she has such an aversion to staying all night without you in that neighborhood. I do not encourage her to go and return the same day. I think it would be unnecessary fatigue without profit. There are a great many whortleberrys. Mrs. [Nancy] Walker said she would like her to go and have some gathered. She has improved very much since she heard from you. Got the first letter last Saturday, the 3d you wrote. We or the Dr. sent every day or two to the office [but] could get no letter. Sent Alick Saturday morning, got one [or] two others advertised, but would not let him have them [as] he had no money with him to pay the advertisement. We thought it bad treatment. They had to be sent for again, so all came the same day. Rebecca and her ma spent the day here together Wednesday. We had sent to the office before they got here, and shortly after [that] your letter got here. We were all very glad to hear from you and hear that you were well.

I saw a touching account of a sick soldier at Norfolk a lady went to see. He was out of his senses; he gazed at her and said, "Go away from me, you are not my mother." Her sympathy kept her with him until his fever abated, when he talked to her about his mother and tears ran down his manly cheeks. I saw another account of a soldier which was mortally wounded. His comrades and officer wished very much to render some comfort to him. He thanked them very much for their offered kindness, told them he was dying [and] there was only one thing they could do: take his testament out of his satchel, and near the end of the fourteenth chapter of John they would find peace. "Will you read it?" he asked. "Peace I leave with you, my peace I give unto you, not as the world giveth, give I unto you. Let not your hearts be troubled neither let it be afraid."[5] He then said, "Thank you, I am dying. I have that peace. I am going to that savior. God is with me; I want no more," and instantly expired. If I know anything of my poor heart, I rejoice to think a Christian can die happy, though his blood may be poured on the battlefield. My child, strive to do your duty honorably in all things, but above all things strive to be in possession of that Christian soldier's glorious peace. Set an example before your comrades worthy of imitation. If you could only know the anxiety your friends have on your account, both as it regards your temporal and spiritual welfare, you would be constrained to watch and pray that you might not enter into temptation. I trust you do not forget the frailty of poor sinful man.

Saturday morning, July 13. We are all about, though your pa is very poorly, threatened with flux, Bettie also. I feel better today and wished to go to see Cousin Daniel this evening, if the rest are well enough. We had rain last night [and] have had a fine season so far this summer. Just finished laying by the corn and garden at home, have that at Bell Branch[6] to plow. George says tell you he would write but Ma writes every thing and leaves nothing for him. He goes to muster every Saturday [and] is gone today. Mr. Hendrick called and stayed sometime waiting for him, was quite chatty. Alexander is gone to mill. I would not be surprised if your grandpa was to break up; the children are in favor of it. Your Uncle Tommy was up there two weeks past. Nathan had got crippled so he could not help any about the harvest (fixing about putting away hay). I want to go up and see how they are getting on. I always am distressed about them. If I had my choice, I would rather they would spend their time among their children than stay there by themselves. The last I heard from Wm. Snow, he was in the hospital sick with measles. How glad I am I had the nursing of you with that disease. I look upon measles as a dangerous disease for grown people not well attended to.

I have commenced making up the servants' winter clothes. I have a piece of cloth in for the women's dresses.[7] I have not made out to get my wool to the machine yet; when I get it corded, I would I give Rebecca some if I knew she wished to make any cloth. Her Ma told me she told her she could spin some thread and make some tablecloths with her if she wished, said she thought it would occupy her mind and she would be better satisfied employed at something of that sort. Your Pa would like to know if you had made up in your mind what land you thought most suitable on Goose Creek to sow in wheat. All join me in love to you. Give my love to your messmates. Tell Stephen or Jo or some of them that has no wife to write to me. How glad I would be to divide milk, butter, and vegetables with you; I had cucumbers for dinner.

I fear the war will be on hand a long time. I just heard Congress had sanctioned Lincoln's proposal to call out four hundred thousand. I suppose they are fighting rapidly in Missouri; I have had no letter from there and despair of getting any soon if ever.[8] I have probably written more than you will be interested in. [I] wrote to you about a week past. You may never get the letter; I did not know how to direct it. I wish to hear from you all often. Yours with all the affectionate regard of a devoted mother,

F. H. Parker

[Hester Parker to Robert Parker]
Dear Brother,

I take my pen in hand to write you a few lines, though I haven't much news to write. I went to Cousin Jim Burroughs' funeral last Sabbath. I saw Aunt Ann, Cousin Liz, Cousin Booker, Uncle Jack. They all seemed to be very cheerful indeed, more so than I expected. Uncle Tommy preached a mighty good sermon, very appropriate for the occasion. He prayed devoutly for the soldiers. I thought of you while he was praying. I saw Tom Lornard last fourth Saturday and would like to have written to you by him, had I known he would have seen you. Ma, Sis, Cousin Jimmie and Cousin Missouri spent the day with Cousin Tabby Graves not long since and was very much pleased. We heard from her Tuesday; she was out where they were hauling up wheat. She seems to be a woman of an energetic disposition. When did you see the two cousin Georges and cousin Will? Write to me soon, now, let it be understood: write to me and tell me all the news about my kinsfolks. I [have] nothing more, but your affectionate sister until death,

Hester M. Parker

P.S. Give my love to all my in you relations company and receive a portion yourself.

Hester M.

Robert, what did you do with your cousin Sally Parker's ring [that] you was to keep until you married? She says as her brother that gave it to her is gone,[9] she would like to have it for his sake. George did not know anything about it. I thought I would ask Rebecca if she knew, but I don't think of it when I see her.

FHP

[Frances Parker to Robert Parker]
Liberty
Saturday morning, July 26, 1861
My Dear Son,

This is the fifth letter I have commenced to writing you since you left Lynchburg. I had the 4th mailed last Tuesday. I have ardently desired you should get every one when I wrote, if that should be the last, and felt like I could live or die better satisfied if I could know you got and perused my poor attempt to writing, and could give you up, if fall you must, more freely if I knew you had read them. Up to this time, I have not heard of one you got. We have received two directed to us, Rebecca six or seven—no doubt all you have written. I wrote to you to get paper of D. W. Robertson; he promised me to let you have some, he had a ream. I saw five letters directed to you in his letter satchel. I would have sent you something if I could by him or your Uncle Johnson, but the latter must needs go back to Uncle Tom's, could neither call here going nor coming. Your brother George has joined Col. Walker's company. He is not able to do such service, but he thought as he mustered, he might be drafted and compelled to go, and he could but be examined and do the best he could if the worst came. It looks like there will be no men left scarcely, they are all joining so fast. Ches Oaty got enough for three companies.

Well, my son, how did you feel after the battle of the 21st? Did you feel humble, grateful, thankful to your merciful benefactor for the preservation of your own life and the lives of your countrymen and country? No doubt it was our enemy's calculation in the event of that battle to possess our beloved VA.[10] O that I could thank and praise our blessed redeemer with my whole heart, mind, and strength. What are we poor sinful creatures that He should have been mindful of us? What is our strength, with all the means this world can afford, without His almighty arm to support? I fear sin on the part of our Confederacy more than the sword. O that our armies may be humble and not exalted. "They that exalt themselves shall be abased, they that abase themselves shall be exalted"[11]—this is God's word and will assuredly come to pass.

You know how nervous I am and suffer from uneasiness in little matters sometimes. I do not know why it was, but I believed you were safe from harm in the battle. I told Rebecca I did not feel like you was killed, and wanted your shirts made and sent on by some of the recruits. But I found she was not inclined to make them until we heard expressly from you. Taking my past life as a specimen in many things, it was astonishing I should have been willing to go to work upon such an uncertainty. We got your letter Tuesday evening. You can't tell the joy it gave all of [us] to get a letter from your own dear hand. Son, keep in mind, in peace or war we have all got to die and appear before the judge of [the] quick and [the] dead. I have tried the best I could to raise all my dear children[12] to feel their dependence to be on that holy and just Being who does all things right, and who is able and willing to save all to the uttermost who put their trust in Him. May He be ever with you, keep you from all harm, and keep you from wandering in the paths of vice and immorality, [and] fit and prepare you for a mansion in the skies. May it be our happy lot to spend a blessed eternity with the blessed Saviour who died to redeem the world.

Your devoted mother,

F. H. Parker

Sunday morning. Jobe came up last evening. All tolerably well down there. He wants a horse to haul oats and thresh wheat. Your wheat was not as good. As you mention your crop sometimes, I have written about it several times. The neighbors down there say it is the best crop of corn they ever saw on the field. The hogs look well; the sow has a pretty litter of pigs. Inmen has three in family. The cow [is] as roguish as ever; your pa has been trying to sell her. We milk nine cows and could spare as many down there as would be necessary. The dog is so sharp, people dread him as bad as a bear. The servants have enjoyed fine health. I understand Bogy has joined Ed's company. He is on the place yet. Your Pa and all send their love and good wishes to you. Your sister has written to you, I expect Beck will, and you will get most of the neighborhood news if you get any. We were at [Olivet] yesterday. Tell Lil Johnson his pa and ma were there, all well; his wife [is] doing very well, also his son, which was two weeks old yesterday. Tell Jo Burroughs to write to me and his mother. Tell Stephen to try to patronize his father. Tell John Graves Cousin Sallie Talby is getting on finely. Tell John Lipscomb Mattie looks very well. Your mother,

F. H. Parker

[Frances Parker to Joseph Burroughs]

Liberty, VA

August the 10, '61

Mr. Burroughs,

Dear sir, I received your favor yesterday, written the first August, and I assure you I was much gratified indeed, and to let you know it I sit down to write this first opportunity. In the first place, I must tell you myself and some other lady I called on Mrs D. W. this morning. I read your letter. She helped some three or four young ladies and one widow for you, hoping she might hit upon the right one. Said I must give her love to you, also to Robert Wm., and say to you you must write to her and let her know which of the girls was your sweetheart, and she was ready to do you any favor in her power, as she was disposed to be accommodating, particularly to southern soldiers. Among the other girls was one Miss Bet. She told me when I wrote I must give her love to you and tell you to write to her also. She had just received a letter from a cousin soldier and said she would like to get one from any one of you. She was always glad to hear from any or all if she could, [for] nothing gave her more pleasure than to hear of their welfare.

I have no idea, since Liberty was a place, it ever was watched as closely for letters as at this time. We send and keep sending, hoping to get a line from some friend. I wrote to two of my relations in Missouri in May and cannot hear a word from them. I fear it is hard times with them as well as the Virginians, MO is so completely mixed with abolitionists, unionists and Confederates. "A house divided against itself cannot stand."[13]

Does Tom Barnard mess with you? I was sorry to hear you all got so badly sunburnt. I would like to have sent you some cream to cure the burn. I wish you or Robert had written, particularly about Alfred Creasy; the most they have heard lately was from here. The old man calls here occasionally, calls for our letters for us at the office. I could only tell him he was sick at the hospital, I suppose with measles. I hope not very sick—I fear the measles are badly managed. I think everyone should take medicine after having measles to carry off the effects from stomach and lungs. We have a weed called cropwort which is very good for coughs, colds, etc.

Where is George L. Parker? I have not heard a word from him since he left Lynchburg. I saw W. Burton yesterday, he speaks of returning to camp next week. I have not heard from George Lipscomb since he got to Liberty two weeks past. A good many soldiers have come home on account of sickness. A soldier from the South on his way to headquarters got his foot mashed with a car at Liberty a few days past. I have not heard what became of him, poor fellow; how sorry we were to hear of his misfortune.

Who takes Mr. Phelps's place—quartermaster? Who takes the places of Capt. Wilson and T. Nants? How far are you from Jamestown and Leesburg? Did you see Joseph Parker? He did not see his sons, [but] went prepared to bring them home if wounded or sick. They were at Leesburg. How does Missis Murrell Hubbard and Johnson get on with camp life, and my dear brother's boy, Stephen Goggin, is he well and doing well? I hope he will not forget the fervent prayers and admonitions of his parents, and will not be led into any vice which will make their hearts, already wounded by his absence from them, bleed. He has parents worthy of his patronage. I hope he will imitate them. If it were possible, I would like to hear from every relation and acquaintance in the army every day. Just here I will give you and all your mess a hint: if you should ever want to write anything to any individual you do not wish everyone to see, write that something on a separate slip from the letter. All your friends are so anxious to see every letter they hear of, it is a cross if they cannot, and on the other hand it would be a cross to me for one not to let friends see what few I get. I suppose I have written upon an average once a week to my son ever since he left home. I received one from him last Friday and saw one he wrote to Missouri Pullen one day later. I was thankful to hear you were well and had plenty to eat, and some time to rest. Have you any thing to read? I want your leisure hours spent to the best advantage. You know the poet very truly says, "For Satan finds some mischief still / for idle hands to do."

Your cousin Tom Pullen's wife had serious loss on account of hail and freshet two weeks past. She had managed finely; had, I suppose, the best crop almost ever on the farm. It was seriously damaged, the corn dreadfully washed. She is considered one of the best managers for her practice, to be stated as a matter of course. She could not help being distressed at the injury of her crop but I hope she will not be disheartened.

I have written to some of the soldiers at Jamestown, among them Mr. Pullen, but have never received a line from any of them. I suppose they have enough to write without poor unworthy me, and I do not think the least hard of it. I am old enough to have long since learned all persons have their special favorites, in peace or war, at home or abroad, on land or sea.

Tuesday, August 13. As paper is scarce and I have not sent this, I must write again. We have had a thundershower almost every day for a week. Corn looks fine, some have commenced fallowing for wheat. I regret to tell you Mr. Isaac Cundiff and Capt. Minter's only child were both buried last Saturday. I understand Cundiff died with fever, Mollie Minter with diphtheria in the same neighborhood. The fever is still raging in the Berger neighborhood. Col. Arthur's wife is dead, also Capt Bitty Austin.

There has another gang of Leftwich's company come home sick: Dick Nants, Wm. Snow, and John Scott, the two first a little unwell, Scott very low. [They] called here yesterday to get some refreshment and a horse. They did not take Mr. Scott out of the carriage. He has been sick three weeks. Tom Saunders's son very low, David [Henesly] mending. [T. W.?] Robertson returned from Manassas last Friday, gives an account of great waste of provisions, which we are sorry to hear. Bacon is worth 22 cts. per lb., salt $7 per sack, coffee 30 cts. per lb. at Lynchburg. We fear waste will cause want. He did not see any of your company; had no conveyance to get about, only when he could walk. George went to Franklin's last Saturday. Says his uncle Jo Parker speaks of going again shortly to see you all. Ben Burroughs has just left Bedford, has been here to bring his children and negroes to get them more out of the way of the Yankees. He lives in Nicholas Cty. I understand Wise keeps retreating this direction to get out of the mountains before fighting.

Well, Jo, I reckon by this time you are ready to say, "Will the woman never get through? I did not expect to be bothered with such a long epistle." I wrote to Robert Wm. a few days past, since I got your letters. If you read his letter and he reads yours, you will get perhaps more news than will be interesting to you, as an old person who is seldom out of hearing of home would be vain to expect to interest the young much, who are ever in a crowd amid the bustle of camp life.

My love to all your company. May you all be blessed with health and strength to perform your duty and return to your friends with unspotted characters, good health, warm friends to each other, and above all, with a heart overflowing with gratitude to your benefactor.

Frances H. Parker

[William Walker to Rebecca Parker]
Camp McCullock, Highland Co., VA
Nov. 19th, 1861
Dear Sister,

I will now try and write you a few lines, though I have nothing of interest to write. This leaves the most of us sick. There is only about sixteen of us able for duty. As to myself and Ed, we are well except cold. We are going to take up winter quarters here. Beck, you must write to me as soon as you get this and write me word when you heard from Bob and where he is. Tell Charley he must write to me. It is reported here that the snow is three feet deep on the [Suel] Mountains and three hundred Yankees froze to death. Tell Sarah and Bet to write to me. Direct your letters to Monterey. I must bring my letter to a close, so nothing more at present. Write soon and write long letters. I remain your brother,

Wm. R. Walker

[George Parker to Ammon and Frances Parker]
Camp Mccullock, Highland Cty.
Decem. the 3, '61
Dear Parents,

I seat myself this evening to write you a few lines, though I have nothing to interest you. I am well as common. I had a very hard race last Sunday. There came a man by our company with a wagon, and a drunken man got out of his wagon and the guards took him to the officer of the day. He did not give a good account of himself and they told me to take some of the relief guard and bring him back. I got 4 of the guards and started on the double-quick after him. I ran him 4 miles and overtook him. He didn't like to go with me, but I told him he had to go and he went without any trouble. We had gone a mile when we met a man. They sent him to tell me to question him, and if he gave a good account of himself, to let him go. I questioned him; he told me he was a volunteer, a member of the Charlotte cavalry stationed at Franklin, 15 miles below us, and the other one was a Confederate soldier. After questioning him a while I released him. He seemed very glad to get away. I would not have run so far for both of his horses, but they told me "Take him," and I was determined to do so. He said if we had not been armed, he would not have gone, but he was afraid to resist for fear we would shoot him. When we got back to camp, we were wet with sweat. I was afraid it would make me sick but it has not hurt me yet. I saw one of the men today who went with me. He said he was so stiff he could hardly walk. It never made me stiff at all.

We moved our camp yesterday and are situated in a [sugar] orchard on the north side of a mountain. We are in a very cold place, but it is dry. We are in a better place and better [fed] than we have been since we left Staunton, and I hope our men will not be so sickly now.

J. L. Preston is sick, not dangerous. T. A. Wright is very sick. Henry Wills is sick. Dr. Gibbs' trunk arrived here yesterday. I got all of my things. My boots are tight but I can wear them. Everything came straight. I got a letter from your pa and ma yesterday. They are all well. I have never got the letter you wrote about Missouri and yet Grandma sent me the one you wrote to her. I was glad to hear she was willing to die and hope she is better off there.

Has nothing happened here lately strange—some of our regiment keep dying. Holly has lost 5 men [. . .], Walker 2. There has a great many of them died. We are still in our tents and will stay in them all the winter, I expect. We can sleep very warm. There are 5 in my tent and 10 blankets. We have straw in them. We warm good by the fire and then go to bed and sleep warm all night.

Ma, I reckon when you read this you will think I am gone deranged, but it is dark and I have no candle and am writing by starlight on my knee you. [. . .] to keep writing to keep from forgetting. I can't see how to read it [. . .] and the weather is very cold so I can't leave the fire. I never knew Mr. F [. . .] was gone till dark and now I have to do the best I can, as Mr. Fields is to start in the morning.

Ma, there is no news and I can't find anything to write about. I received Sarah Walker's letter a few days ago and will answer it soon. I have never missed any duty yet of any sort. I would like to come home in 2 or 3 months if I can. If you get sick you must write me word and write to the Captain to let me come home, as word from you would do better than one from me. Write whether the militia are drafted in Bedford or not. I will bring my letter to a close. You must send me some wafers by Lieut. [. . .] or some other if you can. [. . .]

G. L. Parker

[Frances Parker to Robert Parker]
At home.
February 9, '62
My Dear Son,

We were very glad to receive your letter written 26 of last month, and always rejoice to hear from you, if we could hear nothing more than you were well. Good health is one of the greatest blessings we can enjoy in this sin-stricken world. I feel that I cannot be as thankful as I wish for your good health. While so many have sickened and died, both in camp and at home, you have been blessed with good health. I trust you have been spared for some good purpose and you will be humbled at the thought of the blessings you have received and be always ready to thank the Giver for every mercy bestowed on you. As my sons are obliged to be engaged in this distressing warfare, it helps a great deal to keep my spirits up to hear they get on well with their companions; to hear they are steady and prudent, not partaking of the vices so common in camp.

George told me he had been often begged to play cards. He told them he did not know how and never intended to know. He had been asked if he had any temper, that he could get on anyway and not swear. He told them swearing done no good, no matter what they had to encounter. He got on better without it than they did with it. There is no wrong way about anything that will do in place of the right way. The right way is the safe and pleasant way in every sense of the word.

George had enjoyed better health until taken sick when he came home, and was more fleshy than at any time of his life. He was four inches thicker around the waist, his cloths all too small. I hardly knew how he could wear them. He stayed four weeks. He had not gotten over his cold and cough entirely. I was in hopes he would not start when he went to town last Monday, but I hear they all, except Joie Preston and John McGee, got on the [train] cars to Lynchburg and started. McGee was examined by Dr. Owen and sent back. I heard Cousin Mary was very sick, cousin Joie to come back. She was at her pa's on Sunday before. I have not heard the particulars of the case.

I understand all the companies have left Monterey except Walkers', Booths', and Meadows'— I would suppose a poor state for defense. I expect you have heard of the late battle in Kentucky, in which it is said the South were very victorious.[14] We do not get any paper now and I have seen no account of it. I hear Capt. Pollard is going to start shortly to act as sutler for your regiment. I always have thought he would get into the matter some way. It is to be hoped peace will be made before all the grain is consumed. There will be so few left to make provisions to carry it on if a drought takes the balance. You asked us what we thought of your being drafted before you left the tented field. We don't know what advice to give in such a case, but think we would not enlist. We think if you could come home and manage right, you could do more for your country than you can there, and be much more comfort to your family. We make a hobbling out, getting on with all the places. Your pa's health has been so bad all the fall and winter, he could attend to but little—no one to help him, and recently others of the family have been sick. We expected Caroline to die last week and the week before, but she has appeared to mend some the last few days. Candace has been very sick; the last week she appears better. Sam has been in the barn helping a little about tramping cloverseed the past few days. Alexander's foot is mending. I wrote to you he had cut it the last letter I started. I long for the time when you could be at home in peace. I am sorry for the servants down there. It appears there is no better way that we can see than for them to stay there. Billy Snow's hogs and cattle are there yet to take care of Mrs. Newman's milk cows there to winter. Her sons are in the army. Poor old Job and Elvy have a [. . .] if they half do their duty. Job keeps the 2 best horses that belong to the farm there to haul his wood and plow—if there was any weather to plow. There has not been a plow started here yet. The mules look about as well as before they went away, all to the hair being off. We don't use old Cit but little. Your pa thinks she is with foal, and she is so old, he tries to take great care of her. We have 2 young lambs and sixteen pigs at home. We have not heard from Job's sows since he was up three weeks past. He had fixed beds for them and expected them to take bed constantly. Bacon is starting at 22cts. per lb. Cow is worth about the same. Wheat, the last account, was worth one dollar thirty-seven-and-a-half cts. There have been more distilleries started, which will make corn much higher than it would have been, and I fear make worse for our army.

15 Feb. I have had no chance to mail my letter. Caroline is mending; Candace professes to be about well. The rest of the sick better, no new case. Sam has plowed three days this week; we have had a few fine days, but it is now snowing fast and bids for a deep snow. Rebecca was here last Monday, all tolerable well. Moorman grows fast. Franklin's Peter is dead, making the 3d in the family since Christmas. Rbt. Walker has been here this week and made me a pair of shoes. Fannie Robertson spent Tuesday here. Uncle John is very poorly. Major mending slowly. John Graves was here last week, speaks of going to camp so soon as able. He has had the mumps and fever lately.

I must close. All join me in love to you. Write often, it is a great pleasure to hear from you. I have not heard from your brother since he left nearly 2 weeks. I hope to hear from you both today if the weather is not too bad for anyone to turn out. Farewell, my son. Never be unmindful of your temporal and spiritual interests.

Your Mother, F.

Your pa is fixing to start to Billy Creasy's sale [. . .] Our men are improving. All well at the Dr.'s. [. . .] We have ice and snow plentiful.

[Written on the Robert Parker letter dated March 22, 1862.]
[Rebecca Parker to Mrs. Walker]
Ma,

Let me know when you heard from George, and whether anyone is going out there or not. I would come down today but am looking for Delia and Doria to stay with me tonight.

Beck

["H." to Rebecca Parker]

Rebecca,

I saw a letter last night from [. . .] written the 23d, stating he was to see George the day before. Said he was very low and low-spirited, and that George and G. Fields were all that were considered dangerous. Mr. Parker talks of going or getting some one to go as soon as he can. Prefer his going if his health will permit. I have written to Brother Harrison. I wrote to George last Tuesday and will write again today. Price says he will take some things to him.

H.

[Rebecca Parker to Robert Parker]

Liberty

May the 16

My dear Robert,

Your welcome letter of the 7th just came to hand yesterday. I assure you I have spent many, many anxious moments about you for the past few days, as I heard there had been a considerable battle over near Staunton,[15] and expected you were engaged in it. We have not heard anything from Ed[16] since the battle, except that twelve or thirteen of his company were wounded. Several of Capt. Wright's company were wounded in the battle of Williamsburg.[17] Joe Dearing was killed. I am very anxious to hear the particulars of the late battles, and more than anxious to hear from you again. I reckon you are getting anxious to hear from poor little Moorman again, as he was very sick when I wrote last. But I am more than glad to inform you he has got well again, and is now playing with his shadow on the wall. I had no idea this time last week that he would live two days longer, but he is still spared to cheer my drooping spirits with his sweet prattle and winning ways. He feels more precious to me than ever. I tried to make up my mind to give him up willingly, but I couldn't do it. I finally concluded I could give him up if you could see him first, but I don't believe that would make any difference, for he seems to be a part of my existence, and it would be almost like tearing life itself away, to take my precious babe from me. Oh if you could only see him. I hope you can come home soon.

Well, Robert, what do you think? Miss Sallie Farris and Mr. Peters (who lives where Ned Jones used to live) were married last night. I would like to take a peep at her tonight, wouldn't you? Poor Mary Whitten was married in Jan. and her husband died last Tuesday with consumption. She is left a widow very soon. Cit Rider's husband is dead also; he belonged to Capt. Wright's company. I hope your horse has reached you and suits better than I expect. Your pa has been working your farm. He has mended considerably, but looks quite badly yet. Job was up last Sunday, all were well. Booker went with him to help drive some cows and plant the corn. Our cow has a calf. They will bring her up tomorrow. Mr. Hendricks wants to buy her; your pa thinks he can get fifty dollars for her. I wish he could sell the calf we carried down with her too, for it jumps as much as the cow. The farmers are doing but little towards making a crop. Wheat and oats look fine. The most of the wheat about here is over knee high, and in some rich places it is waist-high. I never saw such a prospect for fruit. The apple trees are loaded, the peach trees are tolerably full. I reckon we will have to live on fruit principally, for everything else is so backward I fear it will not do much. Pa has planted but very little corn, no potatoes except Irish potatoes, some cotton and flax. It has been raining for three days. The water was from hill to hill on Mr. Phelps's bottoms this evening, all over Henry's corn. I must close as Pa is waiting for my letter to take to the office. My respects to Mr. Phelps, Steve Goggin, John Graves and all inquiring friends. I have not heard from Cousin Fannie's this week. Goodbye. Accept the best love and many kisses from Beck and little sweetie. Please write soon and often to your devoted,

Beck

May 17th, '62

[W. P. Lebo to Robert and Rebecca Parker]
Chimborazo, Richmond
Sept. 25th , '62
Mr. and Mrs. R. W. Parker,

Your letter came happy to hand yesterday, which gave me much inspiration to learn you stand by home. Knowing the difference on a sick man being at home and at a hospital, I am always glad to hear of a friend getting home to enjoy the advantages it has there of over every at a hospital. 'Twas sorry to hear that you was no better, but I guess it was caused by the walk you had in the city before you could get off. So I do hope by this time you are sincerely on the mend, and that a speedy restoration and vigor will [. . .] be affected. My letter from your ma came a few days ago. I took it out, read it, and destroyed it. 'Twas a very interesting letter.

No news here except war news, and that you can hear as fast as I can. It seems that anyone can get home but me. I got a letter from my brother that was wounded, and sure enough he is at home, wounded in the foot. I think they ought to let men who have family go home first, especially when they want to see their folks as bad as I do. We are getting on fully. Is well here as when you left. The sick have come in since and save me have left, so I have but few men now in my ward. Mr. Cameron is still low, don't think he will live long.

I do not know when I will leave here yet, but not for some time yet. My respect to yourselves, your pa and ma.

Yours truly,

W. P. Lebo

[Rebecca Parker to Frances A. Jopling]
Oct. 26th, '62
Dear Aunt Fannie,[18]

No doubt you would like to hear from us once more, but there is nothing of any importance except that the sick are improving some. Ma thinks Charlie is little better, though quite sick yet; Robert is mending some, but very slowly. We came up here yesterday morning and killed two bee hives for Ma, and got the greatest quantity of honey I ever saw. They were very large [gums] and were full of honey from the top to the bottom, with the exception of a few inches. Come down and we will give you apple pie and honey. [. . .]

[Rebecca Parker]

[Samuel Murrill to Robert Parker]
Cavalry Camp 4 miles below Culpeper CH
Feb. 17th , '63
Dear Robert,

I read your kind favor of Feb. 6th and was very glad to learn that you had gotten safe home, but was sorry to hear that Whit was so sick, but hope you may both soon recover and return to the co., though I had much rather the war would end and we all could come home, and you would not have to come anymore. I reckon your ma, and wife too, would be glad to hear that you would not have to come anymore. You wished to know how you were reported. On the morning report it is as I told you, "Absent sick," all right. Don't suffer any uneasiness about that, for it is all right. If you can keep clear of the officers and guards at home, all will be well. I am very much obliged to the Dr. for his respects and well wishes. Please remember mine to him. Pray for me.

My love to all enquiring friends. Write again soon.

Yours truly,

Sam L. Murrill

[Leslie Dinwiddie to Robert Parker]
Camp 2 V Cavalry
Feb. 17th ,1863
Esteemed Friends,

I seat myself this gloomy morning to pen you a few lines, though I have no news of interest. Everything is quiet at present. I suppose you have heard that we were at Culpepper Court House. We landed here Thursday last. We had a dreadful time of it, [I] can assure you—the roads were enforced curfew. I am not sorry we left Hanover CH, for we did not get any roughage for our horses and hasn't yet got any here, but I think the prospect is very good to get some as soon as [. . .] Brigade leaves, which I hope will be soon.

Bob, I have no news to write and I hope you will excuse me for such a short note. I am [. . .] to write anyways.

Steve has written on the opposite side and I suppose has given you the news in general. Bob, you must be sure and go to see my wife as soon as you can. I know she would be glad to see you. I reckon you have seen James Lee ere this, as him and James P. McCabe went home on a 30 days furlough. I reckon he is having a nice time since he was at home. I must close for the present. Hoping to hear [from] you.

Return my best respects to all inquiring friends and more especially to your little family.

Most respectfully yours,

L. Dinwiddie

[Mary Parker to Robert Parker]
Feb. 20, 1863
Dear Robert,

I received your kind letter in due time and would have answered it before this time, but I have not been able. I have another girl, born the 6 of this month. She is quite well except the rash, and I have it in my breasts so bad that it is almost like death when the baby sucks. It makes my back so weak that I can hardly sit up. Mr. Parker is very unwell with a desperate cold and his bowels out of order. I am uneasy for fear he will have a hard spell before he gets over it. He coughs a great deal. The children have very bad colds. The balance of the family are well. Mr. [Enos] Robertson has the smallpox. There is several in the neighborhood that has had a chance to get it. I am fearful it will get here before we get it out of the neighborhood. Report say it [is] at brother Pleasant's. I am in hopes it is a mistake. I have not heard from Father's in a month. They were all tolerable well when I heard. I have not heard from your papa in several weeks. They were sick — some of them which I heard [. . .]

We have had desperate weather in this month and nothing done neither out nor in. People are more backward with their business than I ever knew them in this neighborhood. Robert, please answer this letter as soon as you get it and give us all the news. Mr. Parker is hurrying to send the letter to the office so I must close. I have no paper to write on so you will excuse a short letter this time. We have no gardening done yet. I wish I could send you a hot breakfast this morning. I must close, for I can't send it. Give my love to all enquiring friend and accept a large share yourself. Farewell. I remain your most affectionate aunt,

M. A. Parker

Be sure to send me some butter by Will Parker anyhow, for my throat needs greasing.

[Rebecca Parker to Robert Parker]
Liberty
May 7th, '63
My Dear Robert,

I'll again attempt to write you a few lines, though hardly know what to do about it, as I have not heard from you or any of the co. since the fighting. Oh! the agony and suspense I have endured since I heard of the fighting. I have sent to the office every day this week, but have received no information yet. I don't think I ever wanted to hear from you as bad since you have been in service; I think it very strange that we haven't heard from the company at all. I heard cannon very distinctly Sunday morning; I went up to Ed's Saturday eve and stayed till Sunday evening. Lucy has a very pretty little babe, and Jim is the proudest man I ever saw, the baby is not at all like him.

This leaves all tolerably well except myself and Mory. I have had a dreadful headache with burning fever all the week; Mory has a very bad cold and cough. I fear it will terminate in croup, he is very poorly today: I fear I am bordering on a hard spell [. . .]

[Rebecca Parker]

[John Graves to Ammon Parker]
Bedford Co., Va.
March 13th, 1865
Dear Uncle,

As it is your request and I am compelled to return on any certain day, I will wait until Thursday morning and you can tell what arrangement to make with Robert's horse so you can send his horse to Walter Hopkins Thursday by 9 o'clock, and oblige yours truly,

J. P. Graves

P.S. Come to see us soon.

I will be sure to go there. Let me know that day if you find out where regiment is. Respectfully yours, Jno. P. Graves

[Frances Parker to Rebecca Parker]
Rebecca,

The envelope was worn out when I got your letter. I have now the note, and send you J. Graves note also. We had Laura saddled ready to start this morning when we got word. I have watched for an opportunity to send to the office but have had none. I wish Robert could learn his horse is not to start until Thursday. Perhaps he could get back and take her himself. If we get no other word, I would like for Mr. Graves to know what he has written. Robert

Home of Elizabeth Robertson, behind which Robert W. Parker may have been killed and initially buried in 1865. Courtesy of Appomattox Court House National Historic Park.

was in Lynchburg Saturday night. Two men have passed here and say they saw him and his brother.

Respectfully,

F. H. P.

[Anon. to Anon.]

19th

My Dearest Sister,

Many, many have been the changes since last we heard from each other, and often wished to hear from you and yours, but there has been but little passing to town. Had I have written last Monday to you, I could have sent it, as Mr. Hurt saw Mr. Phelps in town. He said that you were all as well as usual. The sad news of the death of dear Robert[19] disturbed me much. Oh, how I felt for dear Rebecca. [Her] soul seemed centered in her dear Robert who was worthy of her love. Indeed, the more I knew of him, the more highly I esteemed him. May the good Lord comfort and sustain her in this great affliction. I was glad to hear that your dear sons were safe at home. I feared that Ellick had gone, as I heard that he was in town on his way just before. It was a mysterious Providence that such a good young man, with so much to live for, should have been taken after suffering all through this cruel war, after so nobly defending the right. Sister, I wrote the above before I rec'd yours, but had no chance of sending it. Poor dear Beck, my heart aches for her in this sad bereavement. Oh, that I knew how to relieve or comfort! Could the tear of sympathy reach or heal, she has that, for I can safely say that I never heard the death of anyone that hurt me more. But enough. I will write to her too.

Yes, sister, the news of Lee's surrender[20] startled me even more than the fall of Richmond,[21] both was like a clap of thunder in a cloudless sky. Charley got home about day Monday morn after the news got to Lynch of Lee's surrender, Jimmy too. The soldiers commenced passing Monday and continued one constant stream till Friday. We lodged and fed many, and I had a house full all the time. Br. Starr and Mollie Saunders have been with us for nearly 3 weeks. Mollie and her mother started home in Loudoun the day R. was evacuated and could not get on nor go back to [Rr. Crops?]. What is to become of us, we know not. Can do nothing but stand still and see the salvation of the Lord [. . .]

Sister, I had this written before Charley came and could not send at 9 a.m. So glad to see dear Charley. How thankful I am but that he is safe after so much suffering. Oh Lord, how long Thou knowest.

[Anon. to Rebecca Parker]
E. P. Walton's house near Appomattox Depot,[22] and they promised to bury him decently as they could.
My Dear Rebecca,

I can't express to you the heartfelt sympathy I feel for you in your great bereavement. Truly have you lost a noble, worthy husband, one on whom I know that you doted, who promised much usefulness to his family and country, and I often find myself making the inquiry, "Why he was taken, Lord?" It seems a mysterious Providence. But we must remember that He is too wise and good to error, and that He has some wise design to accomplish in all his dealings. Therefore I hope and pray that you may be assisted by His grace to cast all your care and burden on them who has promised to sustain and comfort you, and enable you to say, "The Lord gave and the Lord has taken away. Blessed be His name. Though He slay me, yet will I trust in Him"[23] Though He has taken your dear Robert, He loved him even more than you did and has taken Him from the evil to come, from this world of sin and sorrow to one of bliss and glory.[24]

The more I knew of Robert, the more I loved him. I could see in him the traits of a true Christian and gentleman character. I have heard many of his regiment speak of him in the highest terms. We all regret his death so much and would fain offer you all our sympathy and comfort, but I know all your soul and comfort must come from your kind Heavenly Father. Go to Him and tell Him all your heart's sorrow. He has promised to be a husband and father to your precious little children. Cast your all on Him and claim the promise, dear little boys. May they long live to enjoy the freedom and independence their father fought and bled and died for. It is a day of darkness and wonder to us now, but I can't believe but what we are yet to enjoy that for which there has been so much sacrifice and bloodshed.[25] Only let us do our duty, trusting in the Lord. I hope to get down to see you as soon as I can. Write to me if you can, dear Rebecca, and tell me all. You have my prayers and sympathy. Kiss the dear children for me.

NOTES

Introduction

1. Robert W. Parker, Barboursville, to Rebecca L. Parker, Bedford County, Jan. 20, 1865, Robert W. Parker Papers, No. 5261, Southern Historical Collection, Wilson Library, Univ. of North Carolina at Chapel Hill (hereafter cited as Parker Papers).

2. Karen Lystra, *Searching the Heart: Women, Men and Romantic Love in Nineteenth-Century America* (New York: Oxford Univ. Press, 1987), 17; Stephen W. Berry II, *All that Makes a Man: Love and Ambition in the Civil War South* (New York: Oxford Univ. Press, 2003), 89, 184–85, 224.

3. Drew Gilpin Faust, *Mothers of Invention: Women of the Slaveholding South in the American Civil War* (Chapel Hill: Univ. of North Carolina Press, 1996), 115.

4. Robert W. Parker, Fairfax Court House, to Rebecca Parker, Bedford County, Sept. 3, 1861, Parker Papers.

5. James I. Robertson Jr., *Soldiers Blue and Gray* (Columbia: Univ. of South Carolina Press, 1988), 18.

6. Richard E. Beringer, Herman Hattaway, Archer Jones, and William N. Still Jr., *Why the South Lost the Civil War* (Athens: Univ. of Georgia Press, 1986), 26.

7. Carol K. Bleser, "The Marriage of Varina Howell and Jefferson Davis: A Portrait of the President and the First Lady of the Confederacy," in *Intimate Strategies of the Civil War: Military Commanders and Their Wives*, ed. Carol K. Bleser and Lesley J. Gordon (New York: Oxford Univ. Press, 2001), 3; Robert W. Parker to Rebecca Parker, Bedford County, Nov. 31, 1864, Parker Papers.

8. Robert W. Parker and Rebecca L. Walker, Certificate to Obtain a Marriage License, Dec. 4, 1860, and Marriage License, Dec. 6, 1860, Bedford County Marriage Records, Library of Virginia, Richmond; Mary Denham Ackerly and Lula Eastman Jeter Parker, *"Our Kin": The Genealogies of Some of the Early Families Who Made History in the Founding and Development of Bedford County, Virginia* (Lynchburg, Va.: N.p., 1930; reprint, Harrisonburg, Va.: C. J. Carrier, 1976), 650.

9. Ackerly and Parker, *"Our Kin,"* 650; Bureau of the Census, *Population Schedules of the Seventh Census of the United States, 1850*, Bedford County, Virginia, M432, Roll 935, RG 29, NA; Bureau of the Census, *Slave Schedules of the Seventh Census of the United States, 1850*, for Bedford County, Virginia, M432, Roll 984, RG 29, NA.

10. Bureau of the Census, *Slave Schedules of the Eighth Census of the United States, 1860*, Bedford County, Virginia, M653, Roll 1387, RG 29, NA; Virginia Department of

Taxation, Land Tax, 1861, Bedford County, Virginia, Reel 398, Library of Virginia, Richmond.

11. Nora A. Carter, "Lone Aspen" Survey Report, Bedford County, Va., Works Progress Administration of Virginia Historical Inventory, Mar. 1938, Virginia Conservation Commission, Library of Virginia, Richmond.

12. Frances Parker, Liberty, Va., to Robert Parker, July 26, 1861, Parker Papers; Robert Parker, Culpeper Court House, to Rebecca Parker, Mar. 29, 1863, Parker Papers; Virginia Department of Taxation, Land Tax, 1861, Bedford County, Virginia.

13. Emory M. Thomas, *The Confederacy as a Revolutionary Experience* (Englewood Cliffs, N.J.: Prentice Hall, 1971), 14.

14. Peter S. Carmichael, *The Last Generation: Young Virginians in Peace, War, and Reunion* (Chapel Hill: Univ. of North Carolina Press, 2005), 11, 37, 50; Berry, *All that Makes a Man,* 31.

15. Robert W. Parker and Rebecca L. Walker, Certificate to Obtain a Marriage License and Marriage License.

16. Carter, "Lone Aspen" Survey Report.

17. Thomas, *Confederacy as a Revolutionary Experience,* 21.

18. Robert W. Parker, Orange Court House, to Rebecca Parker, Bedford County, Mar. 13, 1864, Parker Papers.

19. Reid Mitchell, *Civil War Soldiers* (New York: Viking Press, 1988), 23.

20. Berry, *All that Makes a Man,* 9.

21. Robert J. Driver Jr., *2nd Virginia Cavalry,* 2nd ed. (Lynchburg, Va.: H. E. Howard, 1995), 2.

22. James M. McPherson, *For Cause and Comrades: Why Men Fought in the Civil War* (New York: Oxford Univ. Press, 1997), 5.

23. Ibid., 22.

24. Robert W. Parker, Waterford, to Rebecca Parker, Bedford County, Feb. 22, 1862, Parker Papers.

25. Steven Elliott Tripp, *Yankee Town, Southern City: Race and Class Relations in Civil War Lynchburg* (New York: New York Univ. Press, 1997), 90.

26. Mitchell, *Civil War Soldiers,* 18–19.

27. R. W. Parker to R. L. Parker, Feb. 23, 1862, Parker Papers; Mitchell, *Civil War Soldiers,* 19.

28. Robert W. Parker, Orange Court House, to Rebecca Parker, Bedford County, Apr. 25, 1862, Parker Papers.

29. Gary W. Gallagher, *The Confederate War* (Cambridge: Harvard Univ. Press, 1997), 5.

30. Tripp, *Yankee Town,* 50.

31. William Blair, *Virginia's Private War: Feeding Body and Soul in the Confederacy, 1861–1865* (New York: Oxford Univ. Press, 1998), 37–38.

32. Robert W. Parker to Rebecca Parker, Bedford County, Mar. 27, 1864, Parker Papers.

33. Robert W. Parker to Rebecca Parker, Bedford County, [n.d.; approx. June 1864], Parker Papers.

34. Ibid.

35. Robert W. Parker, Waterford, to Rebecca Parker, Bedford County, Dec. 13, 1861, Parker Papers.

36. Faust, *Mothers of Invention*, 45–47.

37. Robert W. Parker, Culpeper Court House, to Rebecca Parker, Bedford County, Oct. 31, 1861, Parker Papers; Frances H. Parker, Liberty, to Robert W. Parker, July 12, 1861, Parker Papers.

38. Richard N. Current, ed., *Encyclopedia of the Confederacy* (New York: Simon & Schuster, 1993), 2:594–97.

39. Robert W. Parker, Waterford, to Rebecca Parker, Bedford County, Jan. 22, 1862, Parker Papers.

40. Robert W. Parker, Oak Shade, to Rebecca Parker, Bedford County, June 10, 1863, Parker Papers.

41. Robert W. Parker to Rebecca Parker, Bedford County, June 7, 1861, Parker Papers.

42. Lystra, *Searching the Heart*, 41–42.

43. McPherson, *For Cause and Comrades*, 11.

44. Bell Irvin Wiley, *The Life of Johnny Reb: The Common Soldier of the Confederacy* (Baton Rouge: Louisiana State Univ. Press, 1979), 192; Robertson, *Soldiers Blue and Gray*, 5.

45. Lystra, *Searching the Heart*, 41–42.

46. Robert W. Parker, Culpeper Court House, to Rebecca Parker, Bedford County, Apr. 5, 1863, Parker Papers.

47. Roger W. Little, "Buddy Relations and Combat Performance," in *The New Military: Changing Patters of Organization*, ed. Morris Janowitz (New York: Russell Sage Foundation, 1964), 219; quoted in McPherson, *For Cause and Comrades*, 133.

48. Faust, *Mothers of Invention*, 115.

49. Wiley, *Life of Johnny Reb*, 197, 201.

50. Robert W. Parker to Rebecca Parker, Bedford County, Mar. 2, 1864, Parker Papers.

51. Robert W. Parker, Manassas Junction, to Rebecca Parker, Bedford County, June 26, 1861, Parker Papers.

52. Lystra, *Searching the Heart*, 25.

53. Carmichael, *Last Generation*, 179.

54. McPherson, *For Cause and Comrades*, 139.

55. Carol K. Bleser and Lesley J. Gordon, eds., *Intimate Strategies of the Civil War: Military Commanders and Their Wives* (New York: Oxford Univ. Press, 2001), xxi–xxii.

56. Faust, *Mothers of Invention*, 116.

57. Robert W. Parker, Orange County, to Rebecca Parker, Bedford County, Oct. 9, 1863, Parker Papers.

58. Robert W. Parker, Waterford, to Rebecca Parker, Bedford County, Jan. 6, 1862, Parker Papers.

59. Faust, *Mothers of Invention,* 116; Richard F. Ridgway, *Self-Sufficiency at All Costs: Confederate Post Office Operations in North Carolina, 1861–1865* (Charlotte: North Carolina Postal History Society, 1988), 50; quoted in Faust, *Mothers of Invention,* 282n6.

60. Robert W. Parker, Centreville, to Rebecca Parker, Bedford County, July 31, 1861, Parker Papers.

61. Berry, *All that Makes a Man,* 185.

62. Robert W. Parker, Fairfax Court House, to Rebecca Parker, Bedford County, July 14, 1861, Parker Papers.

63. Robert W. Parker, Culpeper County, to Rebecca Parker, Bedford County, Oct. 21, 1863, Parker Papers.

64. R. W. Parker to R. L. Parker, Jan. 22, 1862, Parker Papers.

65. Anonymous, Appomattox Depot, to Rebecca Parker, [n.d.; approx. Apr. 11, 1865], Parker Papers.

66. This counters the widely held interpretation that "resistance only flickered in the hearts of a few" soldiers and civilians by 1865 (Carmichael, *Last Generation,* 207).

67. Robert W. Parker, Lynchburg, to Rebecca Parker, Bedford County, Mar. 10, 1865, Parker Papers; Robert W. Parker, Lynchburg, to Rebecca Parker, Bedford County, Mar. 11, 1865, Parker Papers.

68. Carmichael, *Last Generation,* 207.

69. McPherson, *For Cause and Comrades,* 168.

70. Carmichael, *Last Generation,* 187–88.

71. Harry S. Stout and Christopher Grasso, "Civil War, Religion, and Communications: The Case of Richmond," in *Religion and the American Civil War,* ed. Randall M. Miller, Harry S. Stout, and Charles Reagan Wilson (New York: Oxford Univ. Press, 1998), 321.

72. Phillip Shaw Paludan, "Religion and the American Civil War," in *Religion and the American Civil War,* ed. Randall M. Miller, Harry S. Stout, and Charles Reagan Wilson (New York: Oxford Univ. Press, 1998), 30.

73. Anonymous to "Sister," [n.d.; approx. Apr. 11, 1865], Parker Papers.

74. R. W. Parker to R. L. Parker, June 7, 1861, Parker Papers.

75. Drew Gilpin Faust, *The Creation of Confederate Nationalism: Ideology and Identity in the Civil War South* (Baton Rouge: Louisiana State Univ. Press, 1989), 26; Robertson, *Soldiers Blue and Gray,* 173–74.

76. Carmichael, *Last Generation,* 180.

77. Eugene D. Genovese, *A Consuming Fire: The Fall of the Confederacy in the Mind of the White Christian South* (Athens: Univ. of Georgia Press, 1998), 45.

78. R. W. Parker to R. L. Parker, Mar. 13, 1864, Parker Papers.

79. Kurt O. Berends, "'Wholesome Reading Purifies and Elevates the Man': The Religious Military Press in the Confederacy," in *Religion and the American Civil War,* ed. Randall M. Miller, Harry S. Stout, and Charles Reagan Wilson (New York: Oxford Univ. Press, 1998), 132.

80. McPherson, *For Cause and Comrades,* 63.

81. Drew Gilpin Faust, "'Without Pilot or Compass': Elite Women and Religion in the Civil War South," in *Religion and the American Civil War*, ed. Randall M. Miller, Harry S. Stout, and Charles Reagan Wilson (New York: Oxford Univ. Press, 1998), 254.

82. Frances H. Parker, Bedford County, to Robert W. Parker, Lynchburg, June 9, 1861, Parker Papers.

83. Ibid.

84. McPherson, *For Cause and Comrades*, 63.

85. R. W. Parker to R. L. Parker, Nov. 31 [*sic*], 1864, Parker Papers.

86. R. W. Parker to R. L. Parker, Apr. 5, 1863, Parker Papers.

87. R. W. Parker to R. L. Parker, Oct. 21, 1863, Parker Papers.

88. Robert W. Parker, Culpeper Court House, to Rebecca Parker, Bedford County, July 6, 1862, Parker Papers.

89. McPherson, *For Cause and Comrades*, 75.

90. Robert W. Parker to Rebecca Parker, Bedford County, June 1, 1861, Parker Papers.

91. Ibid.; Robert W. Parker, Fairfax Court House, to Rebecca Parker, Bedford County, July 8, 1861, Parker Papers.

92. Robert W. Parker, Waterford, to Rebecca Parker, Bedford County, Nov. 17, 1861, Parker Papers.

93. R. W. Parker to R. L. Parker, Sept. 3, 1861, Parker Papers.

94. Robert W. Parker, Fairfax Court House, to Rebecca Parker, Bedford County, Sept. 8, 1861, Parker Papers.

95. For more on camp vices, see Wiley, *Life of Johnny Reb*, 36–58.

96. Robert W. Parker to Rebecca Parker, Bedford, [post-1862], Parker Papers.

97. Genovese, *Consuming Fire*, 46.

98. F. Parker to R. Parker, July 26, 1861, Parker Papers.

99. F. Parker to R. Parker, June 9, 1861, Parker Papers.

100. Esther 4:1 ("Mordecai rent his clothes and put on sackcloth with ashes, and went out into the midst of the city, and cried with a loud and bitter cry") and Matthew 11:21 ("If the mighty works, which were done in you, had been done in Tyre and Sidon, they would have repented long ago in sackcloth and ashes"), King James Version Bible (hereafter KJV); Genovese, *Consuming Fire*, 54.

101. R. Parker to R. Parker, July 6, 1862, Parker Papers.

102. Robert W. Parker, Culpeper Court House, to Rebecca Parker, Bedford County, May 17, 1863, Parker Papers.

103. Robert W. Parker to Rebecca Parker, Bedford County, June 19, [1861], Parker Papers.

104. Robert W. Parker, Union Mills, to Rebecca Parker, Bedford County, July 25, 1861, Parker Papers; R. W. Parker to R. L. Parker, July 31, 1861, Parker Papers.

105. Robert W. Parker, Culpeper Court House, to Rebecca Parker, Bedford County, June 3, 1863, Parker Papers; R. Parker to R. Parker, Mar. 27, 1864, Parker Papers.

106. Robert W. Parker, near Richmond, to Rebecca Parker, Bedford County, May 14, 1864, Parker Papers.

107. McPherson, *For Cause and Comrades*, 163.

108. R. W. Parker to R. L. Parker, May 14, 1864, Parker Papers.

109. Carmichael, *Last Generation*, 188.

110. R. W. Parker to R. L. Parker, Mar.11, 1865, Parker Papers.

111. R. W. Parker to R. L. Parker, Mar. 10, 1865, Parker Papers.

112. R. W. Parker to R. L. Parker, May 14, 1864, Parker Papers.

113. Berends,"Wholesome Reading,"136.

114. Robert W. Parker, Madison Court House, to Rebecca Parker, Bedford County, May 17, 1862, Parker Papers.

115. McPherson, *For Cause and Comrades*, 68.

116. Driver, *2nd Virginia Cavalry*, 161–66.

117. Patrick A. Schroeder, *The Confederate Cemetery at Appomattox*, rev. ed. (Farmville, Va.: Schroeder Publications, 2005), 4, 17.

118. Driver, *2nd Virginia Cavalry*, 166.

119. Rufus H. Peck, *Reminiscences of a Confederate Soldier of Co. C, 2nd Virginia Cavalry* (Fincastle,Va.: N.p., 1913), 71.

120. "Relatives of Last Man Shot in Battle Here,"newspaper clipping, Bedford newspaper, [Apr. 1935], Parker Papers.

121. Schroeder, *Confederate Cemetery*, 7–9, 17; Ladies Memorial Association in Appomattox,"Constitution of the Association,"in Schroeder, *Confederate Cemetery*, 22.

122. Anonymous to"Sister," [approx. Apr. 11, 1865], Parker Papers; Ackerly and Parker,"*Our Kin*," 651, 654.

123. Carmichael, *Last Generation*, 209–10.

124. Anonymous to R. L. Parker, [approx. Apr. 11, 1865], Parker Papers.

125. Anonymous to"Sister," [n.d..; approx. Apr. 11, 1865], Parker Papers.

Methodology

1. Wiley, *Life of Johnny Reb*, 202.

1861

1. War Department, Records of the Adjutant General's Office relating to military and naval service of Confederates, Collection of Confederate Records, M861, RG 109, NA; Edward G. Longacre, *Lee's Cavalrymen: A History of the Mounted Forces of the Army of Northern Virginia* (Mechanicsburg, Pa.: Stackpole Books, 2002), 5–6, 54–57.

2. This is Rebecca"Beck"Louise Fitzhugh Walker (b. January 6, 1840), also of Bedford County. She and Robert William Parker (hereafter RWP) had grown up near one another and were married on December 6, 1860. Ackerly and Parker, *"Our Kin,"* 651.

3. RWP enrolled for active service in Company F, the Bedford Southside Dragoons, in what would become the Second Virginia Cavalry (hereafter 2nd Va. Cav.) in Davis Mills, Virginia, on May 28 under Capt. James Wilson. The company then traveled to their Lynchburg camp and were mustered into service on May 31. Driver, *2nd Virginia Cavalry*, 2.

4. As a noncommissioned officer of the guard, RWP was responsible for supervising other enlisted members of the guard and inspecting pickets.

5. 3rd Lt. Alexander "Alick" Smith Walker (January 9, 1839–May 25, 1902), Company F, 2nd Va. Cav., was Rebecca Walker Parker's older brother and RWP's brother-in-law. He enlisted on May 28, 1861, at Davis Mills. He was absent on sick leave as of June 30, 1861. In July 1861 he hired Tilghman D. Scott as a substitute and was discharged from the army. He is listed as a private on the postwar roster. Driver, *2nd Virginia Cavalry*, 280.

6. Capt. James Wilson (June 22, 1813–August 11, 1883), Company F, 2nd Va. Cav. He enlisted May 28, 1861, at Davis Mills. A farmer before the war, he resigned his post on September 17, 1861. Driver, *2nd Virginia Cavalry*, 287.

7. This is an abbreviation for Bedford Southside Dragoons, Company F's nickname. Driver, *2nd Virginia Cavalry*, 2.

8. In this usage "muster" means to assemble or gather together, perhaps for inspection.

9. Capt. William Richard Terry (August 14, 1824–September 5, 1889), Company A, 2nd Va. Cav. He graduated from the Virginia Military Institute (VMI) in 1850 and attended the University of Virginia 1850–51. He enlisted at Liberty on May 11, 1861, and was promoted to colonel of the Twenty-fourth Virginia Infantry in September 1861. He was wounded in action at Williamsburg on May 5, 1862, and at Gettysburg on July 3, 1863. He commanded Kemper's brigade at the Wilderness. He was appointed brigadier general on May 31, 1864, and commanded the Stonewall brigade under Gen. Jubal Early. He was wounded at Dinwiddie Court House on March 31, 1865, and surrendered at Appomattox on April 9, 1865. Driver, *2nd Virginia Cavalry*, 275.

10. Pvt. Thomas Stephen Goggin (August 30, 1841–April 3, 1863), Company F, 2nd Va. Cav., was RWP's maternal cousin. A farmer before the war, Goggin enlisted at Davis Mills on May 28, 1861. He died of pneumonia in a Lynchburg hospital in April 1863. Driver, *2nd Virginia Cavalry*, 222.

11. 2nd Sgt. John "Jim" T. Lipscomb (September 4, 1831–January 11, 1912), Company F, 2nd Va. Cav. He worked as a farmer before the war and enlisted at Davis Mills on May 28, 1861. He was absent on sick leave with typhoid fever in August 1861. His rank was reduced to private. He was wounded in action at Cross Keys on June 8, 1862. He was absent with diarrhea in a Charlottesville hospital on June 23, 1862, and was transferred to a Lynchburg hospital on August 11, 1862. He was present through June 1864, when he was hospitalized in a Richmond hospital with diarrhea from July 30 through August 17, 1864. He surrendered at Appomattox Court House on April 9, 1865. Driver, *2nd Virginia Cavalry*, 241.

12. Pvt. George D. Lipscomb (c. 1830), Company F, 2nd Va. Cav. He was a former tanner who enlisted at Davis Mills on May 28, 1861. He was present through August 1861 and was discharged on September 17, 1861, for unknown reasons. Driver, *2nd Virginia Cavalry*, 241.

13. Pvt. Joseph Burroughs (c. 1835–May 20, 1862), Company F, 2nd Va. Cav. He was a farmer before enlisting at Davis Mills on May 28, 1861. He was present through December 1861 and died of typhoid fever in a Liberty hospital. Driver, *2nd Virginia Cavalry*, 202.

14. Many soldiers held deep religious convictions and incorporated them into their daily camp routines. Prayer meetings, church services, and revivals were but some of the ways soldiers forged a religious community in their camps. For more on the religion of ordinary soldiers, see Steven E. Woodworth, *While God Is Marching On* (Lawrence: Univ. of Kansas Press, 2001).

15. Pvt. Henry Chapman Bowles (November 20, 1831–August 6, 1918), Company F, 2nd Va. Cav. He was a minister when he enlisted at Davis Mills on May 28, 1861. He was present through October 1861 and absent on sick leave for most of November and December 1861. No further records document his whereabouts during the war, but he was probably discharged due to illness. Driver, *2nd Virginia Cavalry*, 198.

16. Frances H. Goggin Parker was RWP's mother. She was the third of eight children; she married Ammon Hancock Parker on December 10, 1835. Ackerly and Parker, *"Our Kin,"* 650, 671.

17. Ammon Hancock Parker (March 3, 1807–May 8, 1880) was RWP's father. He was a farmer who married his first wife, Frances H. Goggin, on December 10, 1835. Together they built the home known as Lone Aspen and raised their four children. On the eve of the Civil War he owned 6,793 acres of Bedford County land and seventeen slaves. After Frances's death, Ammon married Elizabeth Parker on June 6, 1878. Ackerly and Parker, *"Our Kin,"* 650; Virginia Department of Taxation, Land Tax, 1861, Bedford County, Virginia; Bureau of the Census, *Slave Schedules of the Eighth Census of the United States*, 1860, for Bedford County, Virginia, M653, Roll 1387, RG 29, NA.

18. Thomas Bennett Joplin (also spelled Jopling) (d. November 1, 1867) was Rebecca Walker Parker's maternal uncle. He married Sarah Webb (April 18, 1829–October 12, 1886) on September 21, 1845, and had twelve children. Ackerly and Parker, *"Our Kin,"* 697–98.

19. Many Civil War soldiers were stationed relatively near their homes, resulting in fluidity between homefront and battlefront. Civilians frequently visited soldiers and regiments from their communities, delivering mail, parcels, messages, and news. Wiley, *Life of Johnny Reb*, 199–201.

20. Rations were varied and plentiful at the beginning of the war. It was not until later, when the amount of food being produced dropped drastically and there were difficulties in transporting food to where it was needed most, that food prices skyrocketed and Southerners resorted to a variety of methods to avoid starvation. For more on the diet of Confederate soldiers, see Wiley, *Life of Johnny*

Reb, 90–107; and John D. Billings, *Hardtack and Coffee* ([Alexandria, Va.]: Time-Life Books, 1982). For civilian diets, see George C. Rable, *Civil Wars* (Urbana: Univ. of Illinois Press, 1989), 96–100.

21. Most newly enlisted soldiers had some difficulty adjusting to the discipline of military life. Pvt. Moses P. Rucker, Company F, seconded RWP's thoughts on this matter, saying, "What a green lot of fellows we were and knew nothing about military discipline" (Driver, *2nd Virginia Cavalry*, 6). For more on discipline, see Gerald F. Linderman, *Embattled Courage: The Experience of Combat in the American Civil War* (New York: Free Press, 1987), 34–60.

22. As a third lieutenant, Alexander Walker was a commissioned officer, whereas RWP's rank of corporal placed him as a noncommissioned officer.

23. Contrary to RWP's belief, disease and infection plagued Civil War soldiers for the duration of the war. Indeed, two-thirds of the more than six hundred thousand deaths among troops were caused by disease. For more on this topic, see Alfred Jay Bollet, *Civil War Medicine: Challenges and Triumphs* (Tucson, Ariz.: Galen Press, 2002), 257–58.

24. Alexander Clark Parker (January 14, 1847–January 15, 1931) was the third son of Ammon and Frances Parker and RWP's younger brother. As he was only fourteen when the Civil War began, he did not enlist in the army for several more years. He married his first wife, Elizabeth Ann Teass, on January 17, 1877; his second wife was Mary M. Crews. He had eight children. Ackerly and Parker, "Our Kin," 650, 654–56; Bedford Cemetery Index, Bedford City/County Museum, Bedford, Va., 874.

25. RWP is referring to an engagement known as the Philippi Races in the mountains of western Virginia (present-day West Virginia) on June 3, 1861. Federal troops caught Confederate forces unawares at the town of Philippi and soon had them fleeing. Although a minor skirmish, the Confederates' poor performance may have contributed to the eventual secession of West Virginia. E. B. Long, *The Civil War Day by Day: An Almanac, 1861–1865* (New York: Da Capo, 1985), 26.

26. Many Confederates believed prayer "could assure one of divine grace and protection and preserve a spiritual connection between soldiers and loved ones." Carmichael, *Last Generation*, 171.

27. RWP was a farmer before enlisting in the army and remained interested in his crops and livestock throughout the war. Although he is not listed on tax records as owning his own land, his father Ammon owned approximately 620 acres in Bedford County. RWP may have farmed some of this land as his own. Virginia Department of Taxation, Land Tax, 1861, Bedford County, Virginia.

28. Thomas Clark Goggin (January 12, 1815–April 19, 1895) was RWP's maternal uncle. He married Elizabeth Jane Johnson on December 4, 1838, with whom he had five children. He became a renowned Baptist preacher and a pillar of the Bedford County community. Ackerly and Parker, "Our Kin," 671.

29. RWP's only sister was Hester Ann Mary Parker (August 13, 1849–November 27, 1907), the fourth and youngest child of Ammon and Frances Parker. She

married William Nicholas Reese on November 22, 1866, and eventually bore him twelve children. Ackerly and Parker, *"Our Kin,"* 650, 675–77.

30. When the war began, most soldiers were eager to engage the enemy, who wanted to demonstrate their honor and manliness, stave off boredom, and participate in a glorious adventure. The experience of combat quickly whetted their appetite for battle. For more on this topic, see McPherson, *For Cause and Comrades,* 30–45.

31. Capt. Andrew Lewis Pitzer (May 29, 1827–April 11, 1896), Company C, 2nd Va. Cav. He attended VMI, served as a captain in the Fifth Virginia Cavalry (Militia), and worked as a farmer before enlisting in Company C at Fincastle on May 17, 1861. Despite suffering an accidental gunshot wound in June 1861, he was present through October 1861. He was not reelected on April 25, 1862. He served as a volunteer aide-de-camp on Gen. Jubal Early's staff in August 1862 and was appointed major on January 21, 1863. No records exist for his service beyond July 1863. Driver, *2nd Virginia Cavalry,* 261.

32. Capt. Giles William Bruce Hale (April 21, 1840–September 8, 1933) commanded Company D, 2nd Va. Cav. Hale claimed to have attended VMI, but no record exists to confirm this. He attended Randolph-Macon College from 1860 to 1861 before enrolling in Company D in Franklin County on May 29, 1861. He was present through August 1861 but absent without leave in September and October 1861. He was not reelected on April 25, 1862, but later served on Gen. Jubal Early's staff. Driver, *2nd Virginia Cavalry,* 224.

33. Col. Richard Carlton Walker Radford (July 8, 1822–November 2, 1896) was not elevated to the rank of brigadier general. He attended VMI in 1840–41, graduated from West Point in 1845, and served with the cavalry on the frontier and in the Mexican War. He resigned in 1856 and became a planter in Bedford County but was reappointed by the Confederate army on May 8, 1861. He commanded the regiment at First Manassas but was not reelected on April 25, 1862. He was appointed colonel in the First Virginia State Line Troops on August 22, 1862. He commanded a brigade in February 1863; beyond that date there are no further records to document his service. Driver, *2nd Virginia Cavalry,* 263.

34. Soldiers' families provided whatever material necessities they could. Making and mending clothing was considered women's work because it fell within the domestic realm. Faust, *Mothers of Invention,* 24–25; George C. Rable, *Civil Wars* (Urbana: Univ. of Illinois Press, 1989), 138–44.

35. "Flying artillery," also known as "flying battery," is a group of two or more horse-drawn cannon that could be moved speedily from one area to another. They were sometimes used to give opponents the impression of facing many more cannon than they actually were. Webb Garrison with Cheryl Garrison, *The Encyclopedia of Civil War Usage: An Illustrated Compendium of the Everyday Language of Soldiers and Civilians* (Nashville: Cumberland House, 2001), 80.

36. The Confederate government attempted to centralize their prison system by locating most of their prisons in or near Richmond. Among the more infamous prisons were Libby Prison, Castle Thunder, and Belle Isle. For more on Civil War

prisons, see Lonnie R. Speer, *Portals to Hell: Military Prisons of the Civil War* (Lincoln: Univ. of Nebraska Press, 2005).

37. Dr. James Alexander Walker (June 15, 1802–May 10, 1869) was Rebecca Walker Parker's father and RWP's father-in-law. He studied medicine in Philadelphia and practiced medicine in Bedford County for many years. He married his first wife, Elizabeth Booth, on August 1, 1827; they had four children before her death. His second wife was Nancy Moorman Jopling. They married on November 13, 1837, and had six children together. Ackerly and Parker, *"Our Kin,"* 683–85.

38. Despite the presence of slavery and most of the populace identifying as Southerners, Maryland did not secede from the Union. As a border state it sympathized with the South but strove to remain neutral. President Abraham Lincoln suspended constitutional rights and stationed Federal troops in Baltimore, thus ending any chance for Maryland to secede. Nonetheless, one-third of white Maryland men served in Southern units. Current, *Encyclopedia* 1:195–97; Robert I. Cottom Jr., *Maryland in the Civil War: A House Divided* (Baltimore: Maryland Historical Society, 1994).

39. The Wise Troop was Company B, 2nd Va. Cav., under Capt. (later Maj.) John Scaisbrooke Langhorne. Driver, *2nd Virginia Cavalry*, 2.

40. 1st Lt. John Whitfield "Whit" Johnson (February 12, 1838–November 2, 1902), Company F, 2nd Va. Cav. He was absent sick for unknown ailments for several weeks at a time throughout the war. He was reelected second lieutenant on April 24, 1862, and commanded a regiment of dismounted men at Fort Harrison on April 3, 1865. Driver, *2nd Virginia Cavalry*, 234.

41. RWP's cavalry regiment was initially organized as the Thirtieth Regiment, Virginia Volunteers, before being reorganized and incorporated into the 2nd Va. Cav. Driver, *2nd Virginia Cavalry*, 2, 6.

42. In this context, "Sunday" refers to a religious observance, not merely a day of the week. The leading religious service in camp took place on Sunday afternoon; informal prayer meetings took place more frequently. Robertson, *Soldiers Blue and Gray*, 183.

43. This is a reference to Lt. Gen. Winfield Scott (June 13, 1786–May 29, 1866), Union general-in-chief at the beginning of the Civil War. Although his age and declining health prevented him from the front lines, his proposed "Anaconda Plan" outlined a strategy the Union eventually used with great success, particularly in the West. Mark M. Boatner III, *The Civil War Dictionary*, rev. ed. (New York: Vintage Books, 1991), 728–29; Timothy D. Johnson, *Winfield Scott: The Quest for Military Glory* (Lawrence: Univ. Press of Kansas, 1998).

44. Pvt. Sandy Wilson, Company F, 2nd Va. Cav. He may have been hospitalized in a Richmond hospital June 1–4, 1864. No further records exist documenting his military service. Driver, *2nd Virginia Cavalry*, 287.

45. This may be Archibald H. Vance, Company D, Tenth Virginia Infantry. Janet B. Hewett, ed., *Virginia Confederate Soldiers, 1861–1865*, vol. 2, *L–Z* (Wilmington, N.C.: Broadfoot, 1998), 948.

46. Cpl. Moses Peter Rucker (March 10, 1837–September 2, 1926), Company F, 2nd Va. Cav. A farmer before the war, he enlisted at Davis Mills on May 28, 1861. Although it is unknown what ailed Rucker, he was absent on sick leave from July 1861 through October 1862, and again through March and April 1864. Driver, *2nd Virginia Cavalry*, 266.

47. George Stephen Parker (September 23, 1842–March 1862) was the second of Ammon and Frances Parker's four children and RWP's younger brother. He enlisted as a second corporal, Company A, Fifty-eighth Virginia Infantry, at Bunker Hill on July 25, 1861. He died of disease in March 1862 and is buried in Bedford. Ackerly and Parker, *"Our Kin,"* 650; Robert J. Driver Jr., *58th Virginia Infantry* (Lynchburg, Va.: H. E. Howard, 1990), 128.

48. This is probably Pvt. Charles Edward Adams (b. ca. 1842), Company G, 2nd Va. Cav. He enlisted as a private at Forest Depot on May 28, 1861. He was promoted to first corporal by December 1862, to fourth sergeant by April 1863, and to third sergeant by May 1864. He was wounded in action near Spotsylvania Court House on May 8, 1864, but was present again in June 1864. He lived in Bedford County until at least 1910. Driver, *2nd Virginia Cavalry*, 191.

49. Pvt. John E. Jones (b. ca. 1843), Company F, 2nd Va. Cav., enlisted at Davis Mills on May 28, 1861. He and his horse were wounded in action at Raccoon Ford on October 11, 1863, but was present November 1863 through June 1864. He was paroled in Richmond on April 28, 1865, as a corporal. Driver, *2nd Virginia Cavalry*, 235.

50. Improper hoof care combined with wet and/or dirty conditions could lead to debilitating diseases of the hoof, such as white line disease or thrush. For this reason, keeping horses in dry areas was essential to maintaining the cavalry. Longacre, *Lee's Cavalrymen*, 157.

51. Just one week later Union troops under General McDowell would advance across the Potomac and engage the Confederates at the Battle of First Manassas.

52. Col. Richard S. Ewell (February 8, 1817–January 25, 1872) was graduated from West Point in 1840 and served in the Confederate army under Gen. Thomas J. "Stonewall" Jackson and Gen. Robert E. Lee. He was a spirited but controversial leader who commanded troops in the battles of First Manassas, the Valley campaign, the Peninsula campaign, and Gettysburg, and he commanded Richmond's defenses for a time in 1865. Ezra J. Warner, *Generals in Gray: Lives of the Confederate Commanders* (Baton Rouge: Louisiana State Univ. Press, 1959), 84–85; Donald C. Pfanz, *Richard S. Ewell: A Soldier's Life* (Chapel Hill: Univ. of North Carolina Press, 1998).

53. Goose Creek runs through the northwestern and southeastern Bedford County. RWP apparently farmed land near this creek. Kenneth E. Crouch, "The Names of the Streams and Mountains in Bedford County, Virginia,""Geography: Rivers and Streams"research file, Bedford City/County Museum, Bedford, Va., 1–2.

54. The town is probably Centreville, Virginia.

55. This is the Battle of Blackburn's Ford, which occurred on July 18, 1861, and was an engagement of the First Bull Run campaign. Brig. Gen. Irvin McDowell was

leading his Union troops deeper into Virginia when he ordered a reconnaissance mission toward Blackburn's Ford. Confederate forces under Brig. Gen. James Longstreet repulsed the Federals. Total casualties: 151 (Union: 83; Confederate: 68). Boatner, *Civil War Dictionary*, 65; Long, *Day by Day*, 96.

56. Gen. Pierre Gustave Toutant Beauregard (May 28, 1818–February 21, 1893) was a well-known and controversial Confederate general. He graduated second in his class from West Point in 1838. He served under Winfield Scott in the Mexican-American War, and was commissioned brigadier general in the Confederate army on February 27, 1861. He was present at the battles at Fort Sumter, First Manassas, and Shiloh. Clashes with his superiors, including Gen. Joseph E. Johnston and President Jefferson Davis, rendered him unpopular for much of the war. He was eventually named second in command to Joseph E. Johnston in the Carolinas campaign. Boatner, *Civil War Dictionary*, 54–55; Current, *Encyclopedia* 1:146–50; T. Harry Williams, *P. G. T. Beauregard: Napoleon in Gray* (Baton Rouge: Louisiana State Univ. Press, 1995).

57. This was the Battle of First Manassas (also known as Bull Run). Fought on July 21, 1861, it was the first major battle of the Civil War. General McDowell led his troops from Washington to the Sudley Ford on Bull Run, where they met and engaged Confederate forces under Generals Johnston and Beauregard. The battle raged throughout the day until Confederate reinforcements arrived and routed the Federals. Confederates carried the day, but both sides realized the war would not be won quickly. Total forces: approx. 60,684 (Union: 28,452; Confederate: 32,232). Total casualties: 4,626 (Union: 2,645; Confederate: 1,981). Boatner, *Civil War Dictionary*, 99–101; Current, *Encyclopedia* 3:996–99.

58. Sgt. George Whitfield "Whit" Fuqua (ca. 1832–July 21, 1861), Company A, 2nd Va. Cav. He enlisted in Lynchburg on May 28, 1861, as a private. He was promoted to sergeant shortly before being killed at First Manassas. Driver, *2nd Virginia Cavalry*, 219.

59. Gen. Joseph E. Johnston (February 3, 1807–March 21, 1891) graduated from West Point and served in the Seminole Wars and Mexican-American War. Johnston had a troubled relationship with Confederate president Jefferson Davis, who continually shuffled Johnston among armies throughout the war. He assumed command of the Army of Tennessee in November 1863 but was replaced by Gen. John Bell Hood in July 1864. He capitulated to Gen. William T. Sherman on April 26, 1865. Warner, *Generals in Gray*, 161–62; Current, *Encyclopedia* 2:859–61.

60. Col. William Tecumseh Sherman (February 8, 1820–February 14, 1891) graduated from West Point in 1840. He accepted a commission as colonel in the Thirteenth U.S. Infantry on May 14, 1861. After distinguishing himself at First Manassas, he was promoted to brigadier general of volunteers. After recuperating in Ohio from a nervous breakdown, he was appointed major general on May 1, 1862. He commanded troops at several prominent battles in the Western Theater, including Shiloh and Vicksburg and undertook his infamous March to the Sea and Carolinas campaign in 1864 and 1865, respectively. Boatner, *Civil War Dictionary*, 750–51; Stanley P. Hirshson, *The White Tecumseh: A Biography of General William T. Sherman* (New York: J. Wiley, 1997).

61. Lt. Gen. Thomas J. "Stonewall" Jackson (January 21, 1824–May 10, 1863) was born into an impoverished family in Clarksburg, (West) Virginia. He graduated from West Point in 1846, served with distinction in the Mexican-American War, and taught natural philosophy and artillery tactics at the VMI in Lexington. After entering Confederate military service as a colonel, his effectiveness on the battlefield rapidly propelled him through the ranks. He won the nickname "Stonewall" for his steely resolve at First Manassas, while his brilliant 1862 Shenandoah Valley campaign derailed Federal plans to subdue Virginia. His own troops accidentally shot him on May 2, 1863; he died of pneumonia on May 10. Warner, *Generals in Gray*, 151–52; James I. Robertson Jr., *Stonewall Jackson: The Man, the Soldier, the Legend* (New York: Macmillan, 1997).

62. Jefferson Davis (June 3, 1807/8–December 5, 1889) was a Kentucky-born planter, soldier, and politician. He served as the Confederacy's first and only president from 1861 to 1865. Current, *Encyclopedia* 2:448–53; William C. Davis, *Jefferson Davis: The Man and His Hour* (New York: Harper Collins, 1991).

63. Pvt. Thomas J. Johnson (b. ca. 1831), Company F, 2nd Va. Cav., was a farmer. He enlisted at Davis Mills on May 28, 1861. He was sick with typhoid fever in a Liberty hospital on August 20, 1861, and absent sick again from August 23 through October 31, 1862. He was wounded at Brandy Station on June 9, 1863, and he was listed as present through June 1864. Driver, *2nd Virginia Cavalry*, 234.

64. Pvt. Tilghman D. Scott (August 3, 1834–April 16, 1905), Company F, 2nd Va. Cav. A farmer before the war, Scott enlisted on May 28, 1861, as a substitute for Lt. Alexander Walker, RWP's brother-in-law. Scott was captured in Loudoun County on March 1, 1862, and exchanged July 5, 1862. He had been conscripted on April 24, 1862, and was absent sick in September and October 1862. He was present through June 1864, with no further records to document his whereabouts after that date. Driver, *2nd Virginia Cavalry*, 268.

65. Isaac Olin Cundiff (June 10, 1830–July 20, 1924) was a civilian visiting friends and family, perhaps on an errand delivering news or goods, when he carried RWP's letter back to Bedford County. He enlisted in Company G, 2nd Va. Cav., on April 1, 1862. He was discharged for unknown reasons on June 20, 1862. Driver, *2nd Virginia Cavalry*, 209.

66. Missouri Rebecca Parker (November 14, 1852–September 18, 1894) was RWP's paternal cousin. She married James Sutherland on November 5, 1878, and bore him five children. Ackerly and Parker, "*Our Kin*," 657, 666–67.

67. Nannie Moorman Walker (September 16, 1852–November 9, 1926) was the youngest of Rebecca's siblings. She died unmarried but was "perhaps the most widely known and universally beloved member of the Bedford branch of Walkers." Ackerly and Parker, "*Our Kin*," 684, 691–92.

68. RWP is referring to Rebecca's pregnancy. She must have informed him in her last letter that they were expecting their first child.

69. 2nd Lt. Waddy Burton (August 2, 1840–April 14, 1914), Company F, 2nd Va. Cav., was a farmer when he enlisted as a fourth corporal on May 28, 1861. He was elected first lieutenant on April 24, 1862. He was court-martialed for violating

civilian property but present through August 1863. He was wounded in action at Raccoon Ford on October 11, 1863. He was promoted to captain on December 7, 1864, and was recorded as present through March 1865. Driver, *2nd Virginia Cavalry*, 202.

70. Pvt. Alfred L. Creasy (ca. 1840–June 14, 1865), Company F, 2ndVa. Cav. He was a farmer before enlisting at Davis Mills on May 28, 1861. He was absent sick July 28 through August 31, 1861, and December 18–31, 1861. After being captured at Kelly's Ford on March 17, 1863, he was sent to the Old Capitol until exchanged on March 29, 1863. He was detailed as wagoner for the Brigade Commissary on April 1, 1864, and transferred to Company G, Twenty-eighth Virginia Infantry, on April 9, 1864, for J. C. Morgan. After being captured at Burkesville on April 6, 1865, he was sent to Point Lookout and there died of disease. Driver, *2nd Virginia Cavalry*, 209.

71. Pvt. Clarence H. Payne (ca. 1843–October 28, 1923), Company F, 2ndVa. Cav. A farmer when he enlisted at Davis Mills on May 28, 1861, he was present until sick in a Liberty hospital in March and April 1863. He was then present until transferring to the Confederate States Navy (CSN) on April 21, 1864. He was captured on February 3, 1865, and held prisoner at Fort McHenry until released on May 2, 1865. Driver, *2nd Virginia Cavalry*, 258.

72. Pvt. Granderson Granville Leftwich (December 28, 1839–April 5, 1905), Company F, 2ndVa. Cav. A wheelwright before enlisting at Davis Mills on May 28, 1861, he was absent on sick leave September 20–December 31, 1861. He was detailed as wagoner upon losing his horse. He was captured at Gettysburg on July 6, 1863, and wounded at Front Royal on August 16, 1864. There are no further wartime records. Driver, *2nd Virginia Cavalry*, 240.

73. The Confederate cavalry had a reputation for aggression, fearlessness, and effectiveness that struck fear in the hearts of many Union soldiers. For more on Confederate cavalry, see Grady McWhiney and Perry D. Jamieson, *Attack and Die: Civil War Military Tactics and the Southern Heritage* (University: Univ. of Alabama Press, 1982), 126–40; Longacre, *Lee's Cavalrymen*.

74. Maj. Thomas Taylor Munford (March 29, 1831–February 27, 1918) graduated from VMI in 1852 and was a cotton planter before enlisting as a first lieutenant in Company G. He was appointed major when the regiment was organized. He was appointed lieutenant colonel on September 30, 1861, and elected colonel on April 24, 1862. He was wounded at Second Manassas on August 30, 1862. He was present until wounded at Turkey Ridge on June 2, 1864, and later promoted to brigadier general. Munford was an able commander who led troops at many engagements throughout the war. Driver, *2nd Virginia Cavalry*, 252–53.

75. Sgt. William Fountain Graves (September 26, 1832–July 3, 1923), Company F, 2ndVa. Cav. Graves enlisted at Davis Mills on May 28, 1861, and was elected second lieutenant on August 1, 1861. He was promoted to captain on September 17, 1861. He was absent on leave for two weeks in October 1861. He was reelected captain April 24, 1862. He was absent sick at home in September and October 1862, and again in March and April 1863. He was wounded in action

at Spotsylvania Court House on May 7, 1864, and at Nance's Shop on June 24, 1864. He commanded the regiment July and August 1864 but was hospitalized with dysentery from July through September 1864. He was promoted to major on December 7, 1864, and commanded the six hundred dismounted men of the brigade on March 28, 1865. He was promoted to lieutenant colonel on April 1, 1865. Driver, *2nd Virginia Cavalry,* 223.

76. Boredom was one of the worst aspects of camp life. Reading and writing letters was one of the most popular ways that literate soldiers could stave off the dullness of camp. Wiley, *Life of Johnny Reb,* 192–216; Linderman, *Embattled Courage,* 118.

77. This is probably Pvt. Jesse L. Board (b. ca. 1837), Company F, 2nd Va. Cav. He enlisted at Davis Mills on May 28, 1861. His horse died September 1, 1861, and he was absent on sick leave September 15–October 31, 1861. He was absent sick again September through October 1862. His horse was killed at Raccoon Ford on October 11, 1863, and he was wounded at Todd's Tavern on May 8, 1864. He transferred to Company B, Twenty-eighth Virginia Infantry, on February 7, 1865. He was a resident of Bedford County as of 1882. Driver, *2nd Virginia Cavalry,* 197.

78. Pvt. Thomas W. Bernard, Company F, 2nd Va. Cav. He enlisted at Fairfax Court House on June 27, 1861 and was present through December 1861. He was absent without leave in March and April 1862. He was absent sick September and October 1862 and listed absent without leave since July 1862 on later rolls. He was dropped as a deserter April 30, 1864. Driver, *2nd Virginia Cavalry,* 195.

79. Pvt. Thomas T. Nichols (ca. 1825–September 19, 1861), Company F, 2nd Va. Cav. A blacksmith before he enlisted at Davis Mills on May 28, 1861, Nichols died at Fairfax Court House on September 19, 1861. Driver, *2nd Virginia Cavalry,* 254.

80. Civilians from surrounding areas had gathered to watch the Battle of First Manassas. It is reported that many of them were dressed in their Sunday finery, and some even brought picnic lunches. Civilian buggies and wagons mingled with the flood of retreating Union troops as they fled from the victorious Confederates. This debacle showed both soldiers and civilians the brutality of war and that the Confederacy would not be easily defeated. Alan Hankinson, *First Bull Run 1861: The South's First Victory* (Westport, Conn.: Praeger, 2004).

81. John M. Goggin was RWP's maternal uncle. He married Sarah J. Carney on November 14, 1849. He apparently enlisted in the CSA in early 1862; he may be the "J. M. Goggin" who enlisted in Company A, Thirty-sixth Virginia Infantry. Ackerly and Parker, "Our Kin," 671; Janet B. Hewett, ed., *Virginia Confederate Soldiers, 1861–1865,* vol. 1, *A–K* (Wilmington, N.C.: Broadfoot, 1998), 354.

82. This is probably Lucy Frances Walker (b. August 14, 1846), Rebecca Walker Parker's younger sister and RWP's sister-in-law. She married Rice McGhee on February 26, 1869, and bore him eleven children. Ackerly and Parker, "Our Kin," 684, 689–90.

83. Charles Pleasant Walker (September 9, 1844–October 26, 1924), Rebecca's younger brother and RWP's brother-in-law. He married Octavia Wells and had seven children. Ackerly and Parker, "Our Kin," 684, 686–89.

84. Prince Napoleon Joseph Charles Paul Bonaparte of France met with President Lincoln in August 1861. He also met with Generals Beauregard and Johnson and visited the Manassas battlefield. Long, *Day by Day*, 104–5; *Harper's Weekly*, Aug. 24, 1861, 531.

85. Despite the Confederate government's high hopes and desperate attempts, neither France nor any other nation recognized the CSA as an independent nation. For more on the role of European diplomacy, see Norman A. Graebner, "Northern Diplomacy and European Neutrality," in *Why the North Won the Civil War: Six Authoritative Views on the Economic, Military, Diplomatic, Social, and Political Reasons Behind the Confederacy's Defeat*, ed. David Herbert Donald (Baton Rouge: Louisiana State Univ. Press, 1960), 58–80.

86. Cpl. John M. Garrett (b. ca. 1838), Company F, 2nd Va. Cav. He was a farmer before enlisting at Davis Mills on May 28, 1861. Garrett was reduced from third to fourth corporal in 1862, following being wounded at Second Manassas. There is no further record of his military service beyond June 1864. Driver, *2nd Virginia Cavalry*, 220.

87. This is probably Pvt. James E. Franklin (b. ca. 1833), Company F, 2nd Va. Cav. He enlisted at Davis Mills on May 28, 1861. He was absent on sick leave November 4–December 31, 1861, and later died at a hospital, although the particulars are unknown. Driver, *2nd Virginia Cavalry*, 219.

88. There were seven men with the last name Morgan in Company F and six more in the other companies of the Second Virginia. For biographical information on these men, see Driver, *2nd Virginia Cavalry*, 251.

89. Inflation of Confederate currency had already begun in 1861, although most Confederates would not begin to notice the effects until early 1862. By March 1865 one gold coin was worth sixty Confederate Treasury notes. Current, *Encyclopedia of the Confederacy* 2:820–21.

90. Clem may have been one of the seventeen slaves owned by Ammon Parker in 1860. It appears that she later served as nurse for the Parkers' children. Bureau of the Census, *Slave Schedules of the Eighth Census of the United States*, 1860, for Bedford County, Virginia.

91. Job may be the name of a slave belonging to Ammon Parker, as RWP was not recorded as owning any slaves on the 1860 slave census. Job may have lived with Robert and Rebecca Parker and helped them farm their land. Bureau of the Census, *Slave Schedules of the Eighth Census of the United States*, 1860, for Bedford County, Virginia.

92. Nancy Moorman Jopling Walker (b. 1814) was Rebecca Walker Parker's mother and RWP's mother-in-law. She was the second wife of Dr. James Alexander Walker. Ackerly and Parker, "*Our Kin*," 684, 696.

93. William P. Fields (1843–1914), Company F, 2nd Va. Cav. Fields would later enlist as a private and wagoner at Centreville on October 29, 1861. He was hospitalized in Charlottesville with acute dysentery from July 10 to August 2, 1862. He recovered and was wounded at Spotsylvania Court House on May 18, 1864. He was listed as absent through June 1864 and present in April 1865. Driver, *2nd Virginia Cavalry*, 217.

94. After Thaddeus Lowe demonstrated how balloons could be used for reconnaissance, Abraham Lincoln established the Balloon Corps under the Bureau of Topographical Engineers in the summer of 1861. The first military balloon, the *Union,* was ready to float above Washington, D.C., by August 28, 1861. Other balloons were eventually produced for the war effort, but none were ready at the time RWP witnessed a balloon in the Washington vicinity. Charles M. Evans, *The War of the Aeronauts: A History of Ballooning during the Civil War* (Mechanicsburg, Pa.: Stackpole Books, 2002).

95. This statement indicates that Rebecca expressed some concern about appearing pregnant before her extended family and friends. Many white women in the nineteenth-century South alluded to their pregnancies only in veiled references. Sally G. McMillen, *Motherhood in the Old South: Pregnancy, Childbirth, and Infant Rearing* (Baton Rouge: Louisiana State Univ. Press, 1990), 31, 33–34.

96. These are probably knee-high leather boots that had a flap that extended over the knee and protruded on the sides, so they could be tied behind the knee. Robin Smith and Ron Field, *Uniforms of the Civil War: An Illustrated Guide for Historians, Collectors, and Reenactors* (Guilford, Conn.: Lyon's Press, 2005), 61.

97. Eastern arborvitae, or the northern white cedar (*Thuja occidentalist*), is an evergreen shrub that is cultivated ornamentally. *Reader's Digest North American Wildlife: Trees and Nonflowering Plants* (New York: Reader's Digest, 1998), 35.

98. Pvt. Thomas T. Martin Jr. (September 16, 1830–June 2, 1898), Company F, 2nd Va. Cav. He was a farmer before the war and enlisted at Davis Mills on May 28, 1861. He was absent on sick leave September 6–October 31, 1861. He was wounded in the arm at an unknown place and date. He was hospitalized in Richmond December 2, 1862, transferred to a Farmville hospital on December 21, and granted a thirty-day furlough on December 31. He was sick in a Liberty hospital April 21, 1863, sick in a Richmond hospital May 28, 1863, and absent sick through August 31, 1863. He was present through June 1864; beyond that date there are no further military records. Pvt. Lewis C. Martin (b. ca. 1842), Company F, 2nd Va. Cav., was also a farmer before enlisting at Davis Mills on May 28, 1861. He was absent on sick leave September 6–December 31, 1861. He died in a Bedford County hospital in 1862 or 1863. Driver, *2nd Virginia Cavalry,* 244.

99. The only Sam Nichols on the 2nd Va. Cav. roster is Pvt. Samuel W. Nichols (b. ca. 1832), who was transferred to Company F, 2nd Va. Cav., on August 15, 1863. As this letter predates his enlistment, it is uncertain to whom RWP was referring. Driver, *2nd Virginia Cavalry,* 254.

100. "Duck" was RWP's nickname for Rebecca. Pet names symbolized an exclusive circle of sender and receiver and was a means of affirming a couple's intimacy. Lystra, *Searching the Heart,* 20.

101. At this time Rebecca was approximately seven months pregnant with their first child.

102. Pvt. Lilborne H. Johnson (January 29, 1842–May 7, 1864), Company F, 2nd Va. Cav., a farmer when he enlisted at Davis Mills on May 28, 1861. He was

absent on sick leave October 17–31, 1861, and present on intermittent records until listed as killed in action at Todd's Tavern. Driver, *2nd Virginia Cavalry*, 234.

103. Many cavalrymen held the infantry in contempt or at least believed they were inferior because they marched on foot and personally carried their equipment. Infantrymen were often just as resentful of cavalrymen. Longacre, *Lee's Cavalrymen*, 27.

104. The Confederate victory at First Manassas made many Northerners realize that Washington was vulnerable to potential attacks. Maj. John G. Barnard of the Corps of Engineers was given the task of extending fortifications around the capitol. By 1865 an extensive system of forts and trenches served as protection. B. Franklin Cooling III, "Civil War Deterrent: Defenses of Washington," *Military Affairs* 29, no. 4 (Winter 1965–66): 164–78.

105. Gen. Robert E. Lee (January 19, 1807–October 13, 1870) finished second in the 1829 class at West Point. After serving in the Mexican-American War and on the Texas frontier, he became a full general in the Confederate army in August 1861. He commanded the Army of Northern Virginia after Johnson was wounded in May 1862 and remained in command for the duration of the war. He presided over such well-known battles as the Peninsula and Pennsylvanian campaigns, Cold Harbor, and the siege of Petersburg before surrendering to Gen. Ulysses S. Grant at Appomattox Court House on April 9, 1865. After the war Lee served as president of Washington College in Lexington, Virginia, and as the legendary symbol of the Lost Cause. Current, *Encyclopedia* 3:916–20; Emory M. Thomas, *Robert E. Lee: A Biography* (New York: W. W. Norton, 1997).

106. This probably refers to the Cheat Mountain campaign, September 11–13, 1861. General Lee planned to attack Gen. J. J. Reynolds's forces at Cheat Mountain Summit and Elkwater. A lack of coordination and unfavorable weather foiled Lee's carefully laid plans. Although casualties were light, the campaign thwarted Confederate hopes of regaining western Virginia and soiled Lee's reputation. RWP is therefore mistaken in viewing it as a Confederate victory. Long, *Day by Day*, 117–18.

107. 1st Lt. William Alexander Parker (March 1, 1840–March 1, 1864), Company D, 2nd Va. Cav., was RWP's paternal cousin. He enlisted in Franklin County on May 20, 1861. He was wounded in action at Second Manassas on August 30, 1862, and Kelly's Ford on March 17, 1863. He was killed in action near Stanardsville. Driver, *2nd Virginia Cavalry*, 257.

108. Sgt. James Chalmers (September 21, 1829–October 1, 1861), Company B, 2nd Va. Cav. He attended the University of North Carolina and University of Virginia and worked as a lawyer and a tobacconist. He enlisted in Lynchburg on May 13, 1861, and was mortally wounded near Annandale on September 29, 1861. Driver, *2nd Virginia Cavalry*, 205.

109. The preceding comments refer to Rebecca's pregnancy. She probably requested RWP to return home when their baby was due but was reluctant to ask family or friends for advice concerning childbirth. For more on pregnancy during the Civil War, see McMillen, *Motherhood in the Old South*, 57–110.

110. 2nd Lt. William Radford Beale (March 12, 1838–February 2, 1917), 2nd Va. Cav. He attended the University of Virginia before enlisting at Forest Depot on May 28, 1861. His horse died at Flint Hill on September 15, 1861. He served as regimental commissary officer October 14–31, 1861, and was absent sick at home November and December 1861. He was not reelected, and there are no military records beyond April 25, 1862. Driver, *2nd Virginia Cavalry*, 195.

111. Written passes were required for a person or group to travel through military lines. Garrison and Garrison, *Encyclopedia*, 187.

112. Pvt. Samuel L. Murrill (August 5, 1836–October 15, 1883), Company F, 2nd Va. Cav. He enlisted at Davis Mills on May 28, 1861. He was absent detailed with quartermaster November 4–December 31, 1861. He was promoted to third sergeant and absent sick September–October 1862. His horse was killed at Bull Run on October 15, 1863, and he was wounded at Spotsylvania Court House on May 8, 864. He was absent wounded through June 1864. There are no military records beyond his being paid on December 23, 1864. Driver, *2nd Virginia Cavalry*, 253.

113. The Battle of Leesburg (also known as Ball's Bluff, Harrison's Landing, or Conrad's Ferry). Union troops poured across the Potomac River, but Confederate forces pinned them with their backs to Ball's Bluff. Many Union troops drowned trying to flee across the river; hundreds were taken prisoner. This Confederate victory prevented Union troops from capturing Leesburg and devastated Northern morale. Total forces: 3,400 (Union: 1,700; Confederate: 1,700). Total casualties: 1,076 (Union: 921; Confederate: 155). Long, *Day by Day*, 129–30.

114. Sallie Fannie Parker (b. May 3, 1844) was RWP's paternal cousin. She eventually married Moses Peter Rucker, who served as a corporal in the 2nd Va. Cav., Company F, on February 14, 1866, and bore him three children. Ackerly and Parker, *"Our Kin,"* 660.

115. This refers to the biblical long-suffering Job. According to the Book of Job, God allowed Satan to torment Job to test his righteousness. Despite losing his family, riches, and health, Job remained devoted to God and Satan lost the wager.

116. Robert Moorman Parker, the first child of Robert and Rebecca Parker, was born on November 4, 1861. He grew up at his grandfather's home, Lone Aspen, and worked in the town of Liberty. He married Sallie Viola Wappett in Wytheville, Virginia, on May 8, 1888, and had five children. He moved to Roanoke to work for the Norfolk and Western Railway and died November 11, 1902. Ackerly and Parker, *"Our Kin,"* 651–52.

117. It appears that Rebecca went to the home of her father, who was a doctor, to give birth to their son.

118. "Press master" is shorthand for "impressment officer" or "impressment agent." These officers were responsible for confiscating goods and slaves for Confederate government use. Current, *Encyclopedia* 2:809–10.

119. Sam is probably a slave belonging to RWP's father, Ammon Parker, who owned 17 slaves in 1860. The Confederate government impressed a range of materials required to sustain the war effort, from cotton to slaves. Bureau of the Census,

Slave Schedules of the Eighth Census of the United States, 1860, for Bedford County, Virginia; Thomas, *Confederacy as a Revolutionary Experience*, 65–66; Mitchell, *Civil War Soldiers*, 162–64.

120. RWP is mistaken: a General Butler was not present at this engagement.

121. Col. Edward Baker (1811–1861). Born in England, Baker served as a U.S. congressman and senator before being commissioned colonel of the Seventy-first Pennsylvania Infantry in May 1861. He was mortally wounded at the Battle of Leesburg on October 21, 1861, without having accepted the offer of major general. Boatner, *Civil War Dictionary*, 39.

122. "Temptations" include drinking, gambling, swearing, and breaking the Sabbath. The monotony of camp life and the stress of war induced many enlisted men to take up one or more of these vices. Most civilians and soldiers cautioned against indulging in such activities for moral and religious reasons, as well as to help the army gain God's favor. Robertson, *Soldiers Blue and Gray*, 64–74; Wiley, *Life of Johnny Reb*, 36–58.

123. Matthew 7:16.

124. Matthew 13:45.

125. There was indeed a scuffle at Falls Church on November 18. Long, *Day by Day*, 141.

126. Although there had not been a large-scale battle in Kentucky for some time, there was a skirmish at Cypress Bridge, near Rumsey in McLean County, Kentucky. Long, *Day by Day*, 140–41.

127. This refers to a diplomatic dispute between the United States and Great Britain known as the Mason and Slidell (or Trent) Affair. On November 8, 1861, Union captain Charles Wilkes removed Confederate commissioner to Britain James Mason and commissioner to France John Slidell from the British steamer *Trent* and took them to Boston. This was against naval warfare policy because Wilkes did not apprehend the *Trent* and forcibly removed the two Confederates. Britain's indignation over the search and seizure nearly erupted in warfare with the United States. Only rapid diplomacy and the release of the prisoners in January 1862 ended the dispute. Current, *Encyclopedia* 4:1619–21.

128. The "sickness" RWP refers to was probably Rebecca's recovery from childbirth. For more on the difficulties of childbirth and raising children during the war, see Rable, *Civil Wars*, 61–62.

129. Although it is unclear what medication RWP was administered to treat his dysentery, Civil War physicians used a variety of (usually ineffective) medications to treat digestive diseases. Current, *Encyclopedia* 2:754–58; Bollett, *Civil War Medicine*, 235, 238.

130. Pvt. Alexander McDaniel Whitten (b. ca. 1826), Companies G and F, 2nd Va. Cav. He was a teacher before he enlisted in Company G at Forest Depot on May 28, 1861. He was wounded at Lewisville and captured at Dranesville on November 21, 1861, then sent to the Old Capitol. He remained there until exchanged on February 14, 1862. He reenlisted for two years or the duration of the war at Oak Shade on April 25, 1862. He was elected third lieutenant of Company F

on May 13, 1862. He was captured at Woodstock June 2, 1862, exchanged on August 5, 1862, and absent sick in a Charlottesville hospital January 30–31, 1863. He was promoted to second lieutenant on May 8, 1863. In February 1865 he was detailed to arrest deserters and never reported back. No further record exists to document his whereabouts. Driver, *2nd Virginia Cavalry*, 285.

131. This was probably a soldier of German descent. Germans called their nation "Deutschland" and themselves "Deutschmen," which many Americans misconstrued to mean they were Dutch.

132. Pvt. Benjamin Bowles Fuqua (May 18, 1822–October 9, 1864), Company F, 2nd Va. Cav., worked as a farmer before enlisting at Davis Mills on May 28, 1861. He was absent on leave December 14–31, 1861, and discharged for overage. He reenlisted at Fredericksburg August 18, 1863, but was killed in action at Tom's Brook in the Shenandoah Valley campaign. Driver, *2nd Virginia Cavalry*, 219.

133. Sgt. John P. Graves (December 3, 1834–March 13, 1907), Company F of the 2nd Va. Cav., was a farmer before he enlisted at Davis Mills on May 28, 1861. He was reduced to a private in late 1861 and was absent on sick leave December 6–31, 1861. No further record exists for Graves after he was detailed in the Ambulance Corps in May and June 1864. Driver, *2nd Virginia Cavalry*, 223.

134. Brig. Gen. Daniel Harvey Hill (July 12, 1821–September 24, 1889) graduated from West Point in 1842, served in the Mexican-American War, and was a mathematics professor at Washington College in Lexington, Virginia. Hill was elected colonel on May 11, 1861, and promoted to brigadier general on July 10, 1861, and later to lieutenant general. He led troops in numerous battles, including the Peninsula campaign and Antietam. In December 1861 he replaced Gen. Nathan "Shanks" Evans as commander of Confederate forces in Loudoun County. He surrendered with General Johnston in North Carolina in 1865. Current, *Encyclopedia* 2:775–76; Leonard Hall Bridges, *Lee's Maverick General: Daniel Harvey Hill* (Lincoln: Univ. of Nebraska Press, 1991).

1862

1. Longacre, *Lee's Cavalrymen*, 51, 66, 72–73, 83, 95, 124–27, 137, 158; Driver, *2nd Virginia Cavalry*, 34–67.

2. Although RWP probably wrote these comments in a humorous vein, they reveal martial tensions created by the war. Affection and intimacy were frequently strained by the long absences of husbands. Rable, *Civil Wars*, 59–61.

3. William J. Walker was the third son of Dr. James A. Walker and Rebecca Walker Parker's half-brother. He enlisted as a private in Company A, 58th Virginia Infantry at Bunker Hill on July 25, 1861. He was present until recorded as dead on January 2, 1862. Ackerly and Parker, *"Our Kin,"* 684; Driver, *58th Virginia Infantry*, 142.

4. On December 20, 1861, General Stuart led Confederates, including Captain Pitzer and fifty men from Company C of the 2nd Va. Cav., on a foraging expedition near Dranesville. They discovered a detachment of Union troops and skir-

mished as they attempted to withdraw their supply wagons to safety. Colonel Munford listed his regiment's casualties at one killed, none wounded, and three prisoners. Driver, *2nd Virginia Cavalry*, 31–32, 178.

5. On January 1, 1862, General Jackson led his Confederate troops north from Winchester in the Romney campaign. They moved toward the town of Romney, intent on destroying railroads, dams, and Union troops. On January 10 Federal troops evacuated Romney in the face of Jackson's advance. Long, *Day by Day*, 156–58; Robertson, *Stonewall Jackson*, 303–40.

6. This was the Battle of Hancock, part of Gen. Jackson's Romney campaign. Jackson's troops reached the Potomac River opposite the Union-controlled town of Hancock, Maryland, on January 5, 1862. After firing on the town for two days in an unsuccessful attempt to force a Union surrender or find a safe river crossing, Jackson withdrew and marched on Romney. Robertson, *Stonewall Jackson*, 308–9; Long, *Day by Day*, 157.

7. Many slaves took advantage of wartime disruptions and the proximity of Federal troops to run away from slaveholders. For more on slaves in the Civil War, see Ira Berlin, Barbara J. Fields, Steven F. Miller, Joseph P. Reidy, and Leslie S. Rowland, eds., *Free at Last: A Documentary History of Slavery, Freedom, and the Civil War* (New York: New Press, 1992).

8. Gen. Felix Zollicoffer was camped on the north side of the Cumberland River in Kentucky in January 1862. Cut off from other Confederate forces and facing a large force of advancing Federal troops, Zollicoffer decided to attack Union troops at their Mill Springs, Kentucky, encampment on January 19. This desperate and disastrous affair ended when Zollicoffer mistakenly rode into Federal lines and was killed. Known as the Battle of Mill Springs or Logan's Cross Roads, this skirmish opened the first gap in the Confederate Kentucky defense line and foreshadowed the rest of the war in the West. Total casualties: 794 (Union: 261; Confederate: 533). Long, *Day by Day*, 162.

9. Maj. Gen. George B. McClellan (December 3, 1826–October 29, 1885) graduated second in his 1842 class at West Point. He served with distinction in the Mexican-American War and was appointed major general of Ohio volunteers at the outbreak of the Civil War. He quickly rose through the ranks and was eventually appointed supreme commander over all Union armies. McClellan was a brilliant administrator and trainer of men but an appallingly bad commander. His poor performance in the Peninsula campaign of 1862 and at Second Manassas led to his demotion and gradual removal from command. Boatner, *Civil War Dictionary*, 524; Stephen W. Sears, *George B. McClellan: The Young Napoleon* (New York: Da Capo Press, 1999).

10. Expecting a swift victory, many Confederate soldiers initially enlisted for one year's service. To maintain the army, the Confederate Provisional Congress passed the first Conscription Act on April 16, 1862. This act promised fifty dollars and up to sixty days' furlough to privates, musicians, and noncommissioned officers who reenlisted for three more years or the duration of the war. It also allowed them the privilege of reorganizing and electing their officers. Current, *Encyclopedia* 1:396–97; Robertson, *Soldiers Blue and Gray*, 37–40.

11. The Battle of Roanoke Island, North Carolina, was an important Federal victory that helped tighten the blockade and provided a vital base for operations against the Confederacy. On February 7 Maj. Gen. Ambrose E. Burnside landed seventy-five hundred Union troops on the island. On February 8 Union troops attacked and overwhelmed Gen. Henry A. Wise's twenty-five hundred Confederate soldiers, under the command of Col. H. M. Shaw. Total casualties: 2,800 (Union: 264; Confederate: 2,500). Long, *Day by Day*, 167–69.

12. Fort Henry was an earthen Confederate fort located in western Tennessee on the Tennessee River. General Grant selected Forts Henry and Donelson as targets because of their strategic importance along major water transportation routes. On February 4–5 Grant landed troops on the banks of the Tennessee River just north of the fort. Outnumbered, outgunned, and facing floodwaters, Brig. Gen. Lloyd Tilghman moved most of his Confederate garrison to Fort Donelson. After a brief gunboat engagement, Tilghman surrendered the remainder of his force on February 6, 1862. Current, *Encyclopedia* 2:764–77; Benjamin Franklin Cooling, *Forts Henry and Donelson: The Key to the Confederate Heartland* (Nashville: Univ. of Tennessee Press, 2003).

13. The Union's effective blockade meant that coffee, sugar, salt and tea quickly became rarities in the South once the war began. Manpower shortages and transportation difficulties eventually affected the availability of meat, butter, and grain, and may have contributed to Confederate morale loss. Blair, *Virginia's Private War*, 6, 33, 39, 55; Mary Elizabeth Massey, *Ersatz in the Confederacy: Shortages and Substitutes on the Southern Homefront* (1952; reprint, Columbia: Univ. of South Carolina Press, 1993).

14. Maj. Gen. Sterling "Old Pap" Price (1809–1867) was born to wealthy slaveholders in Virginia, moved to Missouri in 1830, and became a U.S. congressman in 1844. He served as brigadier general in the Mexican-American War and later as governor of Missouri before offering his services as a military commander to Missouri's secessionist governor. He led troops against Union forces through 1861 and 1862, when he and his men officially joined the Confederate army. Military defeats throughout the rest of the war forced him to retreat as far as Texas. Rather than surrender, he fled to Mexico and founded a colony of former Confederates before returning to Missouri in 1867, where he died soon thereafter. Albert Castel, *General Sterling Price and the Civil War in the West* (1968; reprint, Baton Rouge: Louisiana State Univ. Press, 1993); Current, *Encyclopedia* 3:1251–52.

15. This was untrue. Brig. Gen. Samuel Ryan Curtis led his army of twelve thousand Federals against General Price's Confederate force of seven thousand in Springfield. Price evacuated the city on February 12, 1862, and fled to Cross Hollows, Arkansas, constantly skirmishing along the way. Castel, *General Sterling Price*, 65.

16. General Grant estimated the actual number of Confederate prisoners from Fort Donelson at twelve to fifteen thousand. Grant had pursued Confederates from Fort Henry to Fort Donelson in early February. The Confederates surrendered on February 16, 1862, after failing to break through Grant's lines. This first major Union victory kept Kentucky in the Union, opened Tennessee to Union

advances, and made Grant famous. Total casualties: 17,398 (Union: 2,832; Confederate: 1,500). Long, *Day by Day*, 171–72; Cooling, *Forts Henry and Donelson*.

17. As the capitol of Tennessee and a vital base, Nashville was a prime Union target. After General Grant's victories at Forts Henry and Donelson, Union general Don Carlos Buell was able to capture and occupy Nashville without bloodshed on February 25, 1862. Long, *Day by Day*, 175.

18. This was not true. Federal troops threatened the mouth of the Savannah River and jeopardized local defensives. Its nearest fort, Fort Pulaski, finally surrendered on April 11, 1862. Current, *Encyclopedia* 3:1367.

19. Maj. Gen. James Ewell Brown "Jeb" Stuart (February 6, 1833–May 12, 1864) was an effective and charismatic cavalry leader. He graduated from West Point in 1854 and he served in "Bleeding Kansas" during the 1850s border war. In 1861 he resigned his U.S. commission and secured a Confederate commission as colonel of cavalry. He was promoted to brigadier general on September 24, 1861, and later to major general. He orchestrated a number of brilliant cavalry maneuvers and participated in such large-scale battles as the Seven Days' and Chancellorsville. He was mortally wounded on May 11, 1864, at Yellow Tavern, Virginia, and died the next day. Current, *Encyclopedia* 4:1551–54; Warner, *Generals in Gray*, 296–97.

20. This is either Mary A. Toler Parker or Mary Goggin Parker, who were David Parker's first and second wives, respectively. Ackerly and Parker, *"Our Kin,"* 650.

21. Auville R. Goggin was RWP's maternal uncle. He married Emma Catherine Gray on February 15, 1849. It is unknown what unit he served under. Ackerly and Parker, *"Our Kin,"* 671; Hewett, *Virginia Confederate Soldiers* 1:354.

22. This was the First Battle of Winchester, fought May 25, 1862, as part of General Jackson's Shenandoah Valley campaign. Gen. Nathaniel P. Banks attempted to halt Jackson's Confederate assault at Winchester. Jackson's relentless pursuit and General Ewell's timely arrival pushed Union troops north from Winchester and eventually across the Potomac River, thus preventing the Union from converging on Richmond. Total troops: 24,000 (Union: 8,000; Confederate: 16,000 Confederate). Total casualties: 2,419 (Union: 2,019; Confederate: 400). Long, *Day by Day*, 216; Robertson, *Stonewall Jackson*, 399–412.

23. General Banks lost so many wagons, supplies, and munitions to Confederate forces that Southerners nicknamed him "Commissary Banks." Garrison and Garrison, *Encyclopedia*, 53.

24. Gen. Nathaniel Prentiss Banks (January 30, 1816–September 1, 1894) served as a member of Congress 1853–57 and as governor of Massachusetts 1858–61. President Lincoln mustered him into service as a major general of volunteers on May 16, 1861, and he commanded troops in the Eastern and Western Theaters. His unsuccessful Red River campaign led to his resignation in 1864. Boatner, *Civil War Dictionary*, 42; James G. Hollandsworth, *Pretense of Glory: The Life of General Nathaniel P. Banks* (Baton Rouge: Louisiana State Univ. Press, 2005), 3, 262.

25. This is a conjecture based on RWP's comments in following letters.

26. RWP was actually writing from Rockbridge County, not Rockingham County.

27. The "Bridge" is Natural Bridge, a 215-foot-high natural stone bridge in Rockbridge County, Virginia. *Encyclopedia Britannica,* 11th ed., s.v. "Natural Bridge."

28. On June 17 General Jackson's forces left the Shenandoah Valley for the Peninsula to aid General Lee in his clashes with General McClellan. They would arrive in approximately one week—in time for the Seven Days' campaign. Long, *Day by Day,* 227, 230.

29. RWP is referring to the Seven Days' Battles, which were fought from June 25 to July 1, 1862, and ended the Peninsula campaign. The individual battles are as follows: Oak Grove, Mechanicsville, Gaines's Mill, Garnett's and Golding's Farms, Savage's Station, Allen's Farm, White Oak Swamp, and Malvern Hill. Confederate forces repelled the Federals, crushing Northern morale and reinvigorating sagging Southern spirits. Total casualties: 36,000 (Union: 16,000; Confederate: 20,000). Boatner, *Civil War Dictionary,* 731–32; Long, *Day by Day,* 235.

30. Maj. Roberdeau C. Wheat (April 9, 1826–June 27, 1862) served in the Mexican-American War and practiced law in New Orleans before enlisting in Confederate service. An experienced and inspiring leader, he was killed while commanding the Louisiana Brigade in the Battle of Gaines's Mill. Douglas Southall Freeman, *Lee's Lieutenants: A Study in Command,* vol. 1 (New York: Charles Scribner's Sons, 1944), 87–88, 521–23.

31. Col. Isaac G. Seymour was acting head of the Louisiana Brigade in the Battle of Gaines's Mill, where he was killed in action. Freeman, *Lee's Lieutenants,* 517, 525, 536.

32. If RWP heard cannon on Friday night, he was listening to the Battle of Gaines's Mill (or First Cold Harbor), which occurred June 27, 1862. Cannonading could be heard at great distances, thanks to a phenomenon known as an "acoustic shadow." Long, *Day by Day,* 231–32; Charles D. Ross, *Civil War Acoustic Shadows* (Shippensburg, Pa.: White Mane Books, 2001).

33. This could be 1st Sgt. James Malcolm Jones (ca. 1828–ca. 1900) or 1st Sgt. James Monroe Jones (ca. 1837–December 10, 1917), both of Company F. James Malcolm Jones was a farmer before enlisting as a private at Davis Mills on May 28, 1861. He was promoted to first sergeant before being absent sick in September and October 1862. He was captured at Spotsylvania Court House on May 4, 1864, and sent to Point Lookout before being transferred. He was released June 21, 1865. There is little information on James Monroe Jones, who was simply listed on the postwar roster. Driver, *2nd Virginia Cavalry,* 235.

34. RWP is mistaken; by this date, the Peninsula campaign was over and both armies were resting. General McClellan's attempt to circumvent the Army of Northern Virginia and capture the Confederate capitol of Richmond via an amphibious route ended on July 1, 1862, with the Battle of Malvern Hill. By July 1 McClellan had retreated to Harrison's Landing and established his headquarters at Berkeley Plantation on the James River. Current, *Encyclopedia* 3:1191–94; Long, *Day by Day,* 235.

35. Capt. Thomas Bowker Holland (July 8, 1840–June 15, 1864), Company D, 2nd Va. Cav., enlisted in Franklin County on May 20, 1861, as a second corporal. He was

promoted to first corporal on September 13, 1861, and elected captain April 24, 1862. RWP may have been mistaken, as military records do not indicate that Holland was injured in battle at any point in 1862. He is recorded as wounded at Kelly's Ford on March 17, 1863, and listed as hospitalized in a Gordonsville hospital on March 25. He was absent wounded through April 1863 and was wounded again at Meadow Bridge on May 12, 1864. He died of his wounds in a Richmond hospital on June 15, 1864. Driver, *2nd Virginia Cavalry*, 230.

36. The Battle of Seven Pines (or Fair Oaks) took place May 31–June 1, 1862, as part of the Peninsula campaign. Just a few miles east of Richmond, Gen. Joseph E. Johnston attacked two corps of Union troops that had become separated from the rest of McClellan's forces. Johnston was wounded on the first day of battle, but overall neither side could claim victory. Total forces: 83,613 (Union: 41,797; Confederate: 41,816). Boatner, *Civil War Dictionary*, 272–73.

37. Union Gen. George Archibald McCall (1802–1868) graduated from West Point in 1822 and served in the Seminole Wars and Mexican-American War before being appointed brigadier general in 1861. He led troops in several battles during the Peninsula campaign but was captured at the Battle of New Market Cross Roads on June 30, 1862, and held prisoner in Richmond's infamous Libby Prison. Boatner, *Civil War Dictionary*, 522–23.

38. Union forces did indeed destroy a railroad bridge at Rapidan Station on July 13, 1862. They were probably part of Gen. John Pope's forces, which made a reconnaissance to Culpeper, Orange, and Madison Court Houses from July 12 to 17, 1862. Long, *Day by Day*, 239.

39. On July 13, 1862, General Lee ordered General Jackson's command to Gordonsville to oppose approaching Union forces. Long, *Day by Day*, 239.

40. Pvt. Josiah Martin, Company F, 2nd Va. Cav., enlisted in April 1862. Military records indicate he was present through October but died of unknown causes in Albemarle County in December 1862. Driver, *2nd Virginia Cavalry*, 244.

41. RWP is referring to the Battle of Cedar Mountain (or Slaughter Mountain), which occurred August 9, 1862. General Jackson led his men from Orange Court House to engage General Pope's men under General Banks at Cedar Mountain. The Federals were winning the battle until Confederates were reinforced and successfully counterattacked. Total forces: 24,800 (Union: 8,000; Confederate: 16,800). Total casualties: 3,722 (Union: 2,381; Confederate: 1,341). Current, *Encyclopedia* 1:272–73; Long, *Day by Day*, 249–50.

42. Gen. Charles Sidney Winder (October 18, 1829–August 9, 1862) graduated from West Point in 1850. He resigned his commission to accept an appointment as major in the Confederate army to date from March 16, 1861. He commanded forces in the Valley and Peninsula campaigns before being killed by artillery at the Battle of Cedar Mountain (or Slaughter Mountain). Warner, *Generals in Gray*, 339–40.

43. On August 13 the Army of Northern Virginia had begun moving from the Peninsula toward Gordonsville in an effort to defeat General Pope before he could unite with General McClellan. These were the first movements in what would become the Second Manassas campaign. John J. Hennessy, *Return to Bull Run:*

The Campaign and Battle of Second Manassas (Norman: Univ. of Oklahoma Press, 1999), 30–33.

44. This was somewhat true. In early August 1862 the Union armies of General Pope and General McClellan had Lee's men sandwiched in central Virginia. President Lincoln urged a dual attack, but McClellan was (typically) slow to mobilize his forces. This gave General Burnside's Federal corps time to join Pope in defending against Lee's advance. Long, *Day by Day*, 246–47.

45. Sgt. James Addison Wade (May 11, 1838–April 9, 1865), Company F, 2nd Va. Cav., was a carpenter before enlisting as a private at Davis Mills on May 28, 1861. He was promoted to first sergeant on August 1, 1861, and reenlisted at Liberty Mills on April 24, 1862. He was reduced to a private and wounded at Aldie after reportedly whipping "three Yankees there in a hand to hand fight with the sabre." He was absent hospitalized August 25–31, 1863. He was wounded again at Yellow Tavern on May 11, 1864, and absent wounded through June 1864. He was killed at Appomattox Court House on April 9, 1865. Drive, *2nd Virginia Cavalry*, 279.

46. This refers to Rebecca's possible pregnancy.

47. Just south of Richmond, Chimborazo Hospital was one of the largest military hospitals in the world. It opened in October 1861 and treated over seventy-six thousand patients during the war. It was also an innovative facility with a 20 percent mortality rate, low for the period. Carol C. Green, *Chimborazo: The Confederacy's Largest Hospital* (Knoxville: Univ. of Tennessee Press, 2004).

48. RWP was admitted to Chimbarazo on either September 9 or 10, 1862, and was diagnosed with "camp fever," which was an alternate name for typhoid fever. Garrison and Garrison, *Encyclopedia*, 43; War Department, "Registers of Patients, Chimborazo Hospitals No. 4," RG 109, chap. 6, vol. 74, p. 46, NA.

49. War Department, Compiled Service Records, Collection of Confederate Records.

1863

1. Longacre, *Lee's Cavalrymen*, 167, 169–76, 176, 178, 185, 253–55, 264–66; Driver, *2nd Virginia Cavalry*, 68–105.

2. The Battle of Fredericksburg was fought on December 13, 1862. General Burnside sent one brigade after another against General Lee's strategically placed Confederates, who easily repelled the onslaught. Burnside eventually retreated in a humiliating defeat. Total forces: 186,500 (Union: 114,000; Confederate: 72,500). Total casualties: 18,030 (Union: 12,653; Confederate: 5,309). Long, *Day by Day*, 295–96.

3. 3rd Cpl. George N. Parker (October 20, 1841–January 31, 1930), Company D, 2nd Va. Cav., was RWP's paternal cousin. He enlisted as a private in Franklin County on May 20, 1861. He was promoted to second corporal in 1862. He was captured at Farmville in April 1865, sent to Newport News, and released in July 1865. He married his first wife, Bettie Margaret Rucker, on March 5, 1868, and the two had eight children together. He married his second wife, Mary Catherine Powell, on July 4, 1894. Driver, *2nd Virginia Cavalry*, 257; Ackerly and Parker, *"Our Kin,"* 657–60.

4. Pleasant M. Goggin was RWP's maternal uncle. He married Catherine Stone on January 17, 1850. Ackerly and Parker, *"Our Kin,"* 671.

5. This refers to RWP's preceding letter, which was not lost as he feared.

6. Pvt. Joel L. Preston, Company F, 2nd Va. Cav., enlisted at Culpeper Court House on February 1, 1863. He was wounded at Aldie on June 17, 1863, and retired to the Invalid Corps on October 18, 1864. Driver, *2nd Virginia Cavalry,* 262.

7. RWP appears to have returned to Bedford on furlough and/or sick leave.

8. The per diem ration for Confederate cavalry mounts was originally set at a healthy ten pounds of corn and ten pounds of "long forage," or grain. By spring 1862 the scarcity of fodder dropped subsistence to two to five pounds of corn per day, and often no long forage. Longacre, *Lee's Cavalrymen,* 44.

9. Charles Pleasant Walker had enlisted as a private in the 2nd Va. Cav. at Culpeper Court House on February 1, 1863. He was absent at a horse pasture as of the writing of this letter on March 4, 1863, where context indicates RWP may have accompanied him. He was in Bedford on horse detail from August 25 to 31, 1863. He was sick in a hospital February 7–9, 1864, but present again in March. He was wounded at Todd's Tavern on May 7, 1864. He was hospitalized in Richmond May 10, 1864, and transferred to a Lynchburg hospital on May 24. He was absent wounded through June 1864. He was captured at Strasburg November 7, 1864, and sent to Point Lookout before being exchanged on February 15, 1865. He was present in Camp Lee in Richmond February 19, 1865, after which there is no further record. Driver, *2nd Virginia Cavalry,* 28.

10. Pvt. Robert B. Dinwiddie, Company F, 2nd Va. Cav. He enlisted at Orange Court House on July 16, 1862. He was absent sick in September and October 1862. He was sick again in a Charlottesville hospital on March 7, 1863, and was transferred to a Lynchburg hospital on March 12. He was present in camp in April 1863 through June 1864. Driver, *2nd Virginia Cavalry,* 212.

11. Pvt. Henry C. Ballard, Company F, 2nd Va. Cav., enlisted at Brandy Station November 11, 1862. He was absent sick in a hospital April 24–30, 1864. He was present May and June 1864 but sick June 27–July 2, 1864. He was present through February 1865 and listed as wounded in action on the postwar roster. Driver, *2nd Virginia Cavalry,* 194.

12. Sgt. James Pleasant McCabe (April 8, 1838–May 14, 1912), Company B, 2nd Va. Cav. He enlisted as a private at Davis Mills on May 18, 1861, and was soon promoted to fourth sergeant. His horse was killed and he suffered a shell wound at Raccoon Ford on October 11, 1863. After his leg was amputated, he recovered in a Lynchburg hospital until retiring to the Invalid Corps in August 1864. Driver, *2nd Virginia Cavalry,* 245.

13. RWP is referring to Capt. John S. Mosby's capture of Brig. Gen. E. H. Stoughton and thirty-two other Federals on March 8, 1863. The daring incident mortified the North and delighted the South. Long *Civil War,* 327.

14. RWP is referring to a "hunting case" or "hunter case" watch, which is a pocket watch with a front cover (as opposed to an "open face" watch without a front cover). Dictionary.com Unabridged (v. 1.1), based on the *Random House*

Unabridged Dictionary, available on line at http://dictionary.reference.com/browse/hunting%20case (accessed May 26, 2007).

15. Rebecca's last letter apparently mentioned that she was spinning a great deal of wool and/or cotton into thread. Confederate women were encouraged to manufacture their own textiles during the Civil War. Faust, *Mothers of Invention,* 24–25; Rable, *Civil Wars,* 138–44.

16. Pvt. Leslie T. Dinwiddie (d. March 19, 1863), Company F, 2nd Va. Cav., enlisted in Company I, Twenty-eighth Virginia Infantry, on May 13, 1861. He transferred to Company F, 2nd Va. Cav., on October 1, 1861, and died of typhoid fever in a Charlottesville hospital. Driver, *2nd Virginia Cavalry,* 212.

17. This is the Battle of Kelly's Ford (or the Battle of Kellysville), fought March 17, 1863. Brig. Gen. William W. Averell led his Union cavalry across the Rappahannock River and attacked Brig. Gen. Fitzhugh Lee's brigade. This large-scale cavalry fight set the stage for similar battles in the Gettysburg campaign. Total forces: 3,000 (Union: 2,100 Union; Confederate: 800). Total casualties: 211 (Union: 78; Confederate: 133). Longacre, *Lee's Cavalrymen,* 170–75; Boatner, *Civil War Dictionary,* 451.

18. Pvt. John William Burroughs (July 2, 1835–March 17, 1863), Company D, 2nd Va. Cav. He enlisted at Davis Mills on May 28, 1861. He reenlisted for two years or the war and was present until killed in action at Kelly's Ford. Driver, *2nd Virginia Cavalry,* 202.

19. Pvt. James Claytor Leftwich (March 10, 1839–June 10, 1863), Company I, 2nd Va. Cav. He attended the VMI before enlisting in Company B, Fourteenth Virginia Infantry. He served until returning to VMI in 1862. He enlisted in Company I, 2nd Va. Cav. at Campbell Court House on June 9, 1862. His horse was shot and he was captured at Kelly's Ford. He died of his wounds at his father's house in Bedford County. Driver, *2nd Virginia Cavalry,* 240.

20. According to various records documenting the involvement of the 2nd Va. Cav. at Kelly's Ford, between one and four soldiers were killed in action, between ten and twenty-one were wounded in action, and between eleven and eighteen were taken prisoner. Driver, *2nd Virginia Cavalry,* 179.

21. Personal property tax records from 1861 reveal that RWP's horse was valued at sixty dollars. By March 1863 Confederate inflation ensured that horses had become very expensive indeed. Virginia Department of Taxation, Personal Property Tax, 1861, Bedford County, Virginia, Reel 421, Library of Virginia, Richmond; Current, *Encyclopedia* 2:791–93.

22. Pvt. Jesse W. Pollard (b. ca. 1830), Company F, 2nd Va. Cav. A farmer before the war, he enlisted at Davis Mills on May 28, 1861, as a second corporal. He was reduced to a private and reenlisted at Liberty Mills on April 28, 1862. He was promoted to fifth and fourth sergeant before surrendering at Appomattox on April 9, 1865. Driver, *2nd Virginia Cavalry,* 261.

23. Floodwaters would immobilize General Hooker for another two days. Then he would march upstream to cross the Rappahannock River in the hopes of pinning the Army of Northern Virginia. Long, *Day by Day,* 342; Eric J. Wittenberg,

The Union Cavalry Comes of Age: Hartwood Church to Brandy Station, 1863 (Washington, D.C.: Brassey's, 2003), 118, 134.

24. RWP is probably referring to the Battle of Chancellorsville. The 2nd Va. Cav. had been involved in several skirmishes in the first few days of May 1863 as part of Munford's regiment under Jackson against Hooker. Munford was ordered to guard the Confederate left flank and seize Ely's Ford Road, which he did. His troops were not directly involved in the Battle of Chancellorsville, although they performed important duties, such as clearing the roads, to make this daring Confederate offensive a success. Total forces: 194,760 (Union: 133,868; Confederate: 60,892). Total casualties: 30,099 (Union: 17,278; Confederate: 12,821). Driver, *2nd Virginia Cavalry*, 79–80; Boatner, *Civil War Dictionary*, 136–40.

25. Substitutes became increasingly expensive as the war dragged on and the value of Confederate currency decreased. Conscription acts allowed the hiring of substitutes, which exacerbated class tensions. Many Southerners regarded it as a shameful practice that unfairly favored wealthy slaveholders and allowed them to avoid the sacrifices of war. Such practices contributed to the popular belief that it was a "rich man's war and a poor man's fight" and represented an extreme act for a confederation devoted to state sovereignty. Current, *Encyclopedia* 1:396–99; Blair, *Virginia's Private War*, 57–60, 81–84.

26. Rebecca may have just discovered she was pregnant (approximately three months so) with their second child and probably wanted RWP to return home to tell him and/or assist her. Ackerly and Parker, *"Our Kin,"* 651, 653.

27. The battle and siege of Vicksburg were the final events in the Vicksburg campaign. It occurred May 18–July 4, 1863, when Gen. Ulysses S. Grant led his forces against the fortified city. Although Confederate forces repulsed Grant's direct assault in mid-May, disease and hunger ensured they could not hold out through the long siege that followed. General Johnston failed to relieve the beleaguered Gen. John C. Pemberton, leaving Pemberton with no choice but to eventually surrender 29,511 people and 60,172 arms. Boatner, *Civil War Dictionary*, 876–77; Current, *Encyclopedia* 4:1855–60.

28. RWP was misinformed; Union troops did not fall back from Vicksburg. They remained entrenched outside the besieged city through July 4. Boatner, *Civil War Dictionary*, 877.

29. This is the Battle of Brandy Station, which occurred on June 9, 1863, and is considered the first battle of the Gettysburg campaign. General Hooker sent Maj. Gen. Alfred Pleasonton's cavalry corps to attack Maj. Gen. Stuart's cavalry on the Rappahannock River near Brandy Station. The battle lasted from ten to twelve hours and is widely regarded as the greatest cavalry battle of the war. Stuart barely fended off the attack, which also symbolized the increased strength and confidence of the Union cavalry. Total forces: 17,000 (Union: 8,000; Confederate: 9,000). Total casualties: 1,366 (Union: 866; Confederate: 500). Longacre, *Lee's Cavalrymen*, 178–79, 189–90, 193–95, 199; Long, *Day by Day*, 363–64.

30. Col. Alfred N. Duffié was a French military who led cavalry in the Crimean War before coming to the United States to command Union cavalry in the Civil War.

He was commissioned captain and eventually promoted to colonel. Boatner, *Civil War Dictionary*, 250.

31. Pvt. James Knox Polk Preston (ca. 1845–June 9, 1863), Company F, 2nd Va. Cav. He enlisted at Culpeper Court House on March 5, 1863, and was killed in action at Brandy Station. Driver, *2nd Virginia Cavalry*, 262.

32. Pvt. Benjamin R. Turner, Company F, 2nd Va. Cav., enlisted in Liberty on November 10, 1862. He was wounded in the thigh at Brandy Station on June 9, 1863, and present until wounded in action at Cold Harbor May 31, 1864. He was admitted into a Richmond hospital, transferred to a Petersburg hospital, and absent wounded through June 30, 1864. He surrendered at Appomattox on April 9, 1865. Driver, *2nd Virginia Cavalry*, 278.

33. General Lee's headquarters were at Culpeper Court House. The Army of Northern Virginia was preparing to head north and west toward the Shenandoah Valley and eventually on to Pennsylvania in the Gettysburg campaign. Longacre, *Lee's Cavalrymen*, 189; Boatner, *Civil War Dictionary*, 331–40.

34. On June 16, 1863, General Stuart led the cavalry from Brandy Station to screen the right flank of General Longstreet's column, which was bringing up Lee's rear on the march north. Longacre, *Lee's Cavalrymen*, 196.

35. This was the Second Battle of Winchester, which was fought June 14, 1863. Major General Ewell's Confederate corps roundly defeated Maj. Gen. Robert H. Milroy's forces at Winchester and opened the lower Shenandoah Valley to Lee's advance. Total casualties: 3,769 (Union: 3,500; Confederate: 269). Current, *Encyclopedia* 4:1732–33; Long, *Day by Day*, 365–66.

36. The siege of Port Hudson, Louisiana, lasted from May 21 to July 9, 1863. Confederate forces had fortified the town of Port Hudson in spring 1862 to protect its access to the Mississippi River. Confederates held out for forty-eight days before lack of food and ammunition forced them to surrender on July 9. Current, *Encyclopedia* 3:1238–39; Lawrence Lee Hewitt, *Port Hudson, Confederate Bastion on the Mississippi* (Baton Rouge: Louisiana State Univ. Press, 1994).

37. This was the Battle of Aldie, which occurred June 17, 1863. Munford and his troops, including the 2nd Va. Cav., were marching north through Aldie Gap under Stuart's orders. Brig. Gen. Judson Kilpatrick's brigade attacked Munford's men near the village of Aldie. When reinforcements arrived for Kilpatrick after several hours of inconclusive fighting, Munford withdrew. Longacre, *Lee's Cavalrymen*, 197–99.

38. After his stunning success in the Battle of Second Winchester cleared the Shenandoah Valley for the rest of Lee's troops, Ewell led his men to Sharpsburg, Maryland, before continuing into Pennsylvania. Pfanz, *Richard S. Ewell*, 288–92

39. RWP may be referring to Maj. Gen. John A. McClernand being removed from command in Vicksburg. He was replaced by Maj. Gen. E. O. C. Ord. In any case, the siege at Vicksburg continued unabated. Long, *Day by Day*, 368.

40. Brig. Gen. Fitzhugh Lee (November 19, 1835–April 28, 1905) graduated from the U.S. Military Academy at West Point in 1856 while Robert E. Lee, his uncle, was superintendent. He served in the Second U.S. Cavalry and as an instructor at

West Point before resigning from the army in May 1861. He entered Confederate service as an adjutant to General Ewell and received a commission as lieutenant colonel in September 1861. He was later promoted to colonel in the spring of 1862, to brigadier general by July 1862, and to major general in September 1863. He served under General Stuart throughout most of the war. He was wounded at Winchester on September 19, 1864, and was absent wounded until January 1865. Warner, *Generals in Gray*, 145; Current, *Encyclopedia* 2:914–15.

41. The date on this letter is legible but inaccurate, as RWP refers to events that occurred in mid- to late July 1863.

42. Maj. Gen. George G. Meade's forces pursued Gen. Lee's men in the weeks following the Battle of Gettysburg. Lee's rearguard skirmished with Meade as they retreated toward the Potomac, finally crossing at Falling Waters, (West) Virginia. Skirmishing continued as forces trickled through the passes of the Blue Ridge Mountains. Lee finally slipped beyond Meade's reach in late July 1863. Richmond was not Meade's primary objective during this period. Long, *Day by Day*, 384–91; Driver, *2nd Virginia Cavalry*, 92–95.

43. It fell to the Confederate cavalry to protect the Confederate army's wagon train on its retreat from Pennsylvania in early July 1863. They engaged in a series of skirmishes and battles with Union cavalry. Confederates won the Battle of Funkstown on July 7 but continued feinting for several days to lure General Meade's troops away from Lee's retreating rear guard. Longacre, *Lee's Cavalrymen*, 232.

44. Pvt. Creed Thomas Hubbard (1827–1864), Company F, 2nd Va. Cav., was a farmer before enlisting at Davis Mills on May 24, 1861. He was absent sick in a Richmond hospital on November 5, 1861, transferred to a Lynchburg hospital November 23, 1861, and absent sick through December 31, 1861. There are no records of his service in 1862, but he was listed as present in March and April 1863. He was wounded nine times in action at Boonsboro, Maryland, and absent wounded through August 31, 1863. He was wounded in action and captured at Todd's Tavern on May 7, 1864. He was left with the enemy and died of his wounds. Driver, *2nd Virginia Cavalry*, 231.

45. Retreating from Gettysburg, the Army of Northern Virginia had gathered at the high-running Potomac River on July 10. It would be three more days before the river receded enough to allow troops to cross. Long, *Day by Day*, 382.

46. According to various military reports, the 2nd Va. Cav. had one to three men killed in action, six to twelve wounded in action, and between two and thirty-six taken prisoner at Gettysburg. Driver, *2nd Virginia Cavalry*, 179.

47. By this time the Army of Northern Virginia had returned from Pennsylvania, but Union commanders continued pressing south, as if intending to attack Lee's rear. Skirmishes continued along the Rappahannock River for weeks to come, but with little effect. Longacre, *Lee's Cavalrymen*, 237–43.

48. August 1, 1863, saw the last engagement of the Gettysburg campaign. Union cavalry pushed across the Rappahannock River at Kelly's Ford and engaged Confederate forces near Brandy Station in an attempt to discover General Lee's plans. Long, *Day by Day*, 393.

49. Louise was Rebecca's middle name. Ackerly and Parker, *"Our Kin,"* 651.

50. There are two Tuckers listed on the wartime roster from Company B. There is no information on one, Pvt. Brook Tucker; the other is Pvt. Willis T. Tucker (b. ca. 1837), 2nd Va. Cav. He enlisted in Lynchburg on May 13, 1861, and was a brick mason before the war. He was detailed with General Jackson's ordnance train July 1 to October 31, 1862. He was absent with camp itch in a Richmond hospital October 2, 1863, and transferred to a Petersburg hospital on October 7, 1863. He was captured at Meadow Bridge May 12, 1864, and sent to Fort Monroe. He was eventually exchanged on March 15, 1865, and paroled in Lynchburg on April 14, 1865. Driver, *2nd Virginia Cavalry,* 278.

51. Military records indicate RWP was absent on horse detail from August 25 to 31, 1863. He apparently returned home to Bedford for his detail. War Department, Compiled Service Records, Collection of Confederate Records.

52. On September 9 Longstreet's corps of the Army of Northern Virginia departed the Rapidan River area. They were to reinforce Gen. Braxton Bragg, who had recently abandoned Chattanooga, Tennessee, to advancing Union troops and retreated to Georgia. Longstreet traveled as quickly as he could, considering the poor condition of Southern railroads, but it still took him ten days to reach Bragg. Long, *Day by Day,* 407.

53. Brig. Gen. Williams Carter Wickham (September 21, 1820–July 23, 1888) was educated at the University of Virginia, served as a justice of the Hanover County Court for many years, and was elected to the house of delegates and the state senate. He led his militia company into Confederate service when Virginia seceded and served under General Stuart. He was commissioned lieutenant colonel in September 1861, promoted to colonel in August 1862, and promoted to brigadier general to rank from September 1, 1863. He resigned his commission on November 9, 1864. Warner, *Generals in Gray,* 335–36.

54. As Lee withdrew from the Rapidan, the Army of the Potomac pressed forward from the Rappahannock on September 13, 1863. Skirmishing occurred in the area in the days that followed. Long, *Day by Day,* 408–9.

55. On September 23 General Wickham's cavalrymen skirmished with Union troops near Robinson's River. Confederate casualties were indeed low, and Wickham's men captured thirty or forty prisoners and drove the Union cavalry back across the river. Driver, *2nd Virginia Cavalry,* 97.

56. RWP is referring to the Battle of Chickamauga, fought September 19–20, 1864, in northern Georgia. Maj. Gen. William Rosencrans had just forced General Bragg's Confederate forces out of Chattanooga and was pursuing his enemy. In the resulting conflict, Confederates exploited an opening in the Union ranks, divided the Union army, and continued a determined assault. It was a much-needed Southern victory and morale booster. Total forces: 124,548 (Union: 58,222; Confederate: 66,326). Total casualties: 34,624 (Union: 16,170; Confederate: 18,454). Current, *Encyclopedia* 1:302–4; Boatner, *Civil War Dictionary,* 149–53.

57. Nineteenth-century notions of gender roles dictated that mothers were responsible for the religious instruction of their children. Donald G. Mathews, *Religion in the Old South* (Chicago: Univ. of Chicago Press, 1977), 100–102, 112.

58. Colonel Munford later listed thirteen casualties for the Raccoon Ford engagement—seven killed, five wounded, and one taken prisoner. Driver, *2nd Virginia Cavalry*, 179.

59. Adj. Lomax Tayloe (September 22, 1842–October 11, 1863), Company G, 2nd Va. Cav., attended the University of Virginia from 1860 to 1861 and enlisted in the University Guards in April 1861. They were disbanded, and he enlisted in Company G, 2nd Va. Cav. at Forest Depot on May 28, 1861. He was promoted adjutant to rank from June 13, 1862. He was wounded at Bristoe Station on August 23, 1862, and at Shepherdstown on May 16, 1863, and he was killed in action at Raccoon Ford on October 11, 1863. He was buried in Tayloe Cemetery in Roanoke County, Virginia. Driver, *2nd Virginia Cavalry*, 274.

60. Capt. Jesse Irvine Jr. (September 1833–November 16, 1895), Company G, 2nd Va. Cav., was a farmer before enlisting as a first corporal at Forest Depot on May 28, 1861. He was later promoted to first sergeant and elected captain. He was absent sick September 20 through October 31, 1862. He was wounded and had his horse killed at Raccoon Ford on October 11, 1863. He was absent wounded in a Lynchburg hospital through June 1864. He requested retirement October 23, 1864, and beyond that date there are no further service records. Driver, *2nd Virginia Cavalry*, 233.

61. Asst. Surgeon John Alexander Nelson (January 9, 1836–October 11, 1863) graduated from Jefferson Medical College in 1857. He enlisted at Forest Depot May 28, 1861, as a private. He was appointed hospital steward July 7, 1861. He was absent on leave September 6, 1862, and absent without leave September 15 through October 31, 1862. He was appointed assistant surgeon on April 4, 1863, and served in various hospitals. He died of wounds received in a charge at Raccoon Ford on October 11, 1863. Driver, *2nd Virginia Cavalry*, 254.

62. All of this severe skirmishing was prompted by Lee's tentative advance northward, as he attempted to cut Union lines to Washington in the Bristoe campaign, October 9–22, 1863. Long, *Day by Day*, 419–20.

63. October 15, 1863, was the last day of heavy skirmishing and the farthest extent of Lee's northward advance. Fighting was somewhat restrained, as both Union and Confederate commanders tried to determine one another's strength and strategy. Long, *Day by Day*, 422.

64. In October 1863 Gen. George Gordon Meade found his Union army dangerously positioned at the confluence of the Rappahannock and Rapidan Rivers. Meade retreated from Lee's advancing army, just as Gen. Alexander Pope had done the year before, but unlike Pope never mounted a defense because he was under orders to avoid a large-scale battle in his reduced state. Longacre, *Lee's Cavalrymen*, 253–61.

65. Having chased General Meade's forces back across the Rappahannock, General Stuart's cavalry returned to the south side of the river and their encampment. Longacre, *Lee's Cavalrymen*, 260.

66. It was the one-sided Confederate victory in the Battle of Buckland Mills (or the Buckland Races), which occurred October 19, 1863. General Stuart's cavalry was protecting General Lee's withdrawal from Manassas Junction when they

ambushed General Kilpatrick's Union troops and routed them in a five-mile all-out chase. Total casualties: 250. Boatner, *Civil War Dictionary*, 95; Longacre, *Lee's Cavalrymen*, 260–61.

67. A skirmish had occurred at Stevensburg, Virginia, on October 11, 1863, as part of Lee's northward advance. Long, *Day by Day*, 420.

68. On November 7, 1863, General Meade and the Army of the Potomac crossed the Rappahannock River and engaged Confederates at Rappahannock Station and Kelly's Ford. Lee withdrew to the line of the Rapidan. These engagements were not large-scale battles, but it did restore Union troops to the position they held before the Bristoe campaign. Long, *Day by Day*, 431.

69. In April 1863 the Confederate government levied a tax-in-kind on farmers and planters, which required them to contribute a tenth of their annual crop, after setting aside twenty to one hundred bushels of staple foods (depending on the crop), to the government for the war effort. Current, *Encyclopedia* 4:1571.

70. The Army of the Potomac had fallen back across the Rapidan River, but not as far north as the Rappahannock. Meade established winter quarters at Brandy Station on the south side of the Rappahannock. Richard A. Sauers, *Meade: Victor of Gettysburg* (Washington, D.C.: Brassey's, 2003), 67.

71. RWP and Rebecca's second child, a son named George Pleasant Parker, was born on November 17, 1863. It is not clear how RWP learned of his new son's birth. Ackerly and Parker, *"Our Kin,"* 653.

1864

1. Longacre, *Lee's Cavalrymen*, 274, 276–77, 290–91, 296–97, 308–21; Driver, *2nd Virginia Cavalry*, 106–51.

2. Pvt. John W. Krautz (March 18, 1845–June 9, 1887), Company F, 2nd Va. Cav., enlisted at Culpeper Court House on March 5, 1863. He was captured at Kelly's Ford on March 17, 1863, and exchanged. He was wounded at Todd's Tavern May 8, 1864, and absent with wounds through June 1864. His horse was killed at Fisher's Hill on October 5, 1864. Driver, *2nd Virginia Cavalry*, 238.

3. Maj. Gen. Thomas L. Rosser (October 15, 1836–March 29, 1910) attended West Point and was appointed first lieutenant in Regular Confederate service. He was eventually promoted to major general from November 1, 1864. Rosser was praised for his bravery, but his subordinates also complained of his incompetence. Current, *Encyclopedia* 3:1347; Warner, *Generals in Gray*, 264–65.

4. On February 17, 1864, the Confederate government instituted a third conscription act that extended the ages of males eligible for the draft from eighteen to forty-five to seventeen to fifty. It also eliminated several exemptions and offered one hundred dollars in government bonds at 6 percent interest to noncommissioned officers and privates who did not desert. This act would explain the flurry of reenlistment RWP reports here. Current, *Encyclopedia* 1:398.

5. This comment seems to indicate that newly drafted seventeen-year-old soldiers were far more critical of the war and the Confederacy in general than most of

the older, previously enlisted men. Confederate morale was rapidly sinking in 1864, and the unpopularity of conscription merely exacerbated this trend. Blair, *Virginia's Private War,* 108–10.

6. Facing rampant inflation, the Confederacy passed the Currency Reform Act on February 17, 1864. The act repudiated older Confederate notes and required that outstanding Confederate notes be exchanged for bond certificates by April 1, 1864, or for new notes on a 3:2 basis (three old notes for two new ones). RWP encouraged Rebecca to do the latter, as bills and notes that were not spent or exchanged were subject to additional taxes. Richard C. K. Burdekin, and Marc D. Weidenmier, "Inflation Is Always and Everywhere a Monetary Phenomenon: Richmond vs. Houston in 1864," *American Economic Review* 91, no. 5 (Dec. 2001): 1621–30.

7. Pvt. Robert J. Dearing (July 25, 1841–October 15, 1919), Company F, 2nd Va. Cav. He enlisted at Barboursville on August 16, 1862, and was wounded in action at Leesburg September 2, 1862. He was absent wounded in a Charlottesville hospital through March 29, 1863. His horse was killed at Brandy Station on June 9, 1863. The wound RWP mentions occurred near Hartwood Church on February 23, 1864. He was absent wounded in a Liberty hospital through April 30, 1864. He was wounded at Spotsylvania Court House on May 8, 1864, and at Mount Jackson November 21, 1864, with no further military record beyond that date. Driver, *2nd Virginia Cavalry,* 211.

8. On February 28, 1864, Gen. Judson Kilpatrick led a division-sized force of Union cavalry on a raid to Richmond. As a diversionary tactic, he ordered Brig. Gen. George Armstrong Custer's cavalry to ride near Charlottesville. Custer's force of fifteen hundred cavalrymen approached Charlottesville from February 29 to March 1, 1864. The raid eventually sputtered out due to lack of surprise, force, and drive to see it through. The raid was definitively thwarted on March 2, when Kilpatrick's men continued their retreat and Col. Ulric Dahlgren was killed. Longacre, *Lee's Cavalrymen,* 270–71; Long, *Day by Day,* 469–72.

9. Pvt. John Quincey Dickinson (November 20, 1831–November 26, 1923), Company A, 2nd Va. Cav., was an overseer before enlisting in Liberty on April 1, 1862. He was absent sick in a Liberty hospital from July 19 to October 31, 1862. He was captured at Stanardsville on March 1, 1864, and held prisoner at the Old Capitol Prison and Fort Delaware until May 31, 1865. Driver, *2nd Virginia Cavalry,* 212.

10. General Grant instructed General Hunter to advance on Lynchburg and destroy railroads and canals on May 25, 1864, but this plan was not in effect as of March 1864. War Department, *The War of the Rebellion: A Compilation of the Official Records of the Union and Confederate Armies* (Washington, D.C.: GPO, 1891), ser. 1, 34:20–21.

11. This number is exaggerated; about one hundred of Dahlgren's men were captured. Long, *Day by Day,* 471.

12. This quote is attributed to Oliver Cromwell (1599–1658), a military leader, politician, and lord protector of Britain. John Bartlett, comp., *Familiar Quotations,* 10th

ed., rev. and enl. by Nathan Haskell Dole (Boston: Little, Brown, 1919), available on line at www.bartleby.com/100 (accessed June 7, 2007).

13. Capt. Henry Clay Dickinson (February 21, 1830–November 26, 1913), Company A, 2nd Va. Cav., was graduated from Hampden-Sidney College in 1851 and worked as a lawyer in Liberty before enlisting as a private on May 13, 1861. He was promoted through the ranks until being elected captain on April 25, 1862. He was absent on leave January 9, 1863, and absent sick July and August 1863. He was apparently captured and transferred between Union prisons and forts until being released May 30, 1865. Driver, *2nd Virginia Cavalry*, 212.

14. Pvt. Charles D. Nelms (November 17, 1826–June 3, 1887), Company A, 2nd Va. Cav. He enlisted at Liberty on September 7, 1863. His horse was killed and he was captured at the Battle of Stanardsville on March 3, 1863, and was held prisoner at the Old Capitol Prison and Fort Delaware until June 20, 1865. Driver, *2nd Virginia Cavalry*, 253.

15. Pvt. Robert Powell Mattox (January 26, 1820–February 11, 1900), Company F, 2nd Va. Cav., was conscripted on October 27, 1863. He was wounded at Hawes Shop on May 28, 1864, and paroled at Campbell Court House May 30, 1865. Driver, *2nd Virginia Cavalry*, 245.

16. Grant and the Army of the Potomac stood ready to pounce, but when and where remained a mystery. Grant would eventually dispatch his army south in the hopes of skirting Lee's flank and getting between him and Richmond. This hope was dashed, as Lee's troops met them days later at the Wilderness, a tangled forest located ten miles west of Fredericksburg, just south of the Rapidan River. Longacre, *Lee's Cavalrymen*, 275–76; Long, *Day by Day*, 490–92.

17. General Burnside and his Ninth Corps joined General Grant on May 4, 1864. Long, *Day by Day*, 492.

18. The 2nd Va. Cav. fought in the Battle of the Wilderness (or Todd's Tavern), which occurred May 5–7, 1864, as the opening battle of Grant's famed 1864 Overland campaign. They were dispatched to Todd's Tavern on May 5, where they erected breastworks across the road to Spotsylvania Court House. There they engaged Gen. Philip Sheridan's Union cavalry May 6–8. While the Battle of Wilderness was considered a draw, Grant refused to retreat and pushed on toward Spotsylvania Court House. Total engaged: 162,920 (Union: 101,895; Confederate: 61,025). Total casualties: 25,416 (Union: 17,666; Confederate: 7,750). Driver, *2nd Virginia Cavalry*, 111–14; Boatner, *Civil War Dictionary*, 919–25.

19. After fighting in the Battle of the Wilderness, the 2nd Va. Cav. was engaged in the Spotsylvania campaign from May 7 to 20, 1864. Spotsylvania Court House lay about nine miles southwest of Fredericksburg. Throughout this two-week period fighting ceased and then renewed every few days as Grant shifted his armies about, probing for weak spots in Lee's defenses. Grant eventually disengaged and continued his policy of relentless pursuit. Total engaged: 160,000 (Union: 110,000; Confederate: 50,000). Union casualties: 17,500 (Confederate casualties unreliably recorded). Long, *Day by Day*, 505; Current, *Encyclopedia* 4:1518–21; Boatner, *Civil War Dictionary*, 783–89.

20. While it is difficult to ascertain Company F's exact number of casualties, it is possible to estimate the number of casualties suffered by the entire regiment. For the Battles of the Wilderness and Spotsylvania Court House, various records indicate they lost five to fifteen killed, between twenty-three and fifty-three wounded, and one to five taken prisoner. Driver, *2nd Virginia Cavalry*, 179.

21. Pvt. U. W. Fariss, Company I, had enlisted in Campbell County on April 1, 1864. He was slightly wounded in the arm at the Battle of Spotsylvania Court House on May 8 but was recorded as present during that month. He surrendered at Appomattox Court House on April 9, 1865. Driver, *2nd Virginia Cavalry*, 216.

22. Lt. James E. M. Hughes (December 25, 1832–April 11, 1896), Company F, 2nd Va. Cav., was elected third lieutenant at Liberty Mills on April 24, 1862. He was wounded in action at Ashland May 10, 1864, and received a forty-day furlough from his Richmond hospital to Liberty on May 23, 1864. He was wounded in action at Cedar Creek on September 21, 1864. He was present November 29, 1864, but absent sick in a Liberty hospital February 27, 1865, with no further service record beyond that date. Driver, *2nd Virginia Cavalry*, 231.

23. Pvt. John H. Franklin (ca. 1824–December 21, 1918), Company A, 2nd Va. Cav., enlisted at Liberty on March 28, 1862. His horse was killed at Kelly's Ford March 17, 1863. He was captured and paroled at Thompson's Cross Roads on May 4, 1863. He was wounded at the Battle of Spotsylvania Court House on May 8, 1864. Records indicate he was absent due to wounds for the duration of the war. Driver, *2nd Virginia Cavalry*, 219.

24. General Beauregard squared off against General Butler in the Bermuda Hundred campaign, May 1864. Butler's Army of the James was to sever the Richmond and Petersburg Railroad and cut off supplies to Richmond. Confederates successfully cornered Butler's men and won the campaign. Frances H. Kennedy, ed., *Civil War Battlefield Guide*, 2nd ed. (Boston: Houghton Mifflin, 1998), 278–80.

25. Skirmishes and battles were fought at Drewry's Bluff (or Proctor's Creek) on May 4–16, 1864, as part of the Bermuda Hundred campaign. Generals Butler and Beauregard faced off at Fort Darling on Drewry's Bluff above the James River. Beauregard's far smaller force not only mounted a successful defense but also ruined Butler's hopes of capturing Richmond or Petersburg. For operations May 12–14, total forces: 33,825 (Union: 15,800; Confederate: 18,025); total casualties: 6,666 (Union: 4,160; Confederate: 2,506). Boatner, *Civil War Dictionary*, 249; Long, *Day by Day*, 492–503.

26. On May 15 Butler refrained from attacking Beauregard and instead rearranged his defensive lines. Long, *Day by Day*, 502.

27. On July 20, 1864, Gen. John Bell Hood led an ill-fated attack on Gen. William Tecumseh Sherman at Peachtree Creek outside Atlanta. Two days later they met again at the Battle of Atlanta, where Hood's Confederates again suffered defeat. July 28 would see Sherman force Hood to retreat inside Atlanta and the beginning of a siege that would last more than a month. Current, *Encyclopedia* 1:108–11.

28. After General Grant's defeat at Cold Harbor in early June 1864, he moved his troops south to Petersburg. Thinking Grant intended an assault on Richmond,

Lee initially provided General Beauregard with few reinforcements to protect Petersburg. This combined with Union errors on the battlefield ensured that a siege would be necessary for Grant to capture the city. Ernest B. Ferguson, *Not War but Murder: Cold Harbor, 1864* (New York: Vintage, 2001), 243–56.

29. Frustrated with the lengthy entrenchments required to lay siege to Petersburg, Grant enacted a dramatic plan first developed by mining engineer Lt. Col. Henry Pleasants. The plan involved digging a shaft under the Confederate line and detonating explosives directly beneath them, thus creating an opening in their defenses. Digging began on June 25, 1864, and was finished on July 23. Confederates heard rumors of the mine and attempted to discover it, but their countermining attempts proved futile. John Canaan, *The Crater: Petersburg* (New York: Da Capo, 2001), 18, 25, 32.

30. Although military records are silent on RWP's whereabouts during this period, the length of time between this and his previous letter (nearly two months) indicate that he returned to Bedford County, probably on furlough or horse detail. War Department, Compiled Service Records, Collection of Confederate Records.

31. Belle Isle is located in the James River just west of downtown Richmond. During the Civil War it was the site of a prison camp where thousands of Union troops were held. Current, *Encyclopedia* 1:154–55.

32. Chaffin's Farm was a bluff on the James River just south of Richmond. Confederate engineers had created an extensive system of outer line defenses. Kennedy, *Civil War Battlefield Guide*, 362–63.

33. About 4:45 A.M. on July 30, 1864, Union troops detonated eight thousand pounds of explosives beneath Confederate lines. Approximately three hundred troops were killed instantly. The ensuing Battle of the Crater was a hectic and bloody affair that failed to end the siege of Petersburg. Canaan, *Crater,* 27, 84, 87–146, passim.

34. This was true; Union troops suffered far higher casualties than Confederates during the Petersburg mine assault. Total forces: 32,174 (Union: 20,708; Confederate: 11,466). Total casualties: 5,298 (Union: 3,798; Confederate: 1,500). Boatner, *Civil War Dictionary,* 647–49.

35. Union troops under Sherman continued to tighten their lines around Atlanta throughout August. Long, *Day by Day,* 549–57.

36. Maj. Gen. George Stoneman Jr. was granted permission by General Sherman to lead two cavalry divisions to Macon, Georgia, to liberate Union prisoners at Andersonville. On July 27, 1864, he divided his forces and led a small force of twenty-two hundred men on to Macon. Stoneman engaged Confederate troops under Maj. Gen. Howell Cobb on July 30. Several brigades of Confederate cavalry cut off Stoneman's escape. This action was known as the Battle of Hillsboro (or Sunshine Creek), which resulted in the capture of Stoneman and five hundred of his men and deprived General Sherman of almost one-third of his cavalry. Current, *Encyclopedia* 4:1546–47; Boatner, *Civil War Dictionary,* 801–2.

37. Earlier in August Lee sent a number of cavalry divisions, including the 2nd Va. Cav., to reinforce General Early at Front Royal in the Shenandoah Valley against

General Sheridan, whose orders were to destroy the "Breadbasket of the Confederacy." Longacre, *Lee's Cavalrymen*, 309.

38. This was probably the Battle of Guard Hill, fought in Warren County in the Shenandoah Valley on August 16, 1864. A Union division captured a large portion of a Confederate division as they crossed the Shenandoah River, but the battle was ultimately inconclusive. Total casualties: 551 (Union: 71; Confederate: 480). Long, *Day by Day*, 556; Kennedy, *Civil War Battlefield Guide*, 313–14.

39. On August 17 Gen. Fitzhugh Lee led his cavalry in pursuit of the retreating Federal troops. Driver, *2nd Virginia Cavalry*, 133.

40. Maj. (later Col.) Cary Breckinridge (October 5, 1839–May 11, 1918), 2nd Va. Cav., graduated from VMI in 1860. He was a farmer when enlisting as a second lieutenant in Company C, 2nd Va. Cav on May 17, 1861. He was elected captain on January 30, 1862, and major on April 24, 1862. He was wounded in action at Second Manassas August 30, 1862. He was captured at Kelly's Ford on March 17, 1863, sent to the Old Capitol Prison, and exchanged April 6, 1863. He was wounded in action near Berryville on August 20, 1864, and hospitalized in Charlottesville from August 24 to 31, 1864, before being transferred to another hospital and released on an unknown date. He was wounded at Opequan on September 20, 1864. He was eventually promoted to colonel. He was present until the regiment disbanded in Lynchburg on April 11, 1865. Driver, *2nd Virginia Cavalry*, 199.

41. It is unclear to precisely which battle or date RWP is referring. Confederate cavalry were involved in a series of skirmishes and battles throughout the Shenandoah Valley in late August 1864.

42. The Battle of Berryville was fought on September 3–4, 1864, as part of Sheridan's Shenandoah Valley campaign. A Confederate division on reconnaissance encountered and fought Sheridan's divisions. General Early's army prepared to attack but found Sheridan's defensive position too strong. Early retreated beyond Opequon Creek, thus ending the inconclusive battle. Kennedy, *Civil War Battlefield Guide*, 315.

43. The 2nd Va. Cav. had been camped with General Lee in the New Market area of the Shenandoah Valley for some time. Longacre, *Lee's Cavalrymen*, 321.

44. Matthew 6:24–34: "Take therefore no thought for the morrow: For the morrow shall take thought for the things of itself. Sufficient unto the day is the evil thereof" (KJV).

45. Pvt. Bethel K. Wilson, Company F, 2nd Va. Cav., enlisted at Liberty Mills on April 24, 1862. He was dismounted as of July 6, 1863, and present until transferring to the CSN on April 3, 1864. There is no further record of his service beyond being paid in Richmond on August 1, 1864. Driver, *2nd Virginia Cavalry*, 287.

46. Pvt. Charles W. Kidwell, Company F, 2nd Va. Cav., enlisted at Charlestown on September 27, 1862. He was detailed as a wagoner through October 31, 1862. He transferred to the CSN on April 3, 1864. He was in Company A, Ward's Battalion, Confederate prisoners in Lynchburg, on June 11, 1864, but was pardoned

by President Davis on July 11, 1864, for defending Lynchburg. Driver, *2nd Virginia Cavalry*, 237.

1865

1. Longacre, *Lee's Cavalrymen*, 321–22, 328–34; Driver, *2nd Virginia Cavalry*, 152–68; Chris M. Calkins, *The Battles of Appomattox Station and Appomattox Court House* (Lynchburg, Va.: H. E. Howard, 1987), 116–22.

2. It is unclear what the "discouraging" news is to which RWP is referring, for there was much for Confederates to choose from in early 1865. President Lincoln was reelected; Sherman had recently resumed his northward march, setting out from Savanna, Georgia, into South Carolina on January 19, 1865; Union forces attacked Fort Fisher, North Carolina, on January 13 and captured it two days later; and the siege at Petersburg dragged miserably on. Long, *Day by Day*, 618–27; Blair, *Virginia's Private War*, 129.

3. For more on dismounted cavalry, see McWhiney and Jamieson, *Attack and Die*, 134–37.

4. On February 27, 1865, Gen. Philip Sheridan and his force of ten thousand Union cavalrymen headed south through the Shenandoah Valley. They pursued Gen. Jubal Early's depleted cavalry force and all but annihilated the Confederates in the March 2 engagement at Waynesboro. Sheridan's forces then marched north to join Gen. Grant's army at Petersburg. Driver, *2nd Virginia Cavalry*, 154; Long, *Day by Day*, 644–45, 651.

Appendix

1. RWP had already married Rebecca Walker on December 6, 1860. Ackerly and Parker, "Our Kin," 651.

2. Martha Frances Goggin (December 25, 1844–April 19, 1907) was RWP's maternal cousin. She married John Lipscomb. Ackerly and Parker, "Our Kin," 671; Bedford Cemetery Index, 669.

3. This comment reflects Protestant Christianity's emphasis on accepting and developing a personal relationship with God as a precondition to salvation. Because death was always imminent for the Civil War soldier, many women expressed concern for their husbands' and sons' spiritual welfare. Faust, *Mothers of Invention*, 184, 186; Mathews, *Religion in the Old South*, 13.

4. By 1860 Lynchburg's status as the chewing tobacco capital of the United States also made it the second wealthiest city in the nation. Despite its industrial and transportation links to the rest of the country, the centrality of slavery guaranteed it would remain a Southern city. Tripp, *Yankee Town*.

5. John 14:27.

6. RWP's father, Ammon Parker, owned four separate tracts of land in Bedford County, three of which lay along Bell Branch creek. The total acreage for the three tracts is 343 acres, but according to land tax records during the Civil War,

they were not valued as highly as a tract of 329 acres on the Little Otter River. Virginia Department of Taxation, Land Tax, 1861, Bedford County, Virginia.

7. Providing clothing for slaves was among slaveholding women's traditional duties. Elizabeth Fox-Genovese, *Within the Plantation Household* (Chapel Hill: Univ. of North Carolina Press, 1988): 120–29.

8. One branch of the Parker family apparently emigrated from Virginia to Kentucky and then Missouri. Because land and slave prices were higher in the more heavily populated East than on the western frontier, many Southerners moved west in search of socioeconomic opportunities. Ackerly and Parker, "Our Kin," 650; Ted Parker, Peculiar, Mo., to "Reader," Bedford Co., Va., Dec. 11, 1994, "Parker" research file, Bedford City/County Museum, Bedford, Va.

9. Sallie Parker had three brothers (RWP's paternal cousins) who enlisted in the Confederate army, although at this point only two of them had done so: Pvt. (later 2nd Cpl.) George Nicholas Parker, Company D, and 1st Lt. William Alexander Parker, Company D, both of the 2nd Va. Cav. Driver, *2nd Virginia Cavalry*, 257; Ackerly and Parker, "Our Kin," 657, 664.

10. It was not the goal of Gen. Irvin McDowell to capture Virginia. In his proposed plan of operations for First Manassas, he wrote, "The consequences of that battle will be of the greatest importance to the country, as establishing the prestige in the contest, on the one side or that other." He thus felt it would reveal the fighting abilities of both armies, not claim Virginia for the Union.

11. Matthew 23:12: "And whosoever shall exalt himself shall be abased; and he that shall humble himself shall be exalted" (KJV).

12. During the nineteenth century, it was women's duty to instill morals and religion in their children. Any mother who did not do so was considered a failure. Nancy F. Cott, *The Bonds of Womanhood* (New Haven: Yale Univ. Press, 1977), 63–100; Barbara Leslie Epstein, *The Politics of Domesticity: Women, Evangelism, and Temperance in Nineteenth-Century America* (Middletown, Conn.: Wesleyan Univ. Press, 1981), 67–87.

13. This famous phrase is taken both from the Bible and from a speech given by Abraham Lincoln. Matthew 12:25 reads, "And Jesus knew their thoughts, and said unto them, 'Every kingdom divided against itself is brought to desolation; and every city or house divided against itself shall not stand'" (KJV). Lincoln famously paraphrased the last part of this verse in a famous speech given at the Illinois Republican Convention in 1858.

14. Frances Parker is probably referring here to the Battle of Mill Springs (also known as Logan's Cross Roads), which occurred on Sunday, January 19, 1862. Long, *Day by Day*, 162.

15. On April 30, 1862, General Jackson and his troops embarked for Staunton as part of his famed Shenandoah Valley campaign. They arrived in Staunton on May 6 and began fighting just two days later, at the Battle of McDowell (or Bull Pasture Mountain) a few miles west of Staunton. Total forces: 16,000 (Union: 6,000; Confederate: 10,000). Total casualties: 754 (Union: 256; Confederate: 498). Long, *Day by Day*, 205–9.

16. Edward T. Walker (February 5, 1835–March 9, 1911) was Rebecca Walker Parker's half-brother. He attended Washington College before enlisting as a captain in Company A, Fifty-eighth Virginia Infantry at Bunker Hill on July 25, 1861. He was present until wounded in action at Second Manassas on August 29, 1862. He was promoted to major on October 30, 1862. He was absent wounded through November 1, 1864, and retired to the Invalid Corps on December 2, 1864. He farmed in Bedford County and served as county treasurer. Ackerly and Parker, "Our Kin," 684; Driver, 58th Virginia Infantry, 142.

17. The Battle of Williamsburg was the first battle of the 1862 Peninsula campaign. General McClellan's forces under Gen. Joseph Hooker and Gen. Philip Kearny encountered Confederate forces under Gen. James Longstreet and Gen. D. H. Hill on May 5, 1862, just east of Williamsburg. In this inconclusive battle, Federals unsuccessfully assaulted Fort Magruder; Confederate counterattacks were repulsed. Total forces: 71,000 (Union: 40,000; Confederate: 31,000). Total casualties: 3,942 (Union: 2,239; Confederate: 1,703). Long, Day by Day, 207.

18. Frances Amanda Jopling Hurt (January 26, 1819–February 23, 1893) was Rebecca Walker Parker's maternal aunt. She married John Pendleton Hurt on April 3, 1839; they had five children together. Ackerly and Parker, "Our Kin," 696, 698–99.

19. On the evening of April 8 the 2nd Va. Cav. was ordered to Appomattox Court House in order to attack the Union cavalry at the front lines early the next day. They arrived at Appomattox early on the morning of April 9. They attacked at sunrise and routed the enemy but retreated upon the arrival of two corps of Union infantry. With federal troops blocking the road, the 2nd Cav. headed west, riding around the enemy's left flank. They skirmished along the way but managed to reach the Union rear. They began fighting near the Widow Elizabeth Robertson's home, which stood southwest of Appomattox Court House. A Union soldier later reported that "a brave and daring Confederate soldier [who] was far in advance of your line of battle was killed just as we received the order to stop firing," for at that moment "the bearer of a flag of truce was seen coming up the road." This soldier was Robert W. Parker, reportedly "the last man killed in battle in the Army of Northern Virginia." Driver, 2nd Virginia Cavalry, 163–66; Schroeder, Confederate Cemetery, 3–6, 17.

20. On the afternoon of April 9, 1865, Lee surrendered the Army of Northern Virginia to Grant at Appomattox Court House.

21. On April 2 President Jefferson Davis received word that Union troops had finally broken the defensive lines at Petersburg. That night, as Union troops closed in on Richmond, he and his Cabinet evacuated the city. Federal troops overran Richmond, and the city was surrendered early the next morning. Long, Day by Day, 663–64; Nelson Lankford, Richmond Burning: The Last Days of the Confederate Capital (New York: Penguin, 2003).

22. The South Side Railroad used Appomattox Station as its depot in Appomattox County. Robert C. Black III, The Railroads of the Confederacy (Chapel Hill: Univ. of North Carolina Press, 1998), 276.

23. Job 13:15.

24. Historian Phillip Shaw Paludan has argued that the Civil War changed Americans' ideas of heaven. Before the war "books on heaven were few in number and not concrete in meaning and description," but after the war "there was a huge outpouring of books on heaven . . . [that] described in graphic detail what heaven looked like." Paludan, "Religion and the American Civil War," 21–40.

25. This desperate hope proved false. Despite four long years of war and hardship, the Confederacy failed to establish its independence.

BIBLIOGRAPHY

Primary Sources

Bedford Cemetery Index. Bedford City/County Museum, Bedford, Va.

Carter, Nora A. "Lone Aspen" Survey Report. Bedford County, Va. Works Progress Administration of Virginia Historical Inventory. Mar. 1938. Virginia Conservation Commission, Library of Virginia, Richmond.

Parker, Robert W. Papers. No. 5261. Southern Historical Collection. Wilson Library, Univ. of North Carolina at Chapel Hill.

Parker, Robert W., and Rebecca L. Walker. Certificate to Obtain a Marriage License, Dec. 4, 1860, and Marriage License, Dec. 6, 1860. Bedford County Marriage Records, Library of Virginia, Richmond.

Parker, Ted, Peculiar, Mo., to "Reader," Bedford Co., Va. Dec. 11, 1994. "Parker" research file. Bedford City/County Museum, Bedford, Va.

U.S. Bureau of the Census. *Population Schedules of the Seventh Census of the United States,* 1850, Bedford County, Virginia. M432, Roll 935, RG 29, NA.

———. *Slave Schedules of the Seventh Census of the United States,* 1850, Bedford County, Virginia. M432, Roll 984, RG 29, NA.

———. *Slave Schedules of the Eighth Census of the United States,* 1860, for Bedford County, Virginia. M653, Roll 1387, RG 29, NA.

U.S. War Department. Records of the Adjutant General's Office relating to military and naval service of Confederates. Collection of Confederate Records. M861, RG 109, NA.

———. "Registers of Patients, Chimborazo Hospitals No. 4," RG 109, chapter 6, volume 74, pg. 46, NA.

———. *The War of the Rebellion: A Compilation of the Official Records of the Union and Confederate Armies,* ser. 1, vol. 34. Washington, D.C.: GPO, 1891.

Virginia Department of Taxation. Land Tax, 1861, Bedford County, Virginia. Reel 398, Library of Virginia, Richmond.

———. Personal Property Tax, 1861, Bedford County, Virginia. Reel 421, Library of Virginia, Richmond.

Secondary Sources

Ackerly, Mary Denham, and Lula Eastman Jeter Parker. *"Our Kin": The Genealogies of Some of the Early Families Who Made History in the Founding and Development of Bedford County, Virginia.* Lynchburg, Va.: N.p., 1930. Reprint, Harrisonburg, Va.: C. J. Carrier, 1976.

Adams, Michael C. C. *Our Masters the Revels: A Speculation on Union Military Failure in the East, 1861–1865.* Cambridge: Harvard Univ. Press, 1978.

Bartlett, John, comp. *Familiar Quotations.* 10th ed., rev. and enl. by Nathan Haskell Dole. Boston: Little, Brown, 1919. Available on line at http://www.bartleby.com/100. (Accessed June 7, 2007.)

Berends, Kurt O. "'Wholesome Reading Purifies and Elevates the Man': The Religious Military Press in the Confederacy." In *Religion and the American Civil War,* ed. Randall M. Miller, Harry S. Stout, and Charles Reagan Wilson, 131–66. New York: Oxford Univ. Press, 1998.

Beringer, Richard E., Herman Hattaway, Archer Jones, and William N. Still Jr. *Why the South Lost the Civil War.* Athens: Univ. of Georgia Press, 1986.

Berlin, Ira, Barbara J. Fields, Steven F. Miller, Joseph P. Reidy, and Leslie S. Rowland, eds. *Free at Last: A Documentary History of Slavery, Freedom, and the Civil War.* New York: New Press, 1992.

Berry, Stephen W., II. *All that Makes a Man: Love and Ambition in the Civil War South.* New York: Oxford Univ. Press, 2003.

Bridges, Leonard Hall. *Lee's Maverick General: Daniel Harvey Hill.* Lincoln: Univ. of Nebraska Press, 1991.

Billings, John D. *Hardtack and Coffee, or, the Unwritten Story of Army Life.* [Alexandria, Va.]: Time-Life Books, 1982.

Black, Robert C., III. *The Railroads of the Confederacy.* Chapel Hill: Univ. of North Carolina Press, 1998.

Blair, William. *Virginia's Private War: Feeding Body and Soul in the Confederacy, 1861–1865.* New York: Oxford Univ. Press, 1998.

Bleser, Carol K., and Lesley J. Gordon, eds. *Intimate Strategies of the Civil War: Military Commanders and Their Wives.* New York: Oxford Univ. Press, 2001.

Boatner, Mark M., III. *The Civil War Dictionary.* Rev. ed. New York: Vintage Books, 1991.

Bollet, Alfred Jay. *Civil War Medicine: Challenges and Triumphs.* Tucson, Ariz.: Galen Press, 2002.

Burdekin, Richard C. K., and Marc D. Weidenmier. "Inflation Is Always and Everywhere a Monetary Phenomenon: Richmond vs. Houston in 1864." *American Economic Review* 91, no. 5 (Dec. 2001): 1621–30.

Calkins, Chris M. *The Battles of Appomattox Station and Appomattox Court House, April 8–9, 1865.* Lynchburg, Va.: H. E. Howard, 1987.

Campbell, Jacqueline Glass. *When Sherman Marched North From the Sea: Resistance on the Confederate Home Front.* Chapel Hill: Univ. of North Carolina Press, 2003.

Canaan, John. *The Crater: Petersburg*. New York: Da Capo, 2001.

Carmichael, Peter S. *The Last Generation: Young Virginians in Peace, War, and Reunion*. Chapel Hill: Univ. of North Carolina Press, 2005.

Cooling, B. Franklin, III. "Civil War Deterrent: Defenses of Washington." *Military Affairs* 29, no. 4 (Winter 1965–66): 164–78.

Cooling, Benjamin Franklin. *Forts Henry and Donelson: The Key to the Confederate Heartland*. Knoxville: Univ. of Tennessee Press, 2003.

Cott, Nancy F. *The Bonds of Womanhood: "Woman's Sphere" in New England, 1780–1835*. New Haven: Yale Univ. Press, 1977.

Cottom, Robert I., Jr. *Maryland in the Civil War: A House Divided*. Baltimore: Maryland Historical Society, 1994.

Crouch, Kenneth E. "The Names of the Streams and Mountains in Bedford County, Virginia.""Geography: Rivers and Streams"research file. Bedford City/County Museum, Bedford, Va.

Current, Richard N., ed. *Encyclopedia of the Confederacy*. Vols. 1–4. New York: Simon & Schuster, 1993.

Davis, William C. *Jefferson Davis: The Man and His Hour*. New York: Harper Collins, 1991.

Donald, David Herbert. *Why the North Won the Civil War: Six Authoritative Views on the Economic, Military, Diplomatic, Social, and Political Reasons Behind the Confederacy's Defeat*. Baton Rouge: Louisiana State Univ. Press, 1960.

Driver, Robert J., Jr. *2nd Virginia Cavalry*. 2nd ed. Lynchburg, Va.: H. E. Howard, 1995.

———. *58th Virginia Infantry*. Lynchburg, Va.: H. E. Howard, 1990.

Epstein, Barbara Leslie. *The Politics of Domesticity: Women, Evangelism, and Temperance in Nineteenth-Century America*. Middletown, Conn.: Wesleyan Univ. Press, 1981.

Evans, Charles M. *The War of the Aeronauts: A History of Ballooning during the Civil War*. Mechanicsburg, Pa.: Stackpole Books, 2002.

Faust, Drew Gilpin. *The Creation of Confederate Nationalism: Ideology and Identity in the Civil War South*. Baton Rouge: Louisiana State Univ. Press, 1989.

———. *Mothers of Invention: Women of the Slaveholding South in the American Civil War*. Chapel Hill: Univ. of North Carolina Press, 1996.

———. "'Without Pilot or Compass': Elite Women and Religion in the Civil War South." In *Religion and the American Civil War*, ed. Randall M. Miller, Harry S. Stout, and Charles Reagan Wilson, 250–60. New York: Oxford Univ. Press, 1998.

Ferguson, Ernest B. *Not War but Murder: Cold Harbor, 1864*. New York: Vintage, 2001.

Fox-Genovese, Elizabeth. *Within the Plantation Household: Black and White Women of the Old South*. Chapel Hill: Univ. of North Carolina Press, 1988.

Freeman, Douglas Southall. *Lee's Lieutenants: A Study in Command*. Vol. 1. New York: Charles Scribner's Sons, 1944.

Gallagher, Gary W. *The Confederate War*. Cambridge: Harvard Univ. Press, 1997.

Garrison, Webb, with Cheryl Garrison. *The Encyclopedia of Civil War Usage: An Illustrated Compendium of the Everyday Language of Soldiers and Civilians.* Nashville: Cumberland House, 2001.

Genovese, Eugene D. *A Consuming Fire: The Fall of the Confederacy in the Mind of the White Christian South.* Athens: Univ. of Georgia Press, 1998.

Graebner, Norman A. "Northern Diplomacy and European Neutrality." In *Why the North Won the Civil War: Six Authoritative Views on the Economic, Military, Diplomatic, Social, and Political Reasons Behind the Confederacy's Defeat,* ed. David Herbert Donald, 58–80. Baton Rouge: Louisiana State Univ. Press, 1960.

Green, Carol C. *Chimborazo: The Confederacy's Largest Hospital.* Knoxville: Univ. of Tennessee Press, 2004.

Hankinson, Alan. *First Bull Run 1861: The South's First Victory.* Westport, Conn.: Praeger, 2004.

Hennessy, John J. *Return to Bull Run: The Campaign and Battle of Second Manassas.* Norman: Univ. of Oklahoma Press, 1999.

Hewett, Janet B., ed. *Virginia Confederate Soldiers, 1861–1865.* Vol. 1, *A–K.* Wilmington, N.C.: Broadfoot, 1998.

———. *Virginia Confederate Soldiers, 1861–1865.* Vol. 2, *L–Z.* Wilmington, N.C.: Broadfoot, 1998.

Hewitt, Lawrence Lee. *Port Hudson, Confederate Bastion on the Mississippi.* Baton Rouge: Louisiana State Univ. Press, 1994.

Hirschson, Stanley P. *The White Tecumseh: A Biography of General William T. Sherman.* New York: J. Wiley, 1997.

Hollandsworth, James G. *Pretense of Glory: The Life of General Nathaniel P. Banks.* Baton Rouge: Louisiana State Univ. Press, 2005.

Johnson, Robert Underwood, and Clarence Clough Buel. *Battles and Leaders of the Civil War: Being for the Most Part Contributions by Union and Confederate Officers.* Introduction by Roy F. Nichols. 4 vols. New York: T. Yoseloff, 1956.

Johnson, Timothy D. *Winfield Scott: The Quest for Military Glory.* Lawrence: Univ. Press of Kansas, 1998.

Kennedy, Frances H., ed. *Civil War Battlefield Guide.* 2nd ed. Boston: Houghton Mifflin, 1998.

Linderman, Gerald F. *Embattled Courage: The Experience of Combat in the American Civil War.* New York: Free Press, 1987.

Little, Roger W. "Buddy Relations and Combat Performance." In *The New Military: Changing Patterns of Organization,* ed. Morris Janowitz, 195–223. New York: Russell Sage Foundation, 1964.

Long, E. B., with Barbara Long. *The Civil War Day by Day: An Almanac, 1861–1865.* Foreword by Bruce Catton. New York: Da Capo, 1985.

Longacre, Edward G. *Lee's Cavalrymen: A History of the Mounted Forces of the Army of Northern Virginia.* Mechanicsburg, Pa.: Stackpole Books, 2002.

Lystra, Karen. *Searching the Heart: Women, Men and Romantic Love in Nineteenth-Century America.* New York: Oxford Univ. Press, 2001.

Massey, Mary Elizabeth. *Ersatz in the Confederacy: Shortages and Substitutes on the Southern Homefront.* 1952. Reprint, Columbia: Univ. of South Carolina Press, 1993.

Mathews, Donald G. *Religion in the Old South.* Chicago: Univ. of Chicago Press, 1977.

Matthews, James M., ed. *The Statutes at Large of the Provisional Government of the Confederate States of America, from the Institution of the Government, February 8, 1861, to Its Termination, February 18, 1862, Inclusive. Arranged in Chronological Order. Together with the Constitution for the Provisional Government, and the Permanent Constitution of the Confederate States, and the Treaties Concluded by the Confederate States with Indian Tribes.* Richmond: R. M. Smith, 1864. Quoted in *Documenting the American South.* Available on line at Documenting the American South, Univ. of North Carolina at Chapel Hill, http://docsouth.unc.edu/imls/19conf/19conf.html#p223. Accessed 12 January 2007.

McMillen, Sally G. *Motherhood in the Old South: Pregnancy, Childbirth, and Infant Rearing.* Baton Rouge: Louisiana State Univ. Press, 1990.

McPherson, James M. *For Cause and Comrades: Why Men Fought in the Civil War.* New York: Oxford Univ. Press, 1997.

McWhiney, Grady, and Perry D. Jamieson. *Attack and Die: Civil War Military Tactics and the Southern Heritage.* University: Univ. of Alabama Press, 1982.

Mitchell, Reid. *Civil War Soldiers.* New York: Viking Press, 1988.

Paludan, Phillip Shaw. "Religion and the American Civil War." In *Religion and the American Civil War,* ed. Randall M. Miller, Harry S. Stout, and Charles Reagan Wilson, 21–40. New York: Oxford Univ. Press, 1998.

Peck, Rufus H. *Reminiscences of a Confederate Soldier of Co. C, 2nd Virginia Cavalry.* Fincastle, Va.: N.p., 1913.

Pfanz, Donald C. *Richard S. Ewell: A Soldier's Life.* Chapel Hill: Univ. of North Carolina Press, 1998.

Reader's Digest North American Wildlife: Trees and Nonflowering Plants. New York: Reader's Digest, 1998.

Ridgway, Richard F. *Self-Sufficiency at All Costs: Confederate Post Office Operations in North Carolina, 1861–1865.* Charlotte: North Carolina Postal History Society, 1988.

Robertson, James I., Jr. *Soldiers Blue and Gray.* Columbia: Univ. of South Carolina Press, 1988.

———. *Stonewall Jackson: The Man, the Soldier, the Legend.* New York: Macmillan, 1997.

Ross, Charles D. *Civil War Acoustic Shadows.* Shippensburg, Pa.: White Mane Books, 2001.

Sauers, Richard A. *Meade: Victor of Gettysburg.* Washington, D.C.: Brassey's, 2003.

Scarborough, William Kauffman. *Masters of the Big House: Elite Slaveholders of the Mid-Nineteenth-Century South.* Baton Rouge: Louisiana State Univ. Press, 2003.

Schroeder, Patrick A. *The Confederate Cemetery at Appomattox.* Rev. ed. Farmville, Va.: Schroeder Publications, 2005.

Sears, Stephen W. *George B. McClellan: The Young Napoleon.* New York: Da Capo Press, 1999.

Smith, Robin, and Ron Field. *Uniforms of the Civil War: An Illustrated Guide for Historians, Collectors, and Reenactors.* Guilford, Conn.: Lyon's Press, 2005.

Speer, Lonnie R. *Portals to Hell: Military Prisons of the Civil War.* Lincoln: Univ. of Nebraska Press, 2005.

Stout, Harry S., and Christopher Grasso. "Civil War, Religion, and Communications: The Case of Richmond." In *Religion and the American Civil War,* ed. Randall M. Miller, Harry S. Stout, and Charles Reagan Wilson, 313–59. New York: Oxford Univ. Press, 1998.

Thomas, Emory M. *The Confederacy as a Revolutionary Experience.* Englewood Cliffs, N.J.: Prentice Hall, 1971.

———. *Robert E. Lee: A Biography.* New York: W. W. Norton, 1997.

Tripp, Steven Elliott. *Yankee Town, Southern City: Race and Class Relations in Civil War Lynchburg.* New York: New York Univ. Press, 1997.

Warner, Ezra J. *Generals in Gray: Lives of the Confederate Commanders.* Baton Rouge: Louisiana State Univ. Press, 1959.

Wiley, Bell Irvin. *The Life of Johnny Reb: The Common Soldier of the Confederacy.* Baton Rouge: Louisiana State Univ. Press, 1979.

Williams, T. Harry. *P. G. T. Beauregard: Napoleon in Gray.* Baton Rouge: Louisiana State Univ. Press, 1995.

Wittenberg, Eric J. *The Union Cavalry Comes of Age: Hartwood Church to Brandy Station, 1863.* Washington, D.C.: Brassey's, 2003.

Woodworth, Steven E. *While God Is Marching On: The Religious World of Civil War Soldiers.* Lawrence: Univ. of Kansas Press, 2001.

INDEX

Flint Hill, VA, 75

food: civilians provide, 11, 40, 53, 54, 57, 74, 133–34, 134, 144; cooking, 3, 7; destroyed by Union, 140; foraging, 46; insufficiency, 111, 128, 143; scarcity of, 49–50, 67, 68, 72, 155, 159, 176–77n20, 192n13; skirmish over, 24; soldiers' fare, 3, 7, 25, 27–28, 29, 40, 46, 67, 100, 104, 115, 132, 132–33, 133–34, 140, 141

foreign affairs, 26, 48, 53, 189n127

Fort Donelson, TN, 69, 192n12, 192–93n16. *See also* Fort Henry, TN

Fort Henry, TN, 67, 69, 192n12

Franklin, John, 99, 137

Franklin, Pvt. James "Jim" E., 26, 80, 185n87

Franklin, Pvt. John H., 99, 137, 207n23

Frederick County, VA, 139. *See also* Winchester, VA

Fredericksburg, Battle of, 88, 196n2

Fredericksburg, VA: action near, 88, 137; correspondence addressed from, 111, 112, 113, 114; as destination, 71, 132; as military target, 109, 111, 115; reconnaissance near, 135; Second VA Regiment present at, 87

Front Royal, Battle of, 57

Front Royal, VA, 76, 107, 139, 140

Fuqua, Pvt. Benjamin Bowles, 50, 51, 190n132

Fuqua, Sgt. George Whitfield "Whit," 16, 181n58

furloughs: conditions of receiving, 3, 157; denied, 5, 21, 53, 55, 143–44; desire for, 37, 48, 51, 61, 113, 114, 135, 142, 149; hopes for return of those gone, 31, 71, 100; received, 135; uncertainty of receiving, 3, 58, 74, 85, 103, 120, 135, 141

Gainesville, VA, 118

Garrett, Cpl. John, 26, 34, 90, 185n86

Gettysburg campaign, 87, 106–12, 201nn42–43, 201nn45–48

Gills: delivers correspondence, 101; departs for Bedford, VA, 98, 99; receives correspondence, 98; receives horse detail, 96, 98; return to regiment expected, 124; returns to regiment, 124, 125

Goggin, Auville (uncle), 73, 85, 86, 193n21

Goggin, John (uncle), 25, 73, 128, 184n81

Goggin, Martha (cousin), 147–48, 210n2

Goggin, Pleasant (uncle), 88, 111, 121, 125, 127, 197n4

Goggin, Pvt. Thomas Stephen, 175n10; correspondent, 90, 163; Frances Parker inquires about, 154; illness, 31, 34, 36, 38, 50, 51, 90, 93, 95; loves Lucy, 66; as messmate, 2

Goggin, Thomas Clark (uncle), 177n28; departs for Bedford, VA, 4, 24; preaches, 151; with regiment, 25; visits RWP, 108

Gordonsville, VA: box delivered to, 91, 98; correspondence addressed from, 73, 82; departure from, 74; as destination, 73, 77, 82, 128; false report given at, 81; prisoners sent to, 75; reinforced, 71

Grant, Gen. Ulysses S., 127, 135, 138, 139

Graves, John, 138, 144, 159, 164, 190n133

Graves, Sgt. John P.: delivers correspondence, 91; departs for Bedford, VA, 92; en route to pasture near Charlottesville, 77; present in camp, 50; returns to regiment, 74, 124

Graves, Sgt. John P. (cousin), 64

Graves, Sgt. William F., 183–84n75; considers reenlistment, 71; departs for Bedford, VA, 73, 80, 86; elected captain, 36; elected lieutenant, 21; illness, 19, 29, 36, 39, 44, 58, 86, 139; promotion, 97; resignation, 29, 31, 34; returns to regiment, 40, 74; wounded, 137

Guard Hill, Battle of, 139, 209n38

Guinea Station, VA, 88, 89

Lee, Gen. Robert Edward (cont.)
House, 106; headquarters, 200n33;
orders advance, 87, 195n39; surrenders Army of Northern Virginia,
xxvi, 166, 212n20
Lee, Jim, 95, 97, 98
Leesburg, Battle of, 42, 46, 188n113
Leesburg, VA: correspondence addressed
from, 49, 50; departure from, 47, 50;
as destination, 27, 38, 60, 69; evacuation of, 57; false report regarding, 23; fortified, 52, 62; pickets
stationed, 44; prisoners exchanged
across, 68
Leetown, MD, 109
Leftwich, Pvt. Granderson G., 183n72;
furloughed, 92; illness, 19, 26–27;
returns to regiment, 96; wounded,
120, 139–40
Leftwich, Pvt. James C., 94–95, 198n19
Lexington, VA, 79
Liberty, VA: correspondence addressed
from, 13, 152, 153, 164; correspondence addressed to, 13, 117, 154,
118; material support sent from,
97–98; sick sent to, 88; soldiers pass
through, 154
Lindon Station, VA, 107
Lipscomb, Pvt. George D., 176n12; illness, 11, 17, 19; Martha Goggin
visits, 147; as messmate, 2
Lipscomb, Sgt. John "Jim" T., 175n11;
borrows socks, 8; illness, 11, 19,
21, 24, 25, 27, 84; as messmate, 2;
returns to regiment, 40, 78; rumor
regarding marriage, 147; scouts, 100
Lone Aspen, xiv, xv, **xv**
Longstreet, Gen. James, 136, 202n52
Loudoun County, VA: as destination, 91,
99, 100, 109, 166; as military target,
95, 108. *See also* Waterford, VA
Louisiana "Tigers" Brigade, 78
Luray, VA, 75
Lynchburg, 132, 144, 145, 210n4

Madison County, VA, 125. *See also* Madi-
son Court House, VA
Madison Court House, VA, 75, 84
Manassas, First Battle of, xxii, 1, 15–16,
17–18, 152, 181n57, 184n80, 211n10.
Manassas Junction, VA: correspondence
addressed from, 5; as destination, 5,
22, 25, 119; expects engagement, 6;
prisoners sent to, 34
Manassas, Second Battle of, 84, 195–96n43
marriage, 174n2
Martin, George, 134
Martin, Pvt. Josiah, 84, 195n40
Martin, Pvt. Lewis C., 31
Martin, Pvt. Thomas T., Jr., 31, 88, 186n98
Martinsburg, VA, 76
Maryland, 8, 27, 36, 68, 108, 179n38
Maryland campaign, 57
Mason-Slidell Affair, 48, 53, 189n127
Massaponax Church, VA, 87, 88, 89
Mattox, Pvt. Robert, 134, 206n15
McCabe, Sgt. James P., 90, 118, 121, 163,
197n12
McCall, Gen. George, 80, 195n37
McClellan, Gen. George B., 66, 80, 191n9
Meade, Gen. George, 87, 119, 127, 201n42
Mechanicsville, VA, xxvi
Middlebrook, VA, 127, 128
Mill Springs, Battle of, 63, 66, 158, 211n14
Minter, Capt., 12, 155
Missouri, 154, 211n8
Monterey, VA, 156, 158
morale: correspondence sustains, xiii,
xiv, xx, xxi, xxv, 37; emotional sup-
port sustains, xviii; material support
sustains, xvii, xviii; religion sustains,
xxi, xxv
Morgan, John O., 136
Mosby, Capt. John S., 197n13
Munford, Col. Thomas Munford, 183n74;
commands Second Regiment Virginia
Cavalry, xxvi, 143; departs regiment,
59; orders RWP to turn over horse to
quartermaster, 84; praise for, 21
Murrill, Pvt. Samuel, 188n112; assistant
quartermaster, 41; correspondent,

Radford, Col. Richard C. W., 178n33;
commands Second Regiment Virginia Cavalry, 1, 35m 60; denies furloughs, 5; denies substitute, 44; no longer commands Second Regiment VA Cavalry, 21; returns to regiment, 39, 59; rumor regarding promotion, 6

railroads: bridge destroyed, 81; construction of, 7; destroyed, 195n38, 205n10; Gen. Sheridan raids, 127; guarded, 110–11; incomplete, 120; leading to Lynchburg, 77; Manassas Cross, 107; Manassas Gap Railroad, 75; Orange and Alexandria, 12

Rapidan Station, VA, 70, 81, 95

Rappahannock County, VA, 75

religion. *See* Christianity

Richmond, VA: battles near, 78, 80, 137; correspondence addressed from, 86, 136; as destination, 139, 145; as military target, 80, 109; prisoners sent to, 8, 16, 132; sick sent to, 40; soldiers home, 114; surrenders, 166

Rixleyville, VA, 6

Roanoke Island, Battle of, 67, 69, 192n11

Robertson, Booker, 3

Robertson, Daniel, 13, 20, 33, 152

Robertson, Elizabeth, xxvi, **165**, 212n19

Robertson, Jim, 22, 88, 109, 124, 138

Robertson, Tom (uncle), 21, 22

Rockbridge County, VA, 77

Romney campaign, 59, 60, 191n5

Rosser, Gen. Thomas, 129, 144, 204n3

Rucker, Cpl. Moses Peter, 10, 11, 136, 177n21, 180n46

Sam (slave?), 46, 120, 158, 188–89n119. *See also* slaves

Sanders, Tom, 106, 139, 155

Savannah, GA, 69

Scott, Gen. Winfield, 9, 179n43

Scott, Pvt. Tilghman D., 17, 19, 58, 70, 74, 182n64

Secession, xv, xvi, 8

Second Regiment Virginia Cavalry: battles engaged in, 42, 46, 72, 76, 80, 87, 94, 106, 108, 110, 120, 136, 137, 139, 141, 164; commanded by Gen. Beverly Johnson, 57; commanded by Gen. Fitzhugh Lee, 57, 87; commanded by Gen. George H. Steuart, 57; commanded by Gen. J. E. B. Stuart, 72, 87; commanded by Gen. John D. Imboden, 87; commanded by Gen. Richard S. Ewell, 57; commanded by Gen. Wade Hampton, 127; commanded by Gen. Williams C. Wickham, 115, 127; court-martial, 87, 88, 89, 97, 128; covers Gen. D. H. Hill's evacuation of Leesburg, 57; covers Gen. Robert E. Lee's evacuation of Maryland, 109; decamps, 5; dismounted, 94, 106, 110, 137, 144, 210n3; flag, **2**; formation, 1; horse detail, 143; illness in, 3, 11, 12, 17, 21, 24, 26, 27, 31, 42, 44, 51, 84, 89, 93, 115, 134; murder in, 117; reorganization, 74, 179n41; rumor regarding, 92; skirmishes, 201n43

Seven Days campaign, 194n29. *See also* Peninsula campaign

Seven Pines, Battle of, 80, 195n36

Seventeenth Regiment Virginia Infantry, 22

Seymour, Col. Isaac G., 78, 194n31

Sharpsburg, MD, 108

Shenandoah Valley campaign, 160, 211n15; Second Regiment Virginia Cavalry reinforces Gen. Jackson, 57; Second Regiment Virginia Cavalry reinforces Gen. Lee, 127

Shenandoah Valley, VA, 57, 87, 127, 143

Sheridan, Gen. Philip H., 127, 143, 210n4

Sherman, Gen. William T., 16, 181n60

Sixtieth Virginia Infantry, 144

skirmishes, 3, 8, 13, 14–15, 24, 25, 27, 28–29, 29, 47, 55, 75, 81, 85, 90, 112, 116, 118, 118–19, 121, 131, 132, 140, 202n54; at Dranesville, 59; false report regarding, 23; at Gordonsville,

skirmishes (cont.)
82; near Alexandria, 5; near Falls
Church, 36, 38, 39, 48; near Georgetown, 33
slavery, xxiv, xv
slaves: brought to Bedford for safety
from Union, 155; children steal
sweetcakes, 128; correspondence
sent by, 53, 109; escape North, 62,
66, 191n7; impressed, 46; owned
by Parkers, xiv, 83, 94, 120, 125,
126, 153, 158, 159, 185n90, 185n91,
188–89n119; respects sent to, 28;
taken by Union, 84
Snow, Billie, 89, 108, 121, 150, 155, 158–59
Sperryville, VA, 75
Spotsylvania County, VA: correspondence addressed from, 87, 88, 89,
136; fight expected, 133. *See also*
Massaponax Church
Spotsylvania Court House, Battle of, 127,
136–37, 206n19, 207n20
Stanardsville, Battle of, xix
states rights, xv
Staunton, VA, 77, 157, 160
Steuart, Gen. George H., 57
Stoneman, 103, 208n36
Stoneman, Gen. George, 139
Stoughton, Gen. E.H., 197n13
Strasburg, VA, 76, 140
Stuart, Brig. Gen. James Ewell Brown,
193n19; commands Second
Regiment Virginia Cavalry, 87;
commands Thirtieth Regiment VA
Volunteers, 1; death, 127; departs
for Peninsula, 57; reinforced by Sec-
ond Regiment Virginia Cavalry, 72;
rumor regarding defeat, 115
substitutes, 36, 199n25; others intend
hiring, 28, 44, 83; RWP considers
hiring, xxv, 102, 103, 142

Tayloe, Adj. Lomax, 118, 203n59
Terry, Capt. William Richard, 2, 5, 16,
175n9

Thirtieth Regiment Virginia Volunteers. *See*
Second Regiment Virginia Cavalry
Todd's Tavern, VA, 127
Turner, Pvt. Benjamin R., 106, 200n32
Tutwiler, Capt., 84

Union Mills, VA, 13, 14, 15, 17
Union: communications with, 55; execu-
tion, 27; fraternization with, 111,
113; in Missouri, 154; Unionists
abandon farms, 10, 11, 25; Unionist
sympathizers, 44

Vance, Archibald H., 10, 11, 12, 27, 93,
179n45
Vance, John, 96, 98, 137
Vance, Lt. T. H., 10
Vance, "Whit": departs for Bedford, VA,
20, 35; expected in camp, 92; falling out with RWP, 90; furlough, 31;
returns to regiment, 93; wounded,
137
vice: military life encourages, xxiv, 33,
47, 54, 86, 148, 153, 158, 189n122;
military service, 68; soldiers engage,
90, 113
Vicksburg, MS, 103, 105, 107, 108,
199n27, 199n28, 200n39

Wade, Sgt. James Addison, 86, 108, 135,
137, 196n45
Walker, Alexander Smith (brother-in-
law), 1, 3, 175n5
Walker, Charles Pleasant, 184n83, 197n9;
arrives in regiment, 93; battles, 108;
camp guard, 92, 134; correspondence
addressed from, 129; correspondence
expected, 26; correspondent, 90, 96,
103–4; departs for Bedford, VA, 166;
detailed, 123; does not want father's
pistols, 99; encouraged to have bul-
let removed, 139; enlistment advice,
83, 85; health monitored by RWP,

91, 94, 99, 99–100, 107, 108, 111,
112, 122, 136; horse detail, 101, 102;
horse shod, 109; horse throws, 95;
horse valued, 106; illness, 100; joins
mess, 90; laundry, 95; in Lynchburg,
137; newspaper sent to, 100; pickets,
134; returns to regiment, 106; taken
to soldiers home in Richmond, 114;
wounded, 136, 137
Walker, James Alexander (father-in-law),
179n37; loans pistols to RWP, 8, 99,
100; sheepskin accidentally taken, 93
Walker, James "Jimmie" (brother-in-
law): departs for Bedford, VA, 3, 4;
engaged, 65; marriage, 70
Walker, Edward (brother-in-law), 160,
212n16
Walker, Ethereel, 85
Walker, Lucy Frances (sister-in-law), 26,
64, 184n82
Walker, Nancy Moorman Joplin
(mother-in-law), 28, 74, 159, 185n92
Walker, Nannie Moorman, 18, 91, 92, 97,
182n67
Walker, William (brother-in-law), 156,
190n3; death, 59, 83; departs for
Bedford, VA, 82; wounded, 80
Walton, E. P., 166
Warrenton, VA, 6, 71
Washington County, MD, 110
Washington, DC, 8, 9, 34
Washington, VA, 75
Waterford, VA: correspondence
addressed from, 44, 45, 47, 48, 51,
52, 54, 57, 59, 59–60, 61, 62, 63, 65,
67, 68; departure from, 49; as desti-
nation, 50

Wentzdale, VA, 6
Wheat, Maj. Roberdeau C., 78, 194n30
White Sulphur Springs, VA, 6
Whitten, Pvt. Alexander McDaniel, 50,
68, 189–90n130
Wickham, Gen. Williams C., 115, 127,
202n53, 202n55
Wilderness, Battle of the, 87, 127, 136,
206n18, 207n20
Williamsburg, Battle of, 160, 212n17
Wilson, Capt. James, 1, 8, 27, 63, 175n3,
175n6
Wilson, Pvt. Bethel, 142, 209n45
Wilson, Pvt. Sandy, 9, 98, 179n44
Winchester, First Battle of, 76, 193n22
Winchester, Second Battle of, 107, 200n35
Winchester, VA, 52, 69, 76, 107, 139
Winder, Gen. Charles Sidney, 84, 195n42
winter quarters, 48, 50, 51, 52, 53, 57, 59,
141, 156, 204n70
women: ask RWP for assistance, 40–41;
communicate with Federals, 55;
contribute material support, 57, 74,
93, xvi, xvii; flirtation, 153; manage
farms, 155; refugee, 14; reinforce
morale, xvii, xix, xx; return home
after First Manassas, 23. *See also*
clothing
Wright, T. A., 157

Yellow Tavern, VA, 127
Young, Col. Samuel B. M., xxvi

Zollicoffer, Gen. Felix, 63, 66, 191n8
Zouaves, 18

Lee's Last Casualty was designed and typeset on a Macintosh OS 10.4 computer system using InDesign software. The body text is set in 10/13 Palatino and display type is set in Celestia Antiqua. This book was designed and typeset by Stephanie Thompson.